AF718646

Index Annuities
Power & Protection

Jack Marrion

Advantage Compendium

This book is for educational purposes only and does not provide legal, tax, or investment advice. Readers should consult own advisor for their personal situation. Any laws or regulations cited have been edited and summarized for clarity's sake. Any names used in this publication are fictional and have no relationship to any person living or dead. Information is from sources believed accurate but is not warranted.

"S&P 500®" and "Standard & Poor's 500" are trademarks of The McGraw-Hill Companies Inc., and must be licensed for use. S&P Index-linked products are not sponsored, endorsed, sold or promoted by Standard & Poor's and Standard & Poor's makes no representation regarding the advisability of purchasing these Products.

©2003 by Jack Marrion
Published by Advantage Compendium

All rights reserved. The text of this publication, or any part thereof, may not be reproduced in any manner whatsoever without written permission from the publisher.

Printed in the United States of America

First Printing, February 2003
Second Printing, January 2004
Third Printing, September 2004

ISBN 0-9728251-0-X

Advantage Compendium
2187 Butterfield Court
Maryland Heights MO 63032

(314) 434-6030

webmaster@indexannuity.org

Index Annuities – Power & Protection

The Author

Jack Marrion is the acknowledged guru of index annuities. His comments and analysis have appeared in over 100 publications including *Best's Review, Broker World, Business Week, Kiplinger Magazine, The National Underwriter, Chicago Tribune, Los Angeles Times, The Washington Post* and *The Wall Street Journal.* A frequent speaker at industry conferences, he is the author of three books on financial topics and a regular contributor to many periodicals. *Best's Review* said Mr. Marrion was one of the people to watch and likely to affect the course of the industry. Prior to forming the Advantage Compendium Mr. Marrion was president of an investment broker/dealer with offices in nine states, and formerly vice president of a life insurance company and vice president of an NYSE investment banking firm. He has an M.B.A. from the University of Missouri.

Jack Marrion is president of the **Advantage Compendium. Advantage Compendium** provides research and consulting services to insurance companies, financial institutions and financial service firms in a variety of areas. They publish the **Index Annuities Guide** comparing over 180 index products, the quarterly **Advantage Equity Index Sales & Market Report**, and the **Index Compendium** monthly newsletter. Their web site, www.indexannuity.org , is known as the resource on indexed products.

Neither Jack Marrion nor Advantage Compendium markets or endorses any financial product.

Introduction

Welcome. This is a book about index annuities. It was written because everything I've seen on the subject is either very outdated or very slanted. After you read it you'll have a firm understanding of how index annuities and all the major crediting methods work, where index annuities fit, and some marketing and sales ideas that will help you successfully convey the index annuity concept. I've tried to show all the facts as honestly as possible.

This doesn't mean that I'm not biased. Neither my company nor I sell any financial products, nor will I endorse or recommend anybody's annuity over anybody else's, but I am biased. You see I like the index annuity concept. I've done a lot of research on index annuities and I believe they offer a very realistic shot at earning higher returns than you would get on other instruments that provide the same protection of principal.

If you'd like to jumpstart your learning begin with Chapter 2 – Index Annuity Basics, go to Chapter 8 – Index Annuity Solutions, and Chapter 9 – Sales & Marketing Ideas. Then use the index in the back to investigate future topics as needed.

I arranged it so that you don't need to read every single word to make this book work for you. Key points of each chapter are highlighted in blue, very important ones are in red, and the back of each chapter contains a cheat sheet summarizing the important ideas. If you only look at these highlights, and the rest of this Introduction, you'll still get the basic ideas.

I once said that index annuities are a wonderfully simple concept made complicated by insurance companies. I hope this book makes everything clearer.

Jack Marrion

Index Annuity Q & A

What is an index annuity?

An index annuity is a fixed annuity offered by an insurance company. The index annuity earns a minimum rate of interest and offers the potential for excess interest based on the performance of an index.

There are two major types of annuities in the world – fixed and variable. Variable annuities operate a lot like mutual funds in that most of the investment return (and risk) are passed to the investor. Fixed rate annuities operate more like an account at a bank paying a stated rate of interest. Fixed index annuities pay a minimum guaranteed rate and the potential for more interest depending on the performance of an equity or bond index.

Since interest is based on an index, isn't this like a variable annuity?

No. If a variable annuity account goes down, you could lose principal. Index annuity principal is protected from market risk - you can't lose principal if the index declines. Variable annuity gains are typically not locked in. Once index-linked interest is credited in an index annuity it cannot be lost, even if the index subsequently declines. And variable annuities include reinvested dividends; neither the index nor index annuities reflect reinvested dividends.

So do I get all of the index gains and none of the losses?

No. It costs the insurance company to provide this protection against loss. This typically means that you won't fully participate in all of the gains when the market goes up, but you also won't lose principal in a falling market.

What kind of interest will I earn?

Index annuities are designed to provide a return somewhere between stock market vehicles and savings instruments – somewhere between mutual funds and CDs. Because interest is linked to movements of an index there could be periods when the index annuity credits double digit interest rates and years when zero is credited. But index annuities were created with the intention of providing the realistic potential for higher interest rates than other instruments that protect principal from market risk.

How could I earn zero?

The primary goal of the minimum guarantee is to protect the principal from market risk. So if the market drops, the worse thing an index annuity owner would say is "Gee, I didn't lose any principal". Many companies minimize the minimum guarantee so that if the market stayed down for years, the owner would only get back their money and a few dollars of interest. By minimizing the minimum, and only crediting the minimum guarantee at the end of the term, companies can let index annuities participate in more of the possible index performance. There are index annuities that credit at least a minimum interest rate every year, others that offer the thinnest possible minimum return to maximize participation in the index, and still others in between. You should select the guarantee you are most comfortable with.

How did the Millennium Bear Market Affect Index Annuities?

No index annuity owner lost any principal or credited interest due to the market drop.

Do index annuities have fees?

Not in the same way that a variable annuity or mutual fund does, but more like the way a bank does it. Index annuities have penalties for early withdrawal if you surrender the annuity early. You need to match the period with your goals, keeping in mind that all annuities are designed to be long term savings instruments.

The cost of providing the minimum guarantee and the interest-linked interest means that the index annuity probably won't fully participate in any index increases. So, if the index goes up you won't get all of the upside. This doesn't mean that the insurance company gets the other part of the increase. After protecting the minimum guarantee and covering expenses, any remaining money is used to provide the index-linked interest. Sometimes there could be enough remaining money so that the index annuity fully participates in the index, but today the net effective participation of index annuities — the amount of any index gain that would be credited to the index annuity — is around 45% to 85%. Of course, if the index is lower at the end of the period you have zero participation in any losses.

What interest have index annuities actually credited?

The highest index annuity interest rate credited for one-year was over 40%. During the millennium bear market most index annuities credited 0%.

Index annuities have been around since 1995. During this period we've seen the strongest bull market in ages, with five-years of high double-digit stock market gains, and the worst bear market in three generations; hardly a "normal" period. Index annuities are designed to provide a return somewhere between stock market vehicles and savings instruments and they've been performing as intended.

Are all index annuities the same?

No. Index annuities have differing penalties for early withdrawal, may offer different indices, and one index annuity probably calculates index gain, and credits interest, a little differently from another.

Some index annuities credit interest each year, some wait until the end of a longer period, some average the index values, others set a cap or maximum on the interest that may be paid, and some guarantee all of the fees or moving parts won't change, while others have the flexibility to adjust. What all of this means is one company could offer 100% participation in their way of calculating interest, and still credit less interest than another company that participates in 60% of a different method. Or, a company with a 3% "asset fee" could pay more than another company quoting a 0% fee.

Do some insurance companies intentionally make index annuities complicated?

Yes.

Which type of index annuity is best?

I can't give you a straight answer because different types of annuities work better in different kinds of markets.

For instance, if a market is generally rising over time, index annuities with what I call a "term end point" method should do better. These are annuities that don't lock in interest gains until the very end of the term, and they should credit more interest than other methods.

But, if the stock market of the future posts modest gains each year, then the best method is one that places a cap on the maximum interest credited. The cap method allows you to get "more of a little" instead of "less of more" and works better during periods of general market stability.

However, if the market is very volatile, the best performing index annuity may average index values. Averaging index values means you always wind up at the middle. So with averaging, you won't get the highest possible return, but you are also guaranteed not to get the lowest.

In addition, there are index annuities that use still other interest crediting methods, or a combination of methods, to calculate the return.

If different index annuities perform differently, how do I pick one?

If you believe the index will be heading up, and you can wait until the end of the multiple year period before you see any index-linked interest credited to the annuity, then the "term end point" methods may well provide the highest returns.

If you need to see index derived interest credited to the annuity each year, then you should pick an insurance company you trust and an index annuity with a term and structure that matches your needs, regardless of the crediting method.

I've done enough analysis to see that all of these other crediting methods should produce about the same results if you wait long enough — unless you know for certain how the stock market will move in the future — so the key is picking an index annuity carrier that will treat you well down the road.

Can I get back less cash than I put in an index annuity?

Yes. If you cash in an index annuity, surrender charges are usually deducted from the accumulated value (the accumulated value is the original premium plus any interest credited). If the charges were more than the accumulated value, you would get back less than you put in.

Are index annuities safe?

I think so. Both principal and credited interest are protected from index declines, so the worst thing that could happen is the stock market drops for years and you still get back your principal plus a little interest. The index annuity is as safe as the insurance company issuing the annuity.

Am I worried about the insurance company going under? No. States and independent rating firms on a regular basis examine the financial books of insurance companies, and they look to make sure there's enough money to cover everything, which is why you very rarely hear of an insurance company going bust. What if a company does go belly up? An annuity contract is an asset of the insurer, and in the past another insurer has bought the annuity contracts of the troubled company and life goes on. And every state has a guarantee fund to dip into and protect annuity contract owners (up to a certain limit) if a company tanks. It is possible to lose money if an insurance company fails, but based on history it is not very likely. The way I look at it is my car is insured, my house is insured, and my life is insured. I'm not losing any sleep over these insurance companies, why should the annuity carrier be any different.

Who buys an index annuity?

People purchase an index annuity because they aren't satisfied with the returns from their CDs and fixed rate annuities, but don't have the time or temperament for the stock market. If you have sufficient time to recover from potential losses (and the stomach for it) direct stock market investments should give you a higher return than index annuities. However, if your timeframe is too short to recover from a possible bad market, or you simply don't like the idea of possibly losing principal, index annuities are used as an alternative savings vehicle to bank instruments, fixed rate annuities, bonds and bond mutual funds.

Who are you?

I run The Advantage Group, an independent research and consulting firm that examines financial concepts and products. I neither sell nor endorse any financial product. Sometimes I'll say something nice about a financial concept or specific product, but it isn't intentional.

Chapter 1 – Annuity Basics

An annuity is usually defined as an arrangement between two parties – typically an individual and an insurance company – in which the individual hands over cash, called the premium, and the insurance company promises to pay the individual a regular income for a set period of time, or as long as the individual lives, or whichever is longer.

This arrangement offers certain benefits; the biggest being it can be set it up so that one doesn't outlive one's money. There's nothing more frustrating than failing to die on schedule and running out of cash. Annuities can ensure that income is always available.

Most People Don't Annuitize An Annuity

Today however, most people don't convert the money they've built up in their annuity into a guaranteed income stream (converting an annuity's value into an income is called *annuitization*). Instead, they treat the annuity value they've accumulated as any other asset and evidence suggests that almost all of these accumulated annuity values are passed onto the heirs in a big lump sum and not turned into an income stream by the buyers of the annuities. The consensus is less than 2% of deferred annuities are annuitized.

Think about this for a minute. In 2002 alone over $180 billion of deferred annuities were purchased. And yet it appears that almost no one at least initially intends to use these annuities to provide a guaranteed stream of income, which is why annuities were created in the first place. If most people aren't using annuities to do what they were originally intended for, and annuity sales are much higher today than they were when people were buying them solely to provide an income stream, then there must be another reason why people like annuities.

Some Background

Prior to the late 1970s annuities were primarily used as a retirement income vehicle. If you look at some of the magazines for this and previous decades you'll find ads – usually with a picture of a silver hair gentleman in a fishing boat, telling you how he retired on $200 or $300 a month by contributing so many dollars a month to an annuity plan. Alternatively, instead of paying in a few dollars each month you could pay the cost of the retirement annuity with one check. The 1978 edition of *Personal Finance* stated that "individuals such as entertainers, prizefighters, and others receiving large lump-sum income frequently are the purchasers of single-premium annuities".

A quarter century ago the emphasis changed. Financial counselors began looking at annuities as retirement accumulation vehicles rather than retirement income vehicles. The reason was that while an annuity would provide an income that you couldn't outlive, the annuity also offered guarantees of principal, guarantees of interest and tax-deferral. Sure, you could annuitize the accumulated value down the road and turn the annuity value into an income, but perhaps the real value of an annuity was building assets on a tax-advantaged basis.

In the late 1970s sales of fixed rate annuities took off and have never looked back. Fixed rate annuities pay a stated interest rate and provide a competitive alternative to other traditional savings vehicles, but unlike, say, bank accounts the interest earned is not taxed until withdrawn and used. In addition, fixed rate annuities don't expose the principal or interest to investment risk, and are backed by the full faith and credit of the insurance company. In short, fixed rate annuities offer a safe haven and guarantees.

Variable Annuities Remove Tax Considerations From Market Decisions

Although fixed rate annuities began to be used for building long-term savings, variable annuities initially stayed in the background. Variable annuities have been around for over thirty years, but they spent the first half of their life as a niche vehicle in the tax sheltered annuity arena providing retirement income for teachers. Like fixed annuities, these variable annuities were also sold as retirement income vehicles, but the difference was that while the fixed annuity offered an unchanging guaranteed income for the annuity owner, income from the variable annuity was based on the value of the stocks backing the annuity and would fluctuate.

The First Index Annuity Purchased For $21,000 Had A Value Of $51,779 Five Years Later

A couple of decades ago variable annuities came into their own by broadening the investment choices available within the variable annuity body and providing elements of protection from market uncertainty. Consumers could diversify their money into accounts with different goals and objectives, shift funds from one account to another, and let their money grow, all on a tax-deferred basis.

Perhaps the greatest single variable annuity benefit is the removal of tax considerations from market decisions. How many people have kept a stock or mutual fund too long, or allowed a particular stock or fund position to become too large a percentage of assets, because they didn't want to sell and face the tax consequences? Back in 1999 and early 2000 many people explained to me that although they knew they should sell and take some profits from their equity investments, they didn't want to pay tax dollars on those gains. The reality for those people is that the millennium bear market took care of that gain problem for them. Variable annuities remove tax considerations from decisions on repositioning assets and also offer certain protections from market loss to an individual's estate.

In February 1995 the first fixed index annuity was purchased. Why then? Both fixed rate and variable annuity sales had been doing rather well in the preceding years, and since the financial tools to create index annuities had been around for several years why were index annuities introduced then? One big reason is that the psychology of the times was right. It had been a rocky 1994 - bond fund returns were poor, the S&P 500 ended the year on a down note, and many stock funds and variable annuities had marginal or negative returns. In addition, the 8% and 9% rates consumers had realized on traditional fixed annuities in the previous decade appeared to be over. Interest rates were on a long downward slope, from a historic point of view, and insurers were looking for an annuity that had the potential to deliver respectable returns.

The First Index Annuity

On the ides of February 1995 a 60 year old gentlemen was facing a decision. Retirement was looming on the not too distant horizon and the $21,000 he had placed in certificates of deposit had matured. The gentlemen had been thinking about moving the money to mutual funds. However, he remembered the crash of 87' and how mutual fund values fell. In fact in the previous year, 1994, many mutual funds had lost money. Even though the bank was only paying a little over 6% interest at least that money was safe and it would be there in five years when he retired.

The gentlemen and his agent were discussing alternatives when the agent said, "Keyport Life has developed something that might fit your needs. It's called an equity indexed annuity."

"Tell me more," said the gentlemen.

The agent responded "The way I understand it is they guarantee that if the index goes down you'd at least get your $21,000 back at the end of five years plus a little interest, and if the index goes up you participate in some of the gain."

"That sounds interesting. You mean even if the stock market steadily goes down over the next five years my principal is still protected from market risk?"

"Yes. Your indexed annuity is backed by the insurance company. Now, if the index goes up you're not going to get all of the increase and indexed annuities don't include reinvested dividends. Finally, you'd better count on holding this annuity for the full term because there are penalties for early withdrawal."

"Well, this money is earmarked for retirement and I don't plan on touching it. The main point is that my principal is protected from market risk and I might make more than I'm getting from the bank. Let's put that $21,000 in the Keyport indexed annuity."

The first indexed annuity purchased returned almost five times more than the Certificate of Deposit alternative

Although my conversation is imaginary, the first indexed annuity was purchased February 15, 1995 for a premium of $21,000. If the gentlemen had placed the money in the average CD and kept renewing them his $21,000 would have grown to roughly $27,554. Over the same five-year period the same $21,000 placed in a Keyport indexed annuity grew to $51,779.

How Do Fixed Index Annuities Differ From Fixed Rate Annuities?

Fixed index annuities offer the same guarantees of principal, guarantees of interest and tax-deferral benefits of fixed rate annuities. The difference is fixed index annuities offer the potential for more interest because interest earnings are linked to the performance of an external index. In 2002 roughly $12 billion of index annuities were purchased and over $36 billion have been purchased since 1995 according to The Advantage Group.

Fixed index annuities neither are variable annuities nor are they index funds. Index annuities protect principal and credited interest from market loss and are designed to perform as fixed annuities.

Basic Annuity Concepts

Deferred Annuities

Most annuities purchased are deferred annuities. The word "deferred" means that at least a year will elapse between when the premium or premiums are paid and the annuity is annuitized with a regular income produced. As noted, few deferred annuities are ever annuitized. Deferred annuities can be either fixed or variable.

Deferred Annuities

- Tax-deferral of interest compounding inside the annuity
- Lifetime income options
- Surrender Charges (usually)
- May Be Purchased as Single or Flexible Premium
- Withdrawals Taxed on a LIFO (last-in, first-out) basis as ordinary income
- Subject to IRS "Under Age 59 1/2" Premature Distribution Rules
- Pay a death benefit typically greater of premium or accumulated value
- Annuity proceeds may avoid probate if named beneficiary
- Ability to exchange for other annuities without current taxes

Tax Deferral

Interest remaining inside an annuity is not subject to income tax and grows on a tax-deferred basis. However, tax-deferred doesn't mean tax-free. Interest withdrawn from the annuity is subject to income taxes in the year it is received and upon death of the annuity owner all interest earnings are taxable. In addition, interest withdrawn from an annuity before age 59 1/2 is subject to an additional IRS penalty, unless the distribution meets certain exceptions. Taxes or penalties do not apply on the original principal.

Highest Individual Marginal Income Tax Rates

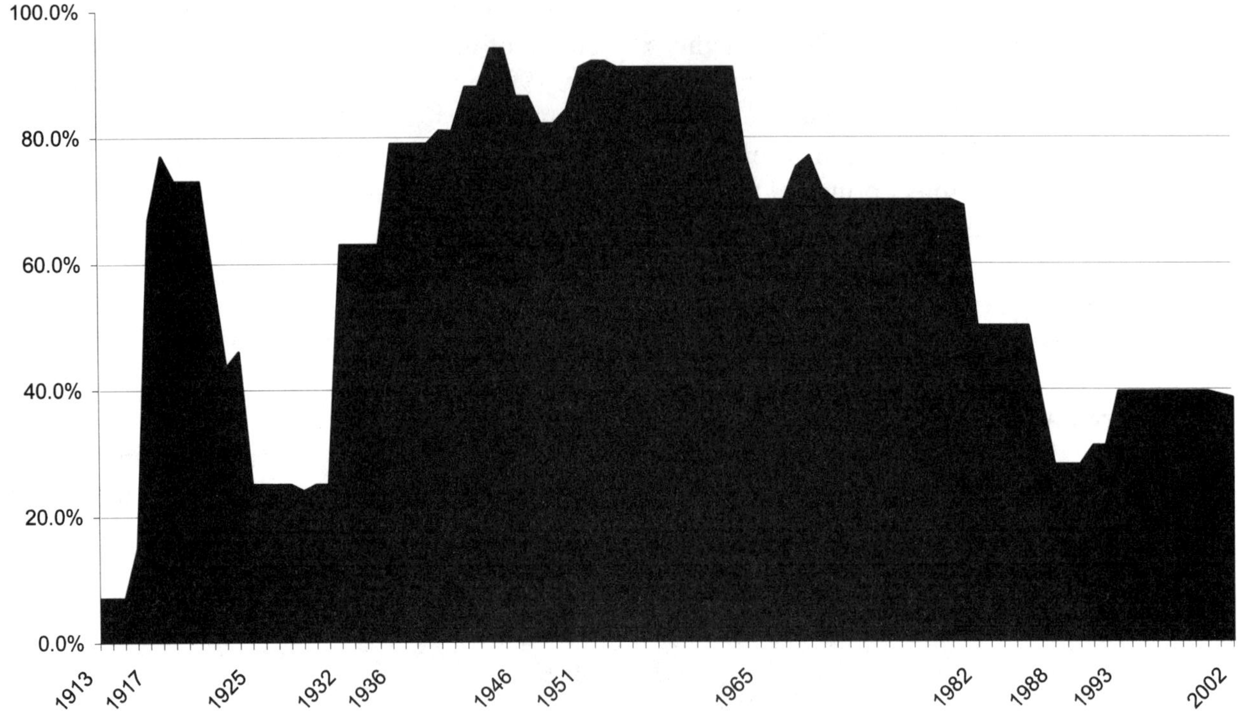

Data Source: Internal Revenue Service

Lifetime Income Options

A deferred annuity policy contains several pages of tables showing the minimum income you'd receive if you annuitized the annuity. Although most annuities are not annuitized it is important to note that only annuities can provide an outcome you can't outlive. An annuity can be set up to provide an income for a set period of time or for the rest of your life or for whichever is longer. An annuity can make sure that an income lasts through two lifetimes or is there to provide money for long term giving.

Surrender Penalties

Almost all deferred annuities charge a surrender penalty if the policy is cashed in prior to the end of the surrender period. Depending on the policy selected, surrender periods vary in length from one to over twenty years. Surrender penalties do not usually apply if the policy is cashed in due to death of the owner or if the policy is annuitized.

Maturity Date

Not to be confused with the surrender period, the maturity date is the longest one can keep annuity interest deferred before it must be taken out. Maturity dates usually occur when the annuitant celebrates their 80th to 90th birthday, but some new policies may be kept until age 100 (the annuitant is the person upon which the annuitization life income is based). The maturity date is not how long the insurance company makes you keep your annuity with them, but how long the insurer will let you keep your money with them.

Withdrawals Taxed on a LIFO (last-in, first-out) basis as ordinary income

The IRS assumes that taxable interest is always withdrawn first from an annuity. Principal is not taxed.

IRS "Under Age 59½" Premature Distribution Penalty

To encourage their use as long-term savings vehicles annuities, just like qualified retirement plans; impose a 10% penalty on withdrawals before age 59½. The penalty is in addition to the normal income taxes owing, and can be avoided if certain conditions are met. In the case of annuities, the penalty only affects earnings on top of the premium.

As an example, if the original annuity premium of $10,000 had grown to $11,000 and you cashed in the annuity contract, the amount subject to taxes and penalty is $1,000 – the amount above the premium. What if the annuity was in a qualified plan? Distributions would fall under qualified plan rules.

Does the "under age 59½" penalty mean younger people should avoid annuities? Not unless the buyer's intention is to use the annuity funds in the near future. Annuities are purchased as long-term savings vehicles and work best when they are given time to work.

Would it ever make sense for a younger person to buy an annuity if they knew they were going to withdraw from it soon? Sure, depending on the return of available alternatives.

In early 2002 some fixed rate annuities were available offering 6.0% interest guaranteed for five years. At the same time the typical five-year certificate of deposit had an annual percentage yield of around 4.5%. Even if the annuity interest was subjected to a 10% under age 59½ penalty, the annuity's after penalty yield is still 5.4% - almost a percent higher than the CD.

Death Benefit & Probate

An annuity is a life insurance contract; therefore proceeds are distributed to named beneficiaries under the terms of the contract and bypass probate. The value of the annuity is generally included in the value of the estate for estate tax purposes.

The death benefit of a fixed rate or fixed index annuity is usually the accumulated value of the annuity with any remaining surrender penalties waived. The death benefit of a variable annuity may be the higher of the account's current value or highest anniversary value.

Tax-Free Exchanges

Section 1035 of the Internal Revenue Code says that one annuity may be exchanged for another annuity without causing a taxable event. You can trade a fixed rate annuity for another fixed rate annuity, swap a fixed rate annuity for a variable annuity, cross a variable annuity with a fixed index annuity, or even get more creative. As long as you let the insurance companies handle the transfer, no current income taxes are due.

Fixed & Variable Differences

Fixed annuities provide a minimum guaranteed return. If the insurance company believes they can pay extra interest from their general account above and beyond this minimum guarantee they will declare a fixed rate of interest and pay the annuity owner a stated interest rate for a period. Or, in the case of a fixed index annuity they could use the extra interest to link the earning of interest to the performance of an external index for a period. The major difference between a fixed rate annuity and a fixed index annuity is in the crediting of excess interest above the minimum guarantee.

Fixed Rate Annuity = Fixed Interest Rate
Fixed Index Annuity = Fixed Index Participation

In a variable annuity the insurance company typically offers a general account with guaranteed returns and separate accounts invested in a wide variety of stocks and/or bonds. Unlike fixed rate and fixed index annuities the investment risk in variable annuities is borne by the annuity owner. Variable annuities are considered securities and require appropriate securities registration.

	Fixed Rate	Fixed Index	Variable
Management Fees	No	No	Yes
Registered as Security	No	No	Yes
Guaranteed Prior Earnings	Yes	Yes	No
Guaranteed Principal	Yes	Yes	No *
Minimum Interest Guarantee	Yes	Yes	No

*yes in time of death

Guaranteed Prior Interest

Interest credited to a fixed annuity cannot be lost if the market declines. Index annuities enable an individual to participate in the upside potential of an index linked return, yet the principal and credited interest earnings can never decrease due to market declines. The percentage of index growth credited depends upon the actual movements of the index and the crediting formula used by the insurance company. Variable annuity gains are typically lost if the separate account values decline, although variable annuities do offer a measure of protection if the annuity owner dies.

Minimum Interest Guarantees

Fixed annuities guarantee payment of a minimum rate of interest. The effective minimum interest guarantee of fixed index annuities may be less than fixed rate annuities.

Immediate (Income) Annuities

Instead of annuitizing a deferred annuity to receive a regular income you may simply purchase an income annuity, also known as an immediate annuity. Immediate annuities are designed to produce a stream of income usually beginning almost as soon as they are purchased. Although all deferred annuities may be annuitized and become immediate annuities, no immediate annuity may become a deferred annuity. Immediate annuity payments are usually fixed and unchanging, but payments may be variable or have both fixed and variable elements. Variable immediate annuities have a fixed number of income units with the value of those units fluctuating because they are based on the value of the underlying investments. The income you receive from a variable immediate annuity will go up and down. An index immediate annuity has a guaranteed payment with additional amounts dependent upon the performance of an external index.

Index Annuity Basics

Index annuities are underwritten by insurance companies. They are usually fixed annuities that provide a minimum guaranteed return with excess interest crediting based on the movement of an external index. Fixed index annuities share the same features, and offer the same protection, of other fixed annuities.

Indexes

Most index annuities base the crediting of excess interest on movements of the S&P 500®. The S&P 500 Index includes a representative sample of 500 common stocks from companies trading on the New York Stock Exchange, American Stock Exchange and NASDAQ National Market System. The objective of the index is to be a benchmark for U.S. stock market performance and represents approximately 80% of the domestic equity market capitalization. Index annuities also base crediting on movements of the Dow Jones Industrial Average, NASDAQ 100®, Russell 2000®, S&P MidCap 400®, and bond and international indices. No index-linked product is sponsored, endorsed, sold or promoted by the respective index provider. Only insurance companies may underwrite index annuities.

Index Annuities Are More Tax-Efficient Than Any Mutual Fund

Unlike an index mutual fund neither dividends nor capital gains are included in the index annuity interest calculation. On the flip side, index annuities do not have the portfolio commissions and transaction costs associated with mutual funds, do not charge management fees, and are more tax-efficient than any mutual fund on the planet.

Minimum Interest Guarantees

Every index annuity guarantees that at the end of the surrender period the original premium will still be there, even if the index steadily declines. Most index annuities currently credit a minimum interest rate of 3% a year, however this is usually credited on less than the full premium so the actual minimum interest earned is less. By calculating the minimum rate on less than the full premium, the insurance company is able to channel more of the premium dollar to providing the potential for more excess interest.

Are Index Annuities Safe?

How safe is the principal in an index annuity? I could talk about the legal reserve system and state guaranty funds and the conservative nature of insurance companies, but reality might be better than theory.

How safe is the principal in an index annuity? No index annuity owner has ever lost money because the insurer failed. I didn't say most people didn't lose...I didn't say almost nobody lost money...I said nobody has ever lost money in an index annuity because the carrier failed, not no how, not no where, not no one.

The Advantage Group unequivocally states that no fixed index annuity customer has ever lost annuity principal due to failure of an insurance company.

Your response might be that the only reason my statement is true is because no carrier has failed since index annuities were introduced. On the contrary, two carriers offering index annuities sought regulatory relief in the '90s, but their customers emerged with both principal and interest intact.

This doesn't mean people don't get hurt if a carrier goes bust. The case most often cited as an example of fixed annuity holders getting back less is Executive Life. After much research I can say that people that surrendered their annuities when Executive Life's business was taken over did take a substantial hit to principal, and even annuity owners staying with the new carrier did not receive 100% of their accumulated account value. However, I cannot find evidence that would support a statement saying that fixed annuity owners ultimately got back less than 100% of their original principal.

Am I saying that every fixed annuity customer that stayed the course throughout the regulatory relief process of every busted carrier got back all of their principal? No. I'm saying that I haven't been able to find any proof that they didn't.

Are Index Annuities Securities?

Stocks, bonds, mutual funds and variable annuities are securities. Fixed annuities are not securities, and are regulated as insurance products by state insurance departments. Because virtually every index annuity is a fixed annuity and not a security, state insurance departments and not the NASD regulate fixed index annuities. The same state licensing required for an agent to sell fixed rate annuities is used with fixed index annuities. Fixed index annuities are regulated as insurance products and not as securities.

Fixed Index Annuities Are Not Securities Because They Meet SEC Safe Harbor Guidelines

Securities Registration

Again, almost every index annuity is classified as an insurance product and not a security. This means that they are not registered as securities with the Securities & Exchange Commission (SEC) nor must an agent be a registered representative of a broker/dealer to sell them. The reason why is because index annuities do not meet the definition of a security under the Securities Act of 1933. In addition, in 1986 the SEC created Rule 151 saying that a product would be deemed an insurance product, and not a security, if the product met three "safe harbor" guidelines.

- The first requirement is that a corporation subject to the supervision of a state insurance commissioner issues the product. Companies subject to state insurance regulation and registration issue all fixed index products.

- The second guideline is that the insurance company assumes the investment risk – not the customer. Unlike variable annuities an index annuity guarantees a minimum annual return and guarantees that once interest is credited it cannot be lost, even if the index declines. In addition to the minimum interest rate an index product may credit additional interest beyond the minimum guarantee. All fixed annuities may credit excess interest above the minimum guarantee. Whether this excess interest is derived from the net investment income of the insurer's portfolio or from the net income attributed to the movements of an index is immaterial. The insurance company still assumes the investment risk.

- The third requirement is that the annuity is not marketed primarily as an investment. Index products are not "index funds with principal protection". Index annuity buyers do not have any direct or indirect ownership of any security or index. Index annuities are long-term retirement savings vehicles.

Index annuities meet the safe harbor definitions and are therefore insurance products and not securities.

The Securities & Exchange Commission (SEC) is a government agency that regulates everything related to securities. The NASD is a self-regulatory body consisting of member broker/dealers and registered representatives. The task of the NASD is to ensure members comply with SEC rules and ones NASD has developed. The NASD has absolutely no authority or say in the marketing of fixed index annuities.

Could the SEC change its mind and say index annuities are securities?

On August 20, 1997 the SEC issued a "Concept Release" (Release No. 33-7438: File No. S7-22-97) requesting comments as to whether index annuities should be registered as securities. In the release the SEC says, "Equity index annuities typically are general account products whose value does not vary according to the investment experience of a separate account. These products therefore appear to satisfy the...Rule 151 investment risk test." The comment period ended January 5, 1998. As of this date the SEC has not said index annuities are securities.

Could an index annuity be registered as a security?

Sure. Index annuities registered as securities have been around almost as long as fixed index annuities; however, until recently they've accounted for far less than one percent of total index sales and were generally designed to be "just in case the SEC changes its mind" index products. Of the 193 active index product variations on the market at the start of the 2002, 191 were fixed index annuities according to The Advantage Group.

Fixed index annuities are fixed annuities and not securities. But there is nothing to preclude a fixed annuity from being redesigned and registered as a security if desired, and more index annuities will be registered in the future because many agents will only sell financial products through their broker/dealer, or are simply more comfortable selling registered products.

Sales Growth

Index annuity sales have set records every year since they were introduced. From annual sales of around $400 million in 1995, index annuity sales exceeded $11 billion in 2002.

Index Annuity Sales (In Billions)

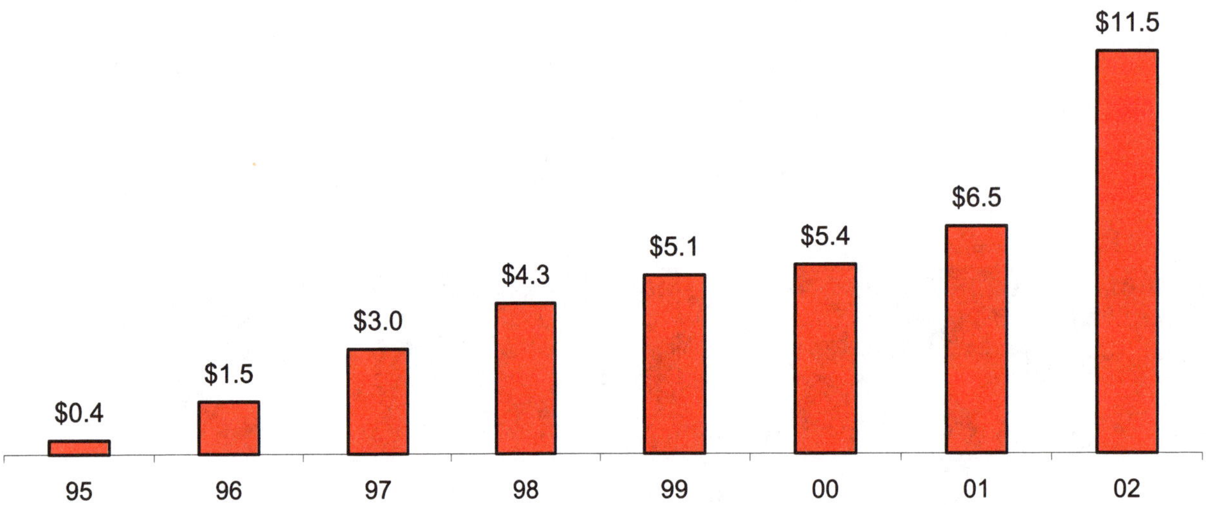

Data Source: The Advantage Group

Summary

Annuities began as retirement income vehicles, but the emphasis changed to using annuities as retirement accumulation instruments due to their tax-deferral benefit and other features. Fixed index annuities offer the same minimum guarantees and protection against market loss of principal associated with fixed rate annuities, but with the potential for excess interest linked to the performance of an external index.

Cheat Sheet

- Most people don't annuitize an annuity. The consensus is less than 2% of deferred annuities are annuitized each year.
- Index annuities are the latest stage in the evolution of the annuity from a retirement income vehicle into a retirement accumulation vehicle.
- Deferred annuities offer tax-deferral, lifetime income options and may avoid probate. Money withdrawn is always taxed as ordinary income and may be subject to IRS "Under Age 59½" Premature Distribution Rules.
- The major difference between fixed and variable annuities is that a variable annuity owner bears the investment risk, while fixed rate and fixed index annuities protect principal and credited interest from investment risk and guarantee a minimum interest return.
- The major difference between fixed rate and fixed index annuities is the crediting of interest earned above and beyond the minimum guarantee.
- Fixed index annuities are insurance products and not securities.
- No one has ever lost principal in an index annuity due to the failure of the insurer.

Universal Disclosure

Investment subject to investment risks, including possible loss of principal, and is not FDIC insured nor a deposit, obligation, or guaranteed by the bank..."S&P 500" is a trademark of The McGraw-Hill Companies, Inc. and must be licensed for use...S&P Index-linked Products are not sponsored, endorsed, sold or promoted by Standard & Poor's and Standard & Poor's makes no representation regarding the advisability of purchasing these Products...A sales charge will apply...Subject to change without notice...Substantial penalty for early withdrawal ...These securities have not been approved or disapproved by the Securities and Exchange Commission nor has the SEC or any state securities commission passed upon the accuracy or adequacy of this prospectus...I understand that the results shown, other than guaranteed values, are not guarantees, promises or warranties...The tax and legal information within is merely a summary of our understanding of interpretations of some of the current tax and other laws and regulations. We suggest that you consult your own attorney, accountant or tax advisor for information concerning your own particular situation...We do not give legal or tax advice...This is for illustrative purposes only... Information obtained from sources believed accurate but is not warranted...Reproduction prohibited without express consent...Past performance is no indication of future results...Any resemblance between persons living or dead is purely coincidental...Void in Wisconsin and Ohio...Always use seatbelts...This is sold by weight, not by volume, contents may settle during shipping...Microwave on premises...Keep out of reach of children...Do not stand on this, this is not a step...Flush immediately with water and contact a physician...Wait four to six weeks for delivery...Do not induce vomiting...Equal Opportunity Lender...Not for use with children under age three...Wait one hour before swimming...Fines doubled in construction areas...If a rash develops discontinue use...Do not operate in bath or shower...Do not operate heavy machinery...Quitting now greatly reduces health risks... The butler did it...If you can read this you don't need glasses...Dispose of gum in wrapper...Close cover before striking.

Discussion Questions

1. What do you see as the key differences between variable, fixed rate and fixed index annuities?

2. Would it ever make sense for a younger person to buy an annuity if they knew they were going to withdraw from it soon?

3. Why do so few people annuitize?

Chapter Quiz

1. The percentage of deferred annuity buyers that annuitize the annuity's value into an income stream are

A. Less than 2%
B. Roughly 50%
C. Roughly 75%
D. More than 98%

2. The first equity index annuity was purchased in

A. 1975
B. 1982
C. 1995
D. 1999

3. The tax-deferral aspect of annuities means

A. The accumulated annuity value passes to heirs tax-free
B. Principal and interest are subject to "under age 59½" penalties when withdrawn
C. Withdrawals from the annuity are taxes on a FIFO (first-in, first-out) basis
D. At least a year passes between the payment of premium and annuitization

4. The index-linked interest earned by an index annuity

A. Includes reinvested dividends
B. Is guaranteed by the index
C. Is excess interest earned above the minimum guarantee
D. All of the above

5. To be considered an insurance product, and not a security, SEC Rule 151 requires

A. The insurance company assumes the investment risk
B. The product be marketed as an investment
C. The product is exempted by the state security commissioner
D. All of the above

Chapter 2 – Index Annuity Basics

Index annuities are fixed annuities. Unlike variable products in which funds are invested in separate accounts and the investment risk is born by the owner, index annuity premium is placed in the insurance company's general account and is backed by the insurer. A dollar of index annuity premium is treated the same as any other premium dollar by the insurer. This means the insurer needs to invest the premium taking into consideration the expenses, contractual guarantees and goals of the annuity. Conceptually, a dollar of premium could be separated into three parts.

Index Annuity Parts

Expenses

Guarantees

Index-Linked

The Expenses Part

Insurance company charges are the first items deducted from a dollar of premium. These charges include the company's operating expenses, agent compensation costs, direct annuity costs and profit objectives.

The Guaranteed Part

All fixed annuities offer a minimum guaranteed return. For fixed index annuities this minimum guarantee promises an accumulated value at least equal to the original principal by the end of the surrender period. To provide this minimum guaranteed return the insurance company invests in bonds or other instruments.

Almost every index annuity sets its minimum guarantee at 3% interest. This is the same minimum rate offered by many traditional fixed annuities. However, eight out of ten available index annuities base this 3% minimum interest rate on less than 100% of the premium received.

If the 3% guaranteed return is calculated on less than the full dollar of premium, then the minimum effective annual return is less than 3%. Why would one accept a minimum return calculated on less than 100% of the premium? Because it may provide the potential for a higher overall return.

Guarantee At 90%

$1.00 Premium
- 0.09 Expenses
- 0.63 Guaranteed Part
$0.28 Available For Options

Say that an index annuity has a nine year term and credited 3% interest on 90% of the premium. The minimum return would be $1.17 at the end of nine years for every $1 of premium ($1.1743 if you want to be exact). If you could find bonds that earn and reinvest at 7% interest, the insurance company would need to invest 63 cents out of this dollar to provide $1.17 in seven years.

The main goal of the minimum guarantee is to preserve the original principal – to give at least a dollar back by the end of term for every dollar put in. A minimum rate of 3% interest compounded on 90% of the premium would give back $1.17 for every $1 put in which means we exceeded our goal.

If we had credited 3% on 100% of the premium, the minimum return would have been $1.30 at the end of 9 years. But even if we could find those same bonds earning and reinvesting at 7%, the insurer would need to invest 71 cents out of each dollar to meet this higher minimum guarantee instead of the 63 cents required when using 90% of the premium.

Guarantee At 100%

$1.00 Premium
- 0.09 Expenses
- 0.71 Guaranteed Part
$0.20 Available For Options

After the premium is placed in the insurer's general account we'll say that 9 cents out of every dollar goes to cover the agent expenses, insurance company expenses and insurance company profits. That means we have 91 cents remaining from our premium (in actuality these expenses are prorated and taken over an extended number of years).

The next step is ensuring that the minimum guaranteed return is met. The amount needed to protect the minimum guaranteed return depends upon what percentage of premium the minimum return is calculated on and the return earned on the insurance company's portfolio. If we go back to our example when the insurance company is earning 7% on the bonds, a minimum return based on 90% of the premium would require 63 cents. But a minimum return based on 100% of the premium would require 71 cents of the dollar.

We have 91 cents remaining after expenses. A 90% guarantee would cost 63 cents leaving 28 cents remaining. A guarantee based on 100% of the premium would cost 71 cents, which leaves 20 cents remaining. A higher guarantee costs more and that means there are a few less pennies available to buy the options, which provide the potential for excess interest.

Which Is Better – A High Or Low Guarantee?

It depends on your comfort level and the way index-linked interest is credited. If an annuity calculates and credits interest annually it would take a very prolonged bad market, and a very poor annuity pricing environment, to average under 3% a year in index-linked interest. But index annuities that don't credit interest until the end of a multiple year term are more likely to only hit the minimum guarantee in a bad patch. From a pricing model viewpoint you gain a little more possible upside in the index if you accept a lower minimum, or you can trade for a little higher minimum return if you accept a little less index participation.

The sizzle behind the Index Annuity Guarantee side is not the minimum return; it's the protection of premium from market risk. Even if the market steadily falls for the next five or ten or twenty years the worst you will get back is your premium". That's the hot story, not earning a measly 1½%, 2% or 3% interest.

How Is The Minimum Interest Credited To The Policy?

Fixed rate annuities credit interest to the policy each year. The credited interest is at least the minimum guaranteed rate, and may include excess interest. On the other hand fixed index annuities – with very few exceptions – physically credit the annuity interest only when there is excess interest earned, or at the end of the term.

In our previous example we calculated that a 3% interest rate paid on 90% of the premium would be worth $1.17 in nine years. If the index steadily dropped for nine years almost every index annuity in existence would credit zero interest each year for eight years and 17 cents in the ninth. The only exception is if you die, the annuity will almost always retroactively give you interest up to that point.

Let's be very clear on this. If the calculated index-linked gains for any year were positive, the annuity owner would receive the credited interest gain. If the calculated index gains were zero for a year, the typical index annuity would not credit the minimum guarantee for that specific year; instead the contract would record 0% interest. The minimum guarantee is normally calculated over the entire term and only applies if the total interest for the entire period is less than the guarantee. So, if the index annuity crediting formula produced returns of zero in year one, zero in year two and ten percent in year three the annuity contract wouldn't credit 3%, 3%, 10%; instead it would show 0%, 0%, 10%.

The minimum guarantee almost becomes irrelevant from a protection point of view after the calculated index-linked gain exceeds it. Using our previous example, say the index annuity credited 20% interest at the end of the first year. This would give the contract an accumulated value of $1.20. The annuity only guarantees a minimum accumulated value of $1.17 after nine years. The interest credited in one year has already exceeded the minimum return requirement for the entire period.

There are index annuities that credit at least a minimum interest rate every year, others that offer the thinnest possible minimum return to maximize participation in the index, and still others in between. You should select the guarantee with which you are most comfortable.

The Index-Linked Part

After covering expenses, the remainder of the fixed rate annuity premium dollar is placed in the insurer's general account where it is invested in bonds and other instruments. If the insurer's net investment return is higher than the annuity's minimum guaranteed return, the insurer declares a fixed or stated rate that essentially reflects guaranteed and excess interest.

A fixed index annuity is treated the same way with one important exception. If the insurer's net investment return is higher than the annuity's minimum guaranteed return, the additional return over the minimum guarantee is used to provide for the linkage enabling the earning of excess interest based on the movements of an index.

Both fixed rate and fixed index annuities have expenses that are deducted from the premium. Both fixed rate and fixed index annuities guarantee a minimum return, the difference is how any remaining cash is used. In a fixed rate annuity any extra cash left after covering expenses and the minimum guarantee is used to buy more bonds, and the insurer announces a stated interest rate. In a fixed index annuity any extra cash is used to buy options, and the insurer announces a stated degree of index participation.

Options

The linkage of index movements to annuity interest is typically accomplished by using options. Most insurance companies buy options on the underlying index. An option gives you the right - not the obligation, to buy or sell something within a period of time.

Buying Options Gives You Rights, Not Obligations

To Use A Specific Stock Example...

Say that you could buy a share of XYZ stock for $50. If you bought the stock and it rose to $60 you could sell it and net a $10 profit. Instead of buying the actual stock we could buy an option that gives us the right to buy the stock for $50 at anytime over the next year. The cost of the option is $2. If the stock price rose to $60 we would use or exercise our option and buy the stock at $50, sell the stock at $60, and make $10 - less the $2 cost of the option.

Buy Stock @ $50	Buy Option for $2 that gives you the right to buy stock at $50
Maximum Profit – Unlimited	Maximum Profit – Unlimited
Maximum Possible Loss - $50	Maximum Possible Loss - $2

Buying an option gives us the right to participate in the growth of the value of the stock, but the real story behind options is what happens if the stock goes down. What would happen if we bought the stock at $50 a share, but instead of going up it went down. If the price of XYZ stock fell to $40 or $30 or $10 a share we'd lose $10 or $20 or $40. However, options give us rights, not obligations. If we had bought an option for $2 instead of buying the stock itself, and the price of the stock fell to $40, $30, $10 or even zero, the most we can lose is $2 - the price of our option.

Stock Options & Index Options

The previous example talked about an option on a specific stock. The options purchased by the insurance company to generate index-linked interest are usually for the entire index and these are called index options. Index options are a bit more complicated because there aren't specific stocks backing the option, but the basic concepts are the same. In either case, the index annuity buyer is not buying options; they are buying an index annuity that derives part of the interest credited from the return on the option purchased by the insurance company.

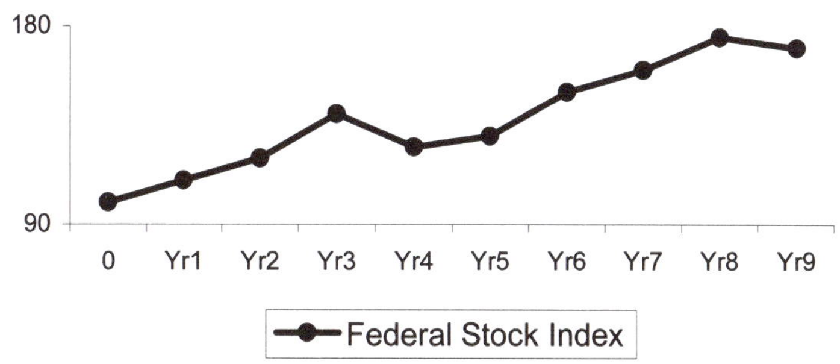

Suppose that an index annuity based the crediting of excess interest on movements of the fictitious Federal Stock Index. Suppose that the index was at a level of 100 and you could purchase an option that would give you the right to buy the index at a level of 100 at anytime prior to the end of the ninth year.

If at the end of the ninth year the Federal Stock Index had a value greater than 100 you'd use (or exercise) the option. If the index was at, say, a level of 170 you'd exercise the option to buy the index at 100, sell the index at 170 and make a gain of 70% [(170-100)/100 = .70].

If the index were at a level of 100 or less you would not use the option. But, even if the index was down 20%, 40% or 100% the most you would lose is the money you paid for the option.

This is how index annuities participate in the index. Option prices are more volatile than direct equity prices, and if the index closed lower than 100 the option would be worthless while the index itself would still have value. But the combination of owning both the option and the bonds means the insurance company can still provide a minimum return even if the index goes down and the option expires worthless.

Where's The Risk?

Most index annuities use options to link index movement to the potential crediting of excess interest above the minimum guarantee. Another name for options is derivatives, and everybody knows that using derivatives may make you go blind and grow hair on your palms. What about the risk?

Index Annuities – What About The Risk?

- The index annuity owner does not directly or indirectly own the index or any stocks
- Both credited interest and principal of the index annuity are protected from market risk
- The index annuity is backed by the insurance company
- The insurance company usually provides the potential for index-linked interest through the purchase of options. Buying options gives you rights, not obligations
- Most of the premium is used to buy bonds to protect the minimum guarantee and only a little is used to buy the options.
- The biggest risk an index annuity owner faces is that they might have earned a higher return in another vehicle (but then again, hindsight's always 20-20)

Both stocks and mutual funds offer the potential for gains, and long-term investors in these vehicles have realized average returns that are higher than safer alternatives, but these vehicles have market risk. The stock market goes up and down and on any given day these investments may be worth more or less than originally paid. Index annuities eliminate this market risk to principal.

When a consumer buys an index annuity their principal is backed by, and is as safe as, the insurance company that issued the annuity. States and rating agencies examine insurance company books on a regular basis, and you rarely hear of an insurance company going bust. What if a company does go belly up? An annuity contract is an asset of the insurer, and historically another insurer simply buys the annuity contracts of the troubled company and life goes on, and every state has a guarantee fund to dip into and protect annuity contract owners up to a maximum account value if a company tanks. It is possible to lose money if an insurance company fails, but based on history it is not very likely. As with all fixed rate insurance products index annuities provide a minimum guaranteed return. Excess interest beyond this minimum guarantee is calculated based on movements on an external index, but the customer is not directly or indirectly involved in buying the index.

The insurance company is also insulated from risk when they buy options on the index and not the underlying securities. Buying an option gives you the right - not the obligation, to buy or sell something. This is how options work. If the index were worth less at the end of period than we paid at the beginning, we would simply let the option expire. We would be out the money we spent on the option – a predetermined and known expense, but that is the limit to our risk.

Why Would The Seller Sell Us The Option?

If buying an option gives the buyer rights to potential gains and the ability to walk away if the index is down, why do sellers sell? Perhaps the seller feels that the index is not heading up during the term of the option. In the meantime the seller continues to receive any dividends that may be paid and the seller receives the fee the buyer paid for the option. In a flat market environment a seller could essentially sell the same option over and over again.

How Much Of The Index Upside Do You Get?

Index annuity owners get the opportunity to earn index-linked excess interest. If the index goes up 10% or 100% or 1000%, how much of the upside could they get? It depends on a number of factors. There are two basic fundamentals affecting how much index participation you get - interest rates that affect the minimum guaranteed side and option prices affecting the index-linked side.

The answer is when general interest rates are rising and/or option prices are falling, insurance companies can buy more options, which lets them increase index participation. When interest rates are falling and/or option prices are rising, insurers have less money available for options so index participation falls.

Interest Rates Affect Index Participation

Guarantee At 90%

$1.00 Premium
- 0.09 Expenses
- 0.63 Guaranteed Part
$0.28 Available For Options

In our earlier example we said that the index annuity had a nine year term and credited 3% interest on 90% of the premium. This resulted in a minimum return of $1.17 at the end of nine years for every $1 of premium. We also said if we could find bonds that earn and reinvest at 7% interest, the insurance company would need to invest 63 cents out of this dollar to provide $1.17 in nine years, and this would leave the insurer 28 cents to buy options.

However, if a bond yield of 9% could be earned you'd only need to invest 54 cents out of each dollar to provide the $1.17 guaranteed return because higher interest rates grow faster (54 cents compounding at 9% equals $1.17 in nine years). This would leave 35 cents to buy options – 9 cents more than we'd have if interest rates were at 7% and we needed 63 cents to provide the guaranteed return – and with more money available to buy options we could raise index participation.

The Rate Of Return Earned On The Bonds Plays A Large Role In Setting Index Participation

To Generate $1.17 In 9 Years

$.75 Is Needed If You Earn 5%

$.63 Is Needed If You Earn 7%

$.54 Is Needed If You Earn 9%

But if we could only realize a bond yield of 5% the money wouldn't grow as fast and you'd need to invest 75 cents out of each dollar to provide the $1.17 guaranteed return. This would leave only 16 cents to buy options – instead of 28 cents – and with less money available to buy options we would have lower index participation.

When interest rates are lower you need to allocate more cents out of each dollar to invest in bonds to provide the minimum guaranteed return. More money spent on bonds leaves less money available to buy options. When rates are higher you need to allocate less money for the bonds, which leaves more money available to buy options.

Option Prices Affect Index Participation

Guarantee At 90%

$1.00 Premium
- 0.09 Expenses
- 0.63 Guaranteed Part
$0.28 Available For Options

In our earlier example we said that we had 28 cents available to buy index options. We'll say that a "full" index option just happens to cost 28 cents. Buying this "full" option means for every 1% increase in the index we'd receive 1% in excess interest credited to our annuity.

If we were fully or 100% linked to the movements of the index and the index was up 10% at the end of the crediting period we'd earn 10% interest; if it was up 20% we'd earn 20%.

But what if we only had 28 cents and the price of a full option shot up to 56 cents? Since we only have half of the money needed to buy a full option we would only be able to buy half of the option and thus participate in only half of any index gains.

What if option prices fell and a full option cost 14 cents? If we still had 28 cents we'd be able to buy two full options and get double whatever the index gained.

Option Prices Also Play A Huge Role In Determining Index Participation

$.52 Buys 1/2 Index or 50% Participation

$.26 Buys 1 Index or 100% Participation

$.13 Buys 2 or 200% Participation

Simply, this determines how much of the index movement an index annuity participates in. If, after covering expenses and the minimum guaranteed return, we have enough left over to buy an option that links 100% of any index gain we'd participate in 100% of any index gain. If we could only buy 60% of a full option, we'd participate in 60% of the gain. If we could afford to buy one and a quarter full options, we'd participate in 125% of any gain.

Other Factors Affect Index Participation

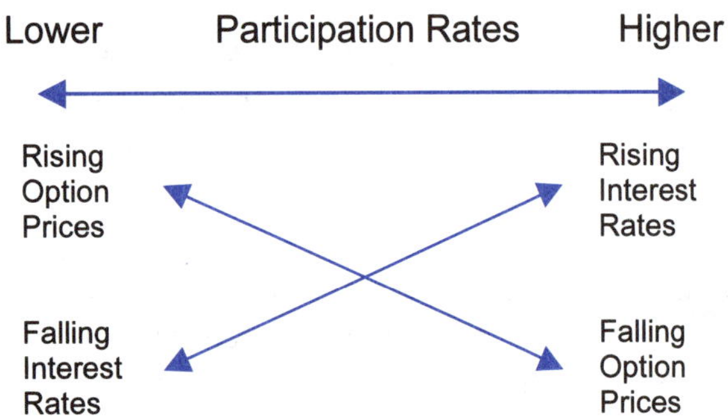

Although interest rates and option prices are the two primary factors in determining index participation, they are not the only ones. If one insurance company's expenses were higher than another then they'd have less money available after paying the expenses and would offer less participation. If one annuity has a longer surrender period than another the insurer can typically earn a little higher return on the guaranteed part by buying longer term bonds, which means a little more money is available for options.

If the degree of index participation in one index annuity can be changed to reflect changes in the market while another annuity locks in index participation, the annuity with the flexibility to change should offer more index participation. If one annuity has a lower minimum guarantee than another, the annuity with the lower guaranty should offer greater index participation because their guaranteed costs are less. And finally, there are different ways used to examine movement of the index itself and calculate how it has moved. Index annuities use many different methods to determine how index movement becomes interest credited.

It's Not Magic - Index Participation

When a company offers greater than 100% participation in an index it isn't magic, like when a magician seems to pour a pitcher of milk into a tiny paper cup. And when an index annuity participates in less than 100% of the index movement it doesn't mean the insurer is skimming options off the top and putting some in their own pocket. Index participation depends upon the amount of options you can afford to buy for your index crediting method.

Index participation depends upon the cost of the option you're buying and how much money you have available to spend. Say you have $1 and you want to buy a quart of milk. If milk at the grocery store costs 50 cents a quart you could buy 2 quarts for your dollar. Just because you wound up with 2 quarts instead of 1 doesn't mean you magically created a fresh quart of milk. You were simply able to buy more milk.

Say you have $1 and milk costs $2 a quart. You'd only be able to buy a pint of milk. When you bring home a pint of milk instead of a quart it doesn't mean that you really had a full quart and put half of it someplace else. Index participation is a matter of available cash and price.

Putting It All Together

We have decided to buy an index annuity. We will earn indexed-linked interest based on the performance of the Federal Stock Index, which is currently at an index level of 100. The insurance company says that at the end of nine years they will credit the greater of the minimum guarantee or 100% of any index-linked interest earned calculated by dividing the ending index value by the beginning index value. The index annuity has a minimum guarantee promising to pay 3% interest on 90% of the premium, meaning that we will at least get back 117% of our premium. We pay our premium to the insurance company.

Behind The Scenes

Guarantee At 90%

$1.00 Premium
- 0.09 Expenses
- 0.63 Guaranteed Part
$0.28 Available For Options

The insurance company was able to find bonds that earn and reinvest at 7% interest, covering the $1.17 minimum guarantee with 63 cents invested today out of our premium dollar. Expenses were 9 cents. After protecting the guarantee and covering expenses the insurer has 28 cents remaining to buy the option on the index.

The insurer is promising to pay 100% of any index-linked gain calculated by computing the difference between the index value today and the index value in nine years. The current level of the Federal Stock Index is 100.

We know that the bonds will provide a minimum return of 117% of premium at the end of nine years, so we don't need to buy an option that starts calculating index gain from today's level. We would buy an option that gives us the right to buy the index at 117 – not at the current level of 100, because the minimum return from the bonds covers the first 17% of increase in the index.

Why don't we simply buy an index that starts from today's index level? We could, and then the annuity buyer would get both the minimum guarantee and any excess interest. However, that would drive up the cost of the option.

A seller might agree to sell us an option so that we would get all potential index gain based on the nine year period starting from today's level of 100, but maybe the seller would charge 35 cents for the option. We only have 28 cents. If we wanted to get index-linked increases from the current level of 100 we would only be able to buy 85% of this option (28 cents divided by 35 cents).

Instead, we tell the seller that he can keep the first 17% of any possible increase and we'll take 100% of the gain after that. In other words, if the index went from 100 to 110 or 115 the seller would keep all of the gain (but we'd still get 17% from the minimum guarantee). If the index went higher than 117 the seller would keep all of the gain from 100 to 117 and we'd keep everything beyond. The seller decides to sell us 100% of the index gain, after he gets the first 17% increase in index value, for a cost of 28 cents, which just happens to be what we have available to spend.

At The End Of The Term

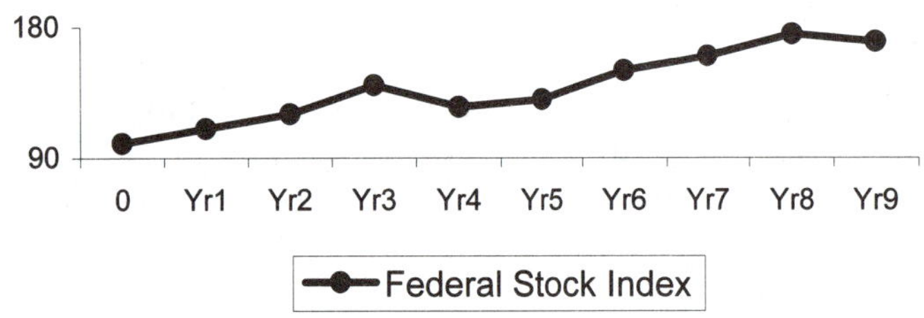

It is now the end of year nine and the Federal Stock Index is at a level of 170. The index annuity divides the current index level by the starting index level [(170/100)-1 = .7] to determine the gain and then multiples the gain by our index participation rate [.7 x 100% = 70%]. The annuity owner earned a total of 70% interest for the nine years.

Behind The Scenes

The insurance company exercises their option to buy the index at a level of 117 and simultaneously sells the index at a current level of 170. This results in an option gain of 53 cents on each dollar of premium. The initial bonds that were purchased nine years ago, and have been growing at 7%, have reached a value of $1.17 and are sold.

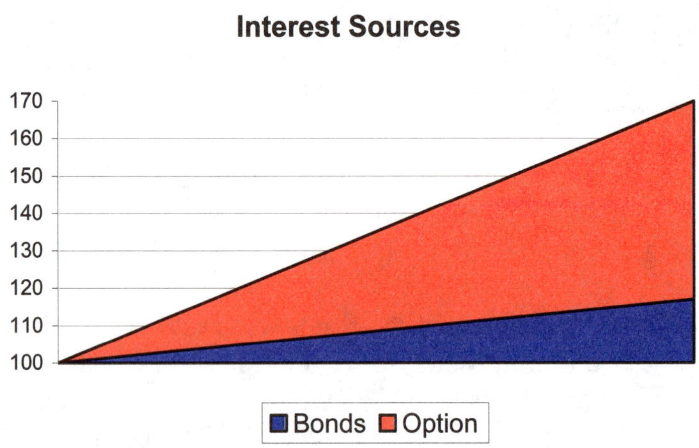

The $1.17 from the sale of the bonds is added to the 53 cents from the sale of the option resulting in a return of $1.70 for each dollar of premium, representing total index annuity interest credited of 70%.

Although overly simplified, these are the concepts involved in an index annuity. There are many ways used to calculate how index movement becomes index credited and we'll examine those at length in the next chapter. Now we'll look at other elements in the index annuity world.

Index-Linked Tradeoffs

This section introduces the fact that there are different ways to structure the index-linked interest of the annuity. We've chosen one alternative that results in the highest index-linked interest if the index grows more than the bonds. But someone else might like the idea of earning more than the guaranteed interest if the index only goes up a little and will settle for less on additional gains. Index annuities calculate index-linked interest in many different ways and are often structured to perform differently under different market conditions. The next chapter talks about the different crediting methods.

Annuity Term

In the example we said that index movement would be calculated over a nine-year period; this could be considered the index-linked term of the annuity. Other index annuities calculate index movement annually and these could be considered annuities with one-year terms. However, typically when someone talks about the term of an annuity they are referring to the length of time that surrender penalties may be charged. So, an annuity with surrender penalties for the first five years after issuance is often referred to as having a five-year term; an annuity with a ten year penalty period is said to have a ten year term.

But all of these references to term are misleading. The real term of an annuity is from the date of purchase until the contract maturity date. At maturity the accumulated value of an annuity must be paid out – either in a lump sum or as a regular income payments. The typical annuity maturity date usually occurs at age 85 or 90 or 100. In effect, the actual "term" of the annuity could be 20, 30 or 50 years depending upon how old the annuity buyer is at time of purchase. But that doesn't mean the annuity owner is locked into the contract for all those years. Although the insurer is required to meet the terms of the annuity until the maturity date, the annuity owner is free to walk away at any time.

Minimum Guaranteed Return

All fixed annuities offer a minimum guaranteed return. For fixed index annuities this minimum guarantee promises an accumulated value at least equal to the original principal by the end of the surrender period. Although most index annuities promise a minimum rate of 3% interest this rate is usually paid on less than the entire premium resulting in an effective rate that is less than 3%.

Minimum Guaranteed Accumulated Return @ 3% Of Premium

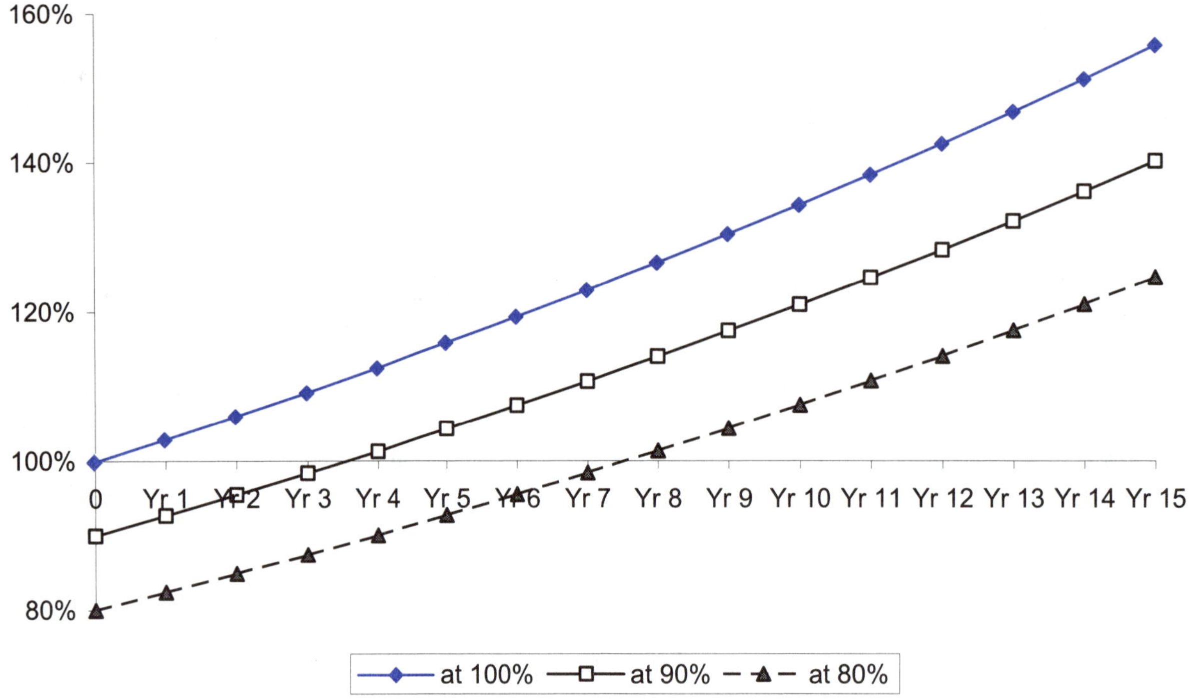

Minimum Guaranteed Return
Effective Interest Rate Is Less Than 3% If Based On Less Than 100% Of Premium
And Is Almost Always Credited At The End Of The Surrender Period And Not Each Year

A lower minimum return may provide the potential for a higher overall return because less of the premium dollar is needed to provide the return, leaving more money for index-lined interest. As the length of time increases, the minimum guarantee becomes less important because the index has more time to perform. Whether you select a higher or lower guarantee is a matter of personal preference.

Effective Annual Return @ 3% Interest Compounded On											
Premium	5 Yrs	6 Yrs	7 Yrs	8 Yrs	9 Yrs	10 Yrs	11 Yrs	12 Yrs	13 Yrs	14 Yrs	15 Yrs
@ 100%	3.00%	3.00%	3.00%	3.00%	3.00%	3.00%	3.00%	3.00%	3.00%	3.00%	3.00%
@ 90%	0.85%	1.21%	1.46%	1.65%	1.80%	1.92%	2.02%	2.10%	2.17%	2.23%	2.28%
@ 80%	negative	negative	negative	0.17%	0.48%	0.73%	0.93%	1.10%	1.25%	1.37%	1.48%

A few index annuities do not state a specific surrender charge, but instead base the net surrender value on the minimum guaranteed value. Although it may not be called a surrender charge the effect is the same.

For example, the minimum guaranteed value based on 3% interest compounding on 90% is 90% during the first contract year, 92.7% during the second, 95.5% during the third and 98.3% during the fourth year. This is really a *de facto* declining penalty of 10%, 7.3%, 4.5% and 1.7% for the first four years of the contract.

Surrender Charges

All fixed index annuities charge a penalty if the policy is cashed in prior to the end of the surrender period. Depending on the policy selected, surrender periods vary in length from one to eighteen years and penalties can be as high as 25% of initial premium. Surrender penalties do not usually apply if the policy is cashed in due to death of the owner or if the policy is annuitized. A typical surrender charge is expressed as either a percentage of the accumulated value of the annuity or a percentage of the original premium. Although index annuity principal is protected from market risk, most index annuities would return less than the original premium if surrendered too early.

Why are there surrender penalties? There are costs involved in issuing an annuity contract and the insurance company wants to ensure these costs are recovered if the annuity buyer cashes in the policy.

What Happens After The Surrender Period Is Over?

For most index annuities nothing happens when the surrender period ends, except there are no more charges on withdrawals. Annuities using term end point designs, which are discussed in the next chapter, may begin a multiple year period with new surrender charges, or they may not.

Reading Annual Statements

The annual statements for annual reset structured annuities tend to look like fixed rate annuity statements with one big difference. Almost every index annuity will show zero interest – not the minimum guaranteed rate – if the index movement is flat or negative. The minimum guarantee only comes into effect if the overall period return is lower, and then minimum interest is retroactively calculated. An annual reset structured annuity might show 7% interest in year 1, 0% interest in year 2, and then 9% in year 3.

Statements from term end point styled annuities are a different matter because interest is usually not credited until the end of the term. So, even if the index were up 40% the first year the statement would only reflect the minimum guaranteed interest. Most insurers also provide a kind of running summary of how their annuity is hypothetically performing if the term ended at the point in time.

It's a good idea to review a sample annual statement at the time of purchase to avoid future surprises.

Why A Fixed Index Annuity Isn't A Variable Annuity

In Chapter 1 I listed the three SEC "safe harbor" guidelines that would ensure an annuity is considered a fixed insurance product and not a security. But the real reasons why fixed annuities are separate and distinct from variable annuities are more fundamental.

Fixed Annuities Don't Have Fees

The way a fixed annuity credits interest may best be compared with the way a bank credits certificate of deposit interest. The bank says they will pay 4% interest on the CD. Okay, what are the bank's fees and expenses on this CD? If your answer is you cannot tell and it doesn't matter because all you really care about is the final rate you get on your money, the same logic applies to fixed annuities.

The insurance company doesn't deduct a management fee and share a net return with the customer. Instead, just like the bank, the insurer pays a fixed return, and this may be stated as a fixed rate or as fixed participation in an index.

Might some banks have lower operating costs or higher revenues than another and thus offer a higher rate? Yes, and an insurer could spend less on office supplies than another insurer and thereby ultimately be able to pay a higher rate on fixed annuities. But I don't know how you translate all of this into fees?

Do some annuities have fees? Yes. These are called variable annuities and they work a lot like mutual funds.

Fixed Annuities Are Not Variable Annuities

A fixed rate annuity pays a stated rate of interest that is no less than the minimum guaranteed rate of interest. A fixed index annuity pays a minimum rate of interest and bases the crediting of excess interest on the movement and participation in an external index. With a fixed index annuity the rate of participation in the index for the crediting period is fixed and known; the minimum guaranteed interest rate is fixed and known; the only unknown is how the index will move. Neither fixed rate nor fixed index annuities can lose principal or credited interest if the stock market goes down

►Variable annuity principal is subject to market risk. Fixed annuity principal is not subject to market risk.

►Variable annuity returns may be lost due to market risk. Fixed annuity credited interest cannot be lost due to market risk.

►Variable annuities have mortality charges and management fees. Fixed annuities do not charge mortality and management fees.

►Variable annuities do not pay minimum interest rates. Fixed annuities do credit minimum guaranteed interest rates.

A fixed annuity is an accumulation vehicle. It should be compared on that basis with other savings instruments.

Fixed Annuities Are Not Subject To Capital Gain Taxes

Savings vehicles are subject to ordinary income tax, not capital gain tax. Fixed annuities, bank savings accounts, savings bonds aren't capital investments; they are interest paying savings instruments.

Fixed Annuities Pay Fixed Annuity Returns

Fixed annuities aim for savings instrument-like returns while providing savings instrument-like protection of principal. Once again, variable annuities and mutual funds are investments; certificates of deposit and fixed annuities are savings instruments. .

If A Dog Quacks, It's A Duck

There are three SEC Safe Harbor guidelines used to determine whether or not an annuity is a security. The first is does an insurance commissioner regulate the company issuing the annuity. The second is does the company assume the investment risk. These seem to be pretty straightforward; it's the third guideline that can be a little confusing.

The third requirement is that the annuity not be marketed primarily as an investment. Now think about that. We have a fixed annuity issued by an insurance company. The customer is not subject to investment risk, in fact the insurance company guarantees both principal and credited interest against investment loss. And investment terms are used to market everything from "invest in your education at our college" to "this fine automobile will provide an exceptional return", and yet colleges are not required to hand out prospectuses detailing the risks of a college education nor are car salespeople required to register with the NASD. But for some reason a fixed annuity can be magically transformed into a security if you speak the wrong incantation. But since I do not write the rules, here is a partial list of what to say and not to say.

- Stress the principal guarantee of the annuity
- Stress the minimum guaranteed interest return
- Mention the annuitization options
- Mention the death benefit
- Emphasize that annuities are long term savings vehicles
- Emphasize that the annuity owner is not directly or indirectly investing in the market
- Don't compare an index annuity with a security, instead contrast the index annuity with a security
- Don't talk about investment performance, instead talk about credited interest
- State the annuity is backed by an insurance company
- State the annuity is not a security or investment, but a fixed annuity

Selecting An Index Carrier

Financial Strength

Pick a carrier with finances you feel comfortable with. If you like to use third party ratings, then pick a carrier evaluated by a rating service you like and define the minimum ratings you will accept. I personally look at a lot of elements when I am evaluating insurance companies and I might feel a "B+" carrier offered the same relative safety as one rated "A+", but that's me.

Renewal History

I strongly believe that the carrier's treatment of renewal rates in much more important than the crediting method, or even the index performance, in realizing the ultimate interest credited. It's one thing to have low index participation because of market forces, it is another to get intentionally nicked with poor index participation.

By renewal history I do not mean interest credited to the policy, I mean the degree of index participation applied to index movement that results in interest credited. An index annuity could have a couple years of high interest credited to the policy and still have uncompetitive renewal rates, because a high rolling stock market offset poor rates, but being lucky in the market cannot offset poor renewal rates forever. At the other end, very good renewal rates could find a bad market and produce poor interest returns. Most index annuities produced zero returns in the years of the millennium bear market, but that was not a reflection of their renewal rates. You need to see if the annuity's renewal participation rates or caps or yield spreads are fair. I determined fairness by developing the Advantage Index Participation Rate Indicator model to measure and compare financial market and renewal rate correlation. You may wish to use an easier approach and simply ask if renewal rates are comparable with new money rates.

One solution to renewal rate risk is to avoid annuities that can change any aspect of their index crediting during the surrender period. This works with annuities with term end point crediting methods because the product pricing can to a large part be worked out at policy issue. But locking in all moving parts of an annual reset structure can be so expensive that it makes the product uncompetitive.

The insurance company needs the flexibility to change index participation factors because financial markets change.

Almost every index annuity using annual or biennial reset methods has at least one part that can move during the surrender period. The annuity may guarantee the participation rate for the life of the contract, but the cap can change. Or the cap and participation rate are locked, but the yield spread can change. Even if products have limits on minimum caps or maximum spreads, forced crediting at these limitation levels would produce terrible returns.

The reality is the insurance company needs the flexibility to change annual reset index participation because financial markets change. You do not want to lock the insurance company into a situation where they might be placed in financial jeopardy – forcing a carrier to go belly up is worse than getting a 20% participation rate one year. In addition, if the product pricing environment improves, this flexibility gives the carrier the ability to raise index participation at renewal. And before anyone goes "yeah right, an insurance company actually raising renewal rates" I have been collecting renewal data and every carrier furnishing their renewal data has raised renewal rates at some point in the past.

How do you determine how carriers will treat you at future renewals? See how they've treated their customers in the past. I look at three things:

Will the carrier provide renewal information? If there is a renewal history and the carrier will not furnish it, don't do business with the carrier. You do not need the rate of every policy ever issued; a representative sample is sufficient.

Does the renewal rate reflect market changes? The carrier does not need to raise and lower index participation every time market volatility changes, but if the carrier cut participation when pricing costs went up then the carrier should also raise participation if conditions improve.

Did the carrier keep their promises? A promise could be a company spokesperson saying that they will not change rates for five years, even though the annuity contract permits annual changes – if they drop the rate in year three they broke their promise. Or a promise could be stating a second year "base rate" after a higher initial year rate – unless pricing conditions have worsened the carrier needs to renew at the base rate to keep their promise. Carriers need to keep their promises.

What if the annuity does not have a renewal history? Index products have been around less than a decade and many carriers have very limited or no index annuity renewal histories. If there's insufficient index annuity history look at their fixed rate annuity renewals. If a carrier has treated customers fairly in the past, it's a promising sign.

Questions To Ask

- What crediting parts move before the end of the surrender period and how often can they change?
- What is the minimum guaranteed return and is it credited annually or calculated at the end of the surrender period?
- Is interest compounded annually?
- Give me an example of how the cash surrender value calculated.
- If there is a cap, is it an index or interest cap? What would be the interest credited if the index went up 8%, 14% and 24%?
- What is your renewal history?
- What happens to the policy after the surrender period is over (any new charges)?

Cheat Sheet

- Although every index annuity has a minimum guaranteed interest rate, the interest is usually calculated on <u>less</u> than 100% of the premium received.
- The minimum guarantee is normally calculated retroactively over the entire term and only applies if the total interest for the entire period is less than the guarantee. If the calculated index gain was zero for a year, the contract would record 0% interest.
- Most insurance companies provide the potential for index-linked interest by buying options on the underlying index. An option gives you the right - not the obligation, to buy or sell something within a period of time.
- The index annuity owner does not directly participate in the market. The insurer provides the potential for index-linked interest by buying options; however, most of the premium is invested in bonds. The combination of bonds and options is a conservative approach.
- It is not magic. The degree of index participation depends on general interest rates and option prices. Higher interest rates and lower option prices means index participation may go up; lower interest rates and higher option prices push index participation down.
- A fixed index annuity is a fixed annuity and not a security. One should emphasize the insurance attributes of the annuity.
- The integrity of the insurer is much more important than the crediting method.

What Can Go Wrong?

- Stock Market can be flat or go down for a prolonged period
- Unforeseen political and economic developments can negatively affect the value of stocks in the index and thereby lower the value of the index
- Interest Rate environment can be so low index annuity participation stinks
- Option Prices can be so high index annuity participation stinks
- Economics are fine, but carrier management decides to increase company profits by cutting renewal rates
- Economics are fine, but carrier pricing people did not hedge index annuity properly so renewal rates stay at guaranteed minimum for years
- Annuity Buyer doesn't understand why return is less than expected and sues agent
- SEC decides index annuities are unregistered securities and goes after carriers and agents
- Insurance Company can go out of business
- This List doesn't cover everything and something else goes wrong

Discussion Questions

1. Is a high minimum guarantee better than a low minimum guarantee?

2. What type of economic conditions would be most favorable for index annuities?

3. What do you feel are the key points in selecting an insurance company?

Chapter Quiz

1. Conceptually, a dollar of index annuity premium could be separated into three parts

A. Expenses, guaranteed, index-linked
B. Expenses, safety, options
C. Costs, safety, growth
D. Commissions, costs, capital

2. Risks facing the index annuity owner include

A. Losses from index ownership
B. Obligations from buying options
C. Earning a lower interest rate than another fixed annuity might have earned
D. None of the above

3. You buy an option for a cost of $2 giving you the right to buy XYZ stock for $50 a share. At the end of the option period XYZ stock is $40 a share. How much did you lose?

A. $2
B. $8
C. $10
D. $12

4. Which of the following scenarios would cause index participation to fall?

A. Rising interest rates, falling option prices
B. Falling interest rates, rising option prices
C. Both A and B
D. Neither A nor B

5. If the total minimum guaranteed return was 20% and the index-linked interest for the period was 60%, how much total interest would the typical index annuity credit?

A. 20%
B. 40%
C. 60%
D. 80%

Chapter 3 – Crediting Methods

There are really only two ways to credit index-linked interest to an annuity. One can either measure index movement over a year or two – an annual reset method, or one can measure index movement over a period of years – a term end point method. And yet, there are currently 40 methods used to calculate how index movement becomes interest credited.

Crediting Methods of the *Annuitus Indexia*

Index Annuity Crediting Methods

Term End Point
Term End Point Averages Final 12 Months
Term End Point Averages Final 52 Weeks
Term End Point Averages Final 52 Weeks with Maximum Cap
Term High Point (High Water Mark)
Term Yield Spread Averages Final 12 Months
Term Two Step Capped Averages Final 12 Months
Term Average Annual High Points
Term Average Highest Anniversary
Term Annual Average w/o Interval Crediting
Annual Reset Point-to-Point (Absolute)
Annual Reset Point-to-Point, Simple Interest
Annual Reset Point-to-Point w/ Index-Gross Cap
Annual Reset Point-to-Point w/ Interest-Net Cap
Annual Reset Point-to-Point w/ Minimum Yearly Crediting
Annual Reset Point-to-Point w/ Yield Spread & Administration Fee
Annual Reset Average Month Values
Annual Reset Average Monthly Negative Values
Annual Reset Average Month Values w/ Yield Spread
Annual Reset Average Month Values w/ Yield Spread & Participation Rate
Annual Reset Average Month Values w/ Yield Spread & Gross Cap
Annual Reset Average Month Values w/ Yield Spread & Net Cap
Annual Reset Average Month Values Rebalanced Indexes
Annual Reset Average Month Values w/ Yield Spread & Premium Bonus
Annual Reset Average Daily Values
Annual Reset Average Daily Negative Values
Annual Reset Average Daily Values, Simple Interest
Annual Reset Average Daily Values w/Yield Spread
Annual Reset Average Daily Values w/Yield Spread & Premium Bonus
Annual Reset Binary Crediting
Annual Reset Fixed Rate w/ Equity Component
Annual Reset Monthly Cap w/o Interval Crediting
Biennial Reset Average Daily Values w/ Yield Spread
Biennial Reset Average Month Values w/ Yield Spread & Cap
Biennial Reset Point-to-Point w/ Yield Spread & Participation Rate
Step Forward, Step Back
Triennial Reset Monthly Cap w/o Interval Crediting

This chapter illustrates how all of the major index crediting methods work. In the next chapter I will examine the good and bad aspects of the different methods.

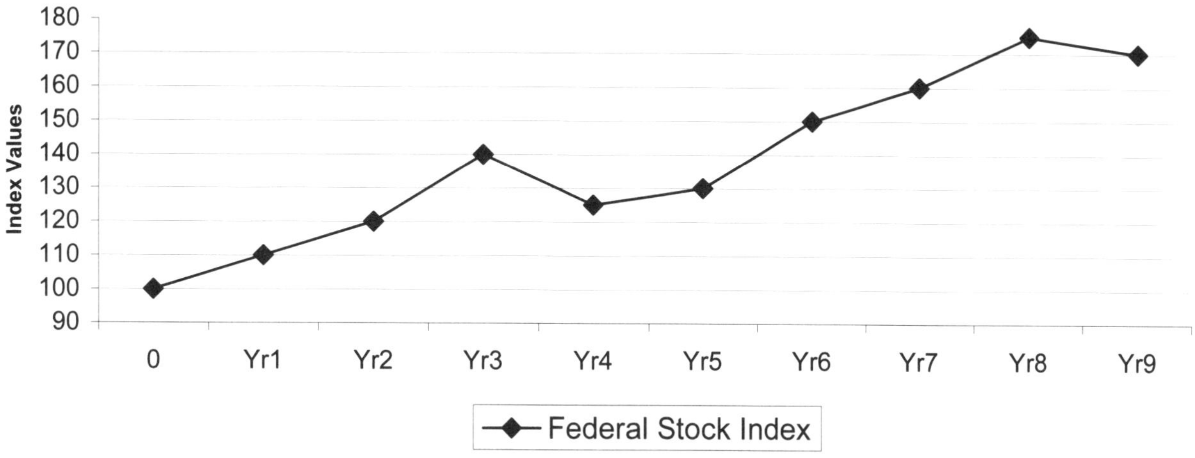

Term End Point (Term Point-to-Point)

A term end point structure measures index movements over a period greater than one or two years.

We have decided to buy an index annuity. We will earn index-linked interest based on the performance of the Federal Stock Index, which is currently at an index level of 100. The insurance company says that at the end of nine years they will credit the greater of the minimum guarantee or 100% of any index-linked interest earned calculated by dividing the ending index value by the beginning index value.

(170 /100) - 1 = 70% Index Gain

70% x 100% participation = 70%

70% = Total Interest Earned

It is now the end of year nine and the Federal Stock Index is at a level of 170. The index annuity divides the current index level by the starting index level and multiples the gain by our original premium. We earned a total of 70% interest for the nine years.

What if the index difference had been negative because the ending index was at a lower level than when we began? The index annuity would credit the minimum guaranteed return.

Term End Point Interest is neither calculated nor credited annually.

A typical term end point index annuity only credits interest realized from index movements at the end of the term. Interest is <u>not</u> calculated and credited annually. Therefore, if the annuity owner surrendered the contract prior to the end of the term they would not usually receive any interest based on positive index movements.

In our chart the Federal Stock Index has reached a level of 140 by the end of year 3 representing a 40% increase in the index from the day the annuity was purchased. If the annuity is then surrendered, how much of this gain does the annuity share in? The almost always answer if the annuity used a term end point crediting structure would be zero, zilch, nada.

Term end point methods do not calculate and credit gain until the end of the period. However, almost every index annuity will treat death as the end of the period and calculate any index gain at that point.

What Happens To Index Gains If I Die?

If you die before the end of the surrender period almost every index annuity will use the greater of the minimum guaranteed value or the accumulated value on the last policy anniversary. With a term end point method, they'll treat the last policy anniversary as the end of the period and calculate interest based on that value, but a few will use the date of death as the end of the period for calculations, and a few will only give the minimum guaranteed return.

Participation Rate

Actual Index Movement = 70%

If Participation Rate	Then Credited Interest
120%	84%
100%	70%
80%	56%
60%	42%

The degree to which one participates in any calculated index gains may be expressed as a percentage. In this example we received 100% of the calculated interest movement. Another way of saying this is that the participation rate was 100%. The participation rate reflects the cost of linking index gains to the annuity and may be more or less than 100%.

Variations - Averaging

A term end point method calculates index movement from a start point to an end point some years away, but only one index annuity on the market uses the actual sole index value on the final day of the period. Every other term end point structured annuity uses an average of the final year's index values as an end point. Averaging of index values means the average final value probably won't reflect the actual final value of the index on that last day.

The next chart takes the index values for the ninth year from the previous chart and magnifies it to show the monthly index movements. You can see the end value of 170, which we used for our calculation.

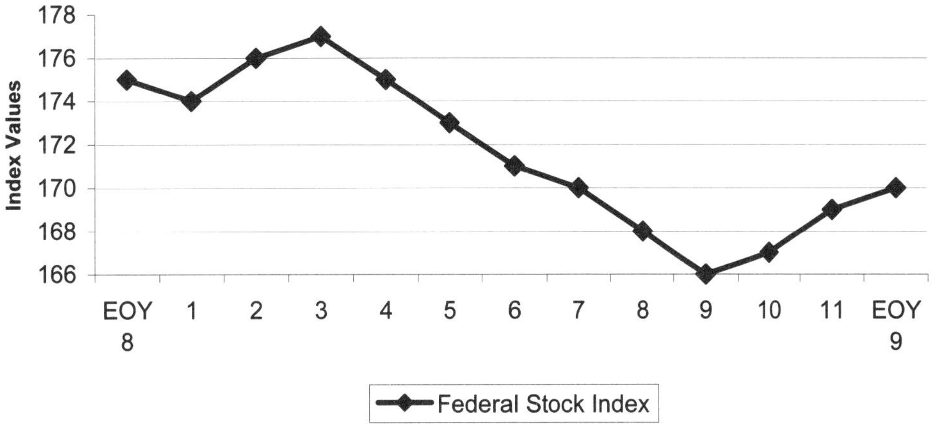

But what if we instead used the monthly average of the final year's values for the period as our end point. If we add up all twelve values and divide by twelve we get a number of 171.33. If we now calculate our index-linked gain based on this new number [(171.33/100) -1 = 71.33%] we find that averaging of the final year's monthly values resulted in a slightly higher value than using the absolute end point. Annuities with term end point structures average the final year's months, weeks, days or final quarter.

Variations - Caps

Insurance companies usually buy options to provide the index linking of interest. The seller of the option is hoping the index increase is less than the money they received from the insurance company to participate in any increase. The greater the exposure the option seller has to unlimited increases in the index, the greater the cost of the option. And the greater the cost of the option the less of the option the insurer can buy, thus resulting in lower participation in index gains.

A cap on index gains lessens the seller's exposure to potential losses and thereby reduces the cost of the option. An index annuity might only be able to offer an 80% participation rate if the potential gains are unlimited, but could offer 100% participation if the cap is double your money back. Caps maximize gains in fair and good markets and stifle gains in great markets.

High Point Term (High Water Mark)

The first successful index annuity used a high point term, also known as high water mark, crediting method. I consider a high point term structure as a type of term end point method with one very important difference. The difference is the ending index number is the higher of the end of the period value or the highest previous anniversary value.

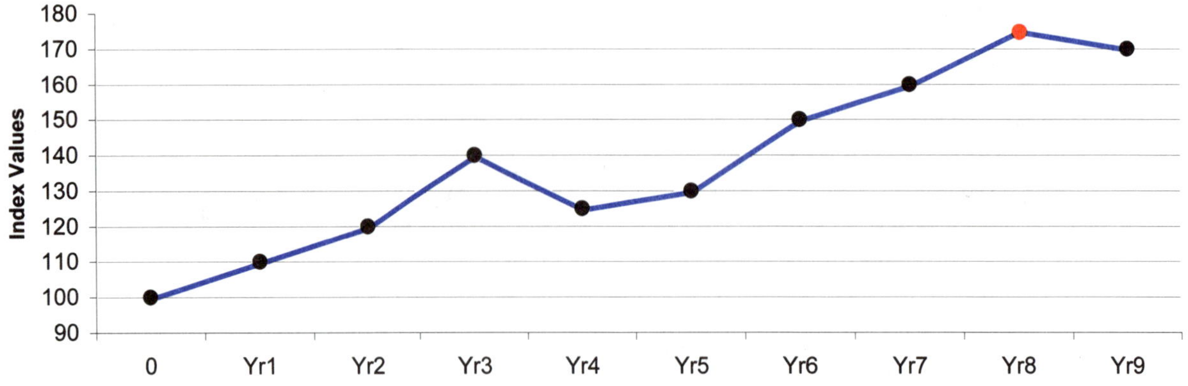

The Federal Stock Index began at a level of 100 and was at 170 nine years later. But the highest value reached on a contract anniversary was 175 on the eighth anniversary (the red dot). The high point term method would base the gain calculation on the higher 175 value rather than the lower 170 end value, and record a total index gain of 75% [(175/100) -1 = 75%]. The index gain would then be multiplied by the participation rate to determine interest credited to the contract.

If the term high point method does a better job of protecting against late period index losses than term end point methods, then why not always use term high point method? The reason is it is more expensive for the insurance company to provide the protection of the high point term method because the cost of the options is higher, and so index participation would be lower than it would be for term end point structures. Of course, if the index does decline at the end of the period the high point term benefit could more than offset the lower participation.

Term Yield Spread (Term Asset Fee)

Another term end point variation is the term yield spread structure. This structure calculates the total gain for the index over the period, determines the annualized return, deducts a spreads from the annualized return to find the index annuity annualized return, then compounds the annualized return to determine the index annuity credited interest.

The Federal Stock Index began at a level of 100 and was at 170 nine years later for a total gain of 70%. A nine-year gain of 70% represents an annualized gain of 6.07%. If there was a 1% yield spread, the carrier would deduct 1% from the index annualized gain of 6.07% and credit an annual interest rate of 5.07%. If you compound 5.07% for nine years the total return becomes 56.11%.

An index annuity asset fee or yield spread is in no way, shape, or form the same as a variable annuity asset fee or mutual fund asset fee. The index annuity "spread" or "fee"is simply another way of saying participation rate. The insurance company <u>does not</u> receive the spread. And the "spread" can never result in a negative value because the lowest return an index annuity pays is zero.

Term yield spread methods usually average the final year's index values, may have a cap on credited interest, or may use the highest contract anniversary level as the end point.

Which approach results in the greatest credited interest to the owner – participation rate or yield spread? It depends. Usually the participation rate method produces more credited interest in fair markets, the yield spread approach maximizes returns in great markets, and they come out about the same in good markets.

Term Two-Step (Stepped Participation)

Another term end point variation is the term two-step. This method credits a higher participation rate on initial index movement and a lower rate on any additional movements.

The Federal Stock Index began at a level of 100 and was at 170 nine years later for a total gain of 70%. A term two-step method might offer a participation rate of 100% on the first 50% of positive index movement and 50% thereafter. Therefore, this annuity would take the first 50% of the gain times the 100% participation rate for a first step subtotal of 50%. The annuity would then multiply any remaining gain – in this case 20% (70%-50%) by the second step participation rate of 50% (20% x 50%) to get a second step sub total of 10%. The first step subtotal (50%) is added to the second step subtotal (10%) to determine total interest credited.

Term Yield Spread		Term Two Step		Term End Point	
70%	Total Index Movement	70%	Total Index Movement	70%	Total Index Movement
6.07%	Annualized Interest Rate	50%	100% of first 50%	x 100%	Participation Rate
- 1.00%	Yield Spread	+ 10%	50% of additional gain		
5.07%	Index Annuity Interest Rate	60%	Index Annuity Interest	70%	Index Annuity Interest

Why use a two-step approach? It is a way for the insurer to lower exposure to a large increase in the index and keep costs down, without resorting to caps or lower participation rates. The approach maximizes returns in fair or good markets.

Annual Reset (Annual Ratchet)

A fixed rate annuity credits interest at the end of each contract year. Index annuities crediting interest each year are known as annual reset or annual ratchet methodologies. Annual reset methods begin the calculation of the next period's index movement using the closing value of the previous period.

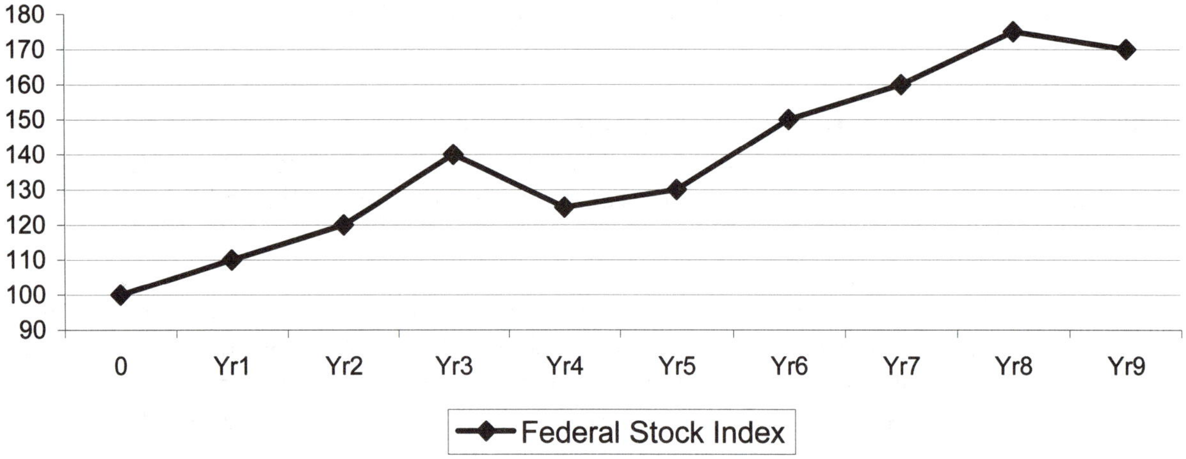

Annual Point-to-Point (APP)

Let's say that an index annuity credits 60% of any positive index movement at the end of the contract year. The Federal Stock Index level is 100 today. One year later the index has reached 110. The way this works is the beginning index value is subtracted from the ending index value (110-100 = 10) and the difference is divided by the beginning value to determine the percentage of index movement (10/100 = 0.10).

How Annual Reset Interest Is Calculated
Annual Point-to-Point

	110	Ending Index Value
-	100	Beginning Index Value
	10	Index Difference
/	100	Divided By Beginning Value
	.10	Index Movement
x	60%	Participation Rate
	6%	Interest Earned

We said our index annuity participates in 60% of any positive movement, so we multiply the percentage of index movement by 60% to determine the actual interest earned by the annuity, which is 6%.

What if the index difference had been negative? If the index difference is negative an annual reset treats it as zero positive interest.

This example shows the way an annual point-to-point crediting method works. The insurance company says in advance to what extent the index annuity will participate in the coming year's index movement. This participation rate is applied to any positive movement produced by the index.

Annual Yield Spread (Asset Fee)

Participation in an index can be expressed as a percentage – like the 60% participation rate used above, or we could deduct an "asset fee" or "yield spread" from the index movement to determine actual interest credited to the index annuity.

Instead of saying that the annuity will credit interest equal to 60% of any positive index movement the insurer could say that 100% of the index movement will be credited minus a 4% "asset fee".

If the index movement were 10% deducting a 4% fee would give us 6% interest – the same credited interest than the 60% participation rate provided.

How Annual Reset Interest Is Calculated
Annual Yield Spread

	110	Ending Index Value
-	100	Beginning Index Value
	10	Index Difference
/	100	Divided By Beginning Value
	.10	Index Movement
-	4%	Yield Spread
	6%	Interest Earned

So which is better, "times a participation rate" or "minus a yield spread"? It depends on the respective rates and the amount of index gain.

In this example the two approaches resulted in the same credited rate, but what if the index increased 15% and one product had a 60% participation rate and another deducted a 4% yield spread? Then the 60% participation rate would result in 9% interest while the 4% yield spread produced 11% interest (15% x 60% = 9%, 15% - 4% = 11%). If the index gained 5% the participation rate structure would credit 3% and the yield spread would credit 1% (5% x 60% = 3%; 5% - 4% = 1%). Yield spread methods can credit more in great markets; participation rate methods can credit more in fair markets.

"Asset fee" and "spread" are just another way of saying participation rate.

As I said before an index annuity asset fee or yield spread is not the same as a variable annuity asset fee or mutual fund asset fee. "Asset fee" and "spread" are just another way of saying participation rate. The insurance company does not receive the spread. And the "spread" can never result in a negative value because the lowest return an index annuity pays is zero.

As examples, if a variable annuity had a 4% asset fee and the index gained 3% the net to the account would be a loss of 1%; if the index lost 3% the net to the account after the 4% asset fee would be a negative 7%. However, if the same numbers were applied to an index annuity the net effect would be 0% because an index annuity cannot lose credited interest.

At These Index Gains	A Participation Rate of 40%	50%	60%	70%	80%
2%	1.2%	1.0%	0.8%	0.6%	0.4%
4%	2.4%	2.0%	1.6%	1.2%	0.8%
6%	3.6%	3.0%	2.4%	1.8%	1.2%
8%	4.8%	4.0%	3.2%	2.4%	1.6%
10%	6.0%	5.0%	4.0%	3.0%	2.0%
12%	7.2%	6.0%	4.8%	3.6%	2.4%
14%	8.4%	7.0%	5.6%	4.2%	2.8%
16%	9.6%	8.0%	6.4%	4.8%	3.2%
18%	10.8%	9.0%	7.2%	5.4%	3.6%
20%	12.0%	10.0%	8.0%	6.0%	4.0%
Is Equal To The Above Yield Spreads					

If They Are Not Really Fees, Why Are They Called That?

Because agents wanted an easier story to tell. When index annuities were introduced a combination of strong bond yields and low option costs enabled insurers to offer high participation rates, often near 100%. When market forces pushed participation rates lower agents asked the insurers if there was a way to keep the rate at 100%. One alternative was to restate the participation rate as a spread. As the graph above illustrates if the index increases 10%, a 4% yield spread provides the same credited interest as a 60% participation rate. And many consumers understand the concept of asset fees, because they own investments. However, an index annuity spread or fee is in truth another way of saying "participation rate".

Averaging

Over 75% of available index annuities average at least some portion of index values. We will look at an index annuity with an annual reset methodology that applies a participation rate to the monthly average of the year's index values. The participation rate in any index increase is 100%.

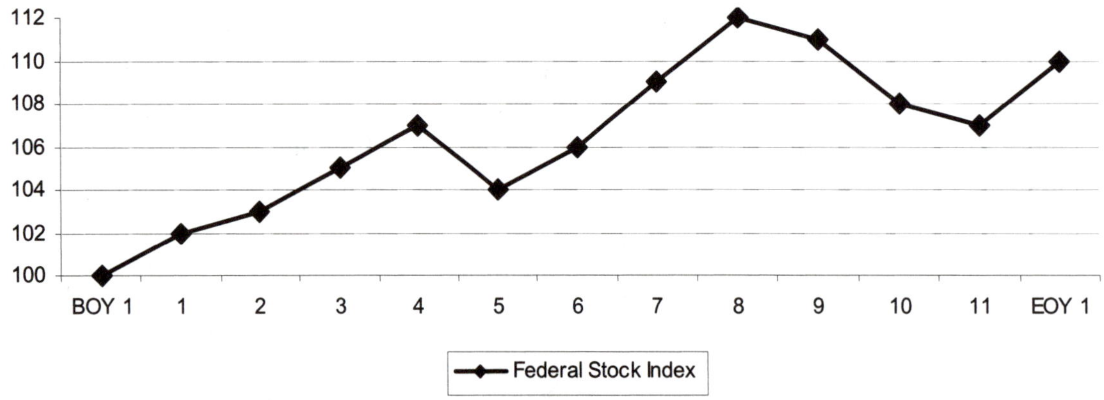

In this chart we have magnified the index values for the first contract year to show the monthly index movements. The year finished at 110, which we used for annual point-to-point calculations.

The Federal Stock Index closing monthly values for the first year are listed below. Although we ended the year at 110, if you add up all the monthly values and divide by 12 you get an averaged ending value of 107.

How Annual Reset Interest Is Calculated

Monthly Averaging

Beginning Value	100
Value Period 1	102
Value Period 2	103
Value Period 3	105
Value Period 4	107
Value Period 5	104
Value Period 6	106
Value Period 7	109
Value Period 8	112
Value Period 9	111
Value Period 10	108
Value Period 11	107
Value Period 12	110
Average End	107

107	Average End Value
- 100	Begin Index Value
7	Index Difference
/ 100	Divided By Begin Value
. 07	
x 100%	Participation Rate
7%	Interest Earned

Averaging always drive numbers to the middle. In a generally rising market averaging usually produces a lower value than an actual end point, in a falling market averaging generally produces a higher ending value than an actual end point.

If you think the index will be rising over the next year, and averaging produces a lower end value in a rising market than an actual ending point, then wouldn't you always want to go with the non-averaged crediting method? The answer is, it depends.

Crediting methods using averaging offer higher index participation. In this example 100% of the monthly index points produced an average end value of 107, or a 7% increase for the year. An annual point-to-point method uses the actual end point of 110, which represents a 10% increase for the year. But in our examples the annual point-to-point method has a participation rate of 60%, resulting in 6% interest credited to the annuity (10% x 60%). The monthly average method has a 100% participation rate, which gives 7% interest (7% x 100%). The averaging method produced higher net interest than the point-to-point method.

Caps

Another variation annual reset crediting structures may use are caps. A Cap is a ceiling or upward limit on the interest that may be credited to the annuity and may be used in conjunction with a participation rate or yield spread structure. A Cap usually reflects the maximum interest that can be credited to the annuity contract - an **Interest (Net) Cap** of 12% would mean that regardless of index movement the maximum interest credited for any one period is 12%. Another type of Cap is an **Index (Gross) Cap** which limits the amount of index movement to which a crediting method is applied - an Index Movement Cap of 12% would mean that any index movement above 12% is ignored.

Interest (Net) Cap of 12%		Index (Gross) Cap of 12%	
10% Index Movement x 60% Participation Rate 6% Interest Is 6%≤12%; Yes 6% Interest Credited 10% Index Movement - 3% Yield Spread 7% Interest Is 7%≤12%; Yes 7% Interest Credited	30% Index Movement x 60% Participation Rate 18% Interest Is 18%≤12%; No 12% Cap Credited 30% Index Movement - 3% Yield Spread 27% Interest Is 27%≤12%; No 12% Cap Credited	10% Index Movement Is 10%≤12%; Yes 10% x 60% Participation Rate 6% Interest 6% Interest Credited 10% Index Movement - 3% Yield Spread 7% Interest	30% Index Movement Is 30%≤12%; No 12% x 60% Participation Rate 7.2% Interest 7.2% Cap Credited 12% Index Movement - 3% Yield Spread 9% Interest

It is very important to note whether it is an interest cap or an index cap. An interest cap says this is the most interest that will be credited; an index cap says this is the most index gain that will be recognized. If you mistake an index (gross) cap for an interest (net) cap you could be negatively surprised.

Caps are used to boost participation rates or minimize yields spreads. Since they limit upside exposure, the cost of providing the index-linked interest is less, so participation in gains up to the cap are higher. Caps enable one to get "more of most" instead of "less of more".

Because caps limit the maximum interest that could be credited to an index annuity the annuity buyer could feel they are missing out on potential gains. However, a cap on interest may help the annuity produce higher earnings.

Index annuities usually buy options on the index to create the potential for excess interest beyond the minimum guarantee. The sellers of the options have to pay off at whatever the market level is when the option is exercised, so the sellers bear the risk of a rising market. If the market only goes up a little, or if their exposure to market gains is limited, the sellers pay out less money. If they sell an option without an upward limit the sellers demand significantly more dollars for the option because they have substantially more risk. If the insurance companies have to pay more for options they cannot buy as many, so the participation rate they credit is lower.

Putting a cap on the potential increase in the value of the option means that the sellers have less risk, so a lower price is charged. Lower option prices means that the insurance company can buy more options and offer a higher participation rate.

Placing a cap on potential gains means the participation rate should be higher for the capped product than for the annuity without a cap. If index gains are modest the capped version will credit more interest. Which annuity will credit more? It depends on the relative rates and how often the interest ceiling is actually exceeded.

Say that one point-to-point annuity had a rate of 55% with no cap and another offers a 100% rate, but will credit a maximum return of 11% for the coming year. What this means is that in any year when the index growth exceeds 20% the non-cap annuity will produce a higher return. We determine this point by dividing the cap (11%) by the non-cap rate (55%). Conversely, whenever the index gains less than 20% the index annuity with a cap will have the higher return.

Index Gain	x 55%	x 100% with 11% Cap
22%	12.1%	11%
21%	11.6%	11%
20%	11.0%	11%
19%	10.5%	11%
18%	9.9%	11%

So which is best? If you plug in these rates and caps into the last fifty years and figure out the average hypothetical return for the two versions over all of these years the average returns are virtually identical!

Biennial Reset

A handful of companies calculate index movement over two years instead of one, and all of the methods and variations available to annual reset structures apply. It is less expensive to buy one two-year option than two successive one-year options, so index participation can usually be higher for a biennial reset.

Annuitization Requirement

Fewer than 2% of index annuities on the market require policy annuitization to receive index-linked interest earned. The minimum payout period is usually 5 years, but may be as long as 10 years and the minimum interest credited during payout can be as low as 2%.

Simple versus Compound Interest

Almost every index annuity using an annual reset structure compounds credited interest.

Length Of Rate Guarantee

In 2002 22% of the index annuities guaranteed the initial index participation factors for the full surrender period, 71% had the ability to reset at least one participation factor each contract year, and a few companies offered something in between. Term end point structures guarantee all moving parts for the multiple year index period. A few annuities with term end point designs have index periods shorter than the surrender period.

An annuity using an annual reset design almost always has at least one crediting part that can be changed prior to the end of the surrender period. The carrier may guarantee a 100% participation rate, but the cap or spread can change.

Most annuities with annual reset designs have at least one moving part that can change each year. An annuity may guarantee that the participation rate never changes, but the cap may be moved or the yield spread may be altered. This means that later caps, spreads or rates may be higher or lower.

The Cost Of Free Withdrawals

The vast majority of index annuities offer some form of surrender penalty free annual withdrawals; typically 10% of the accumulated value after the first contract year. However, taking money out of an index annuity early - whether the annuity uses a term end point or annual reset design - can kill the return. If you look at multiple year index periods the majority of the total gain for most periods are created by a few exceptional years. The index will increase 10%, then go up 7%, then maybe drop 15% and then go up 30%. If you make your withdrawal just before the year with the 30% increase, you have severely limited the total return. Taking money out of an index annuity early is like timing the market with a roulette wheel. Even if the annuity provides liquidity it should be treated as a long-term savings vehicle and with the knowledge that any withdrawals could hurt overall returns.

Vesting

Although the typical term end point structure does not lock in any gain until the end of the term, annuities using the term high point method typically vest a portion of the gain each year and make the vested gain available for withdrawal.

Premium Bonuses & Enhanced Rates

A number of annuities offer bonuses. These are usually applied to the premium and any interest crediting is based on the premium plus the bonus. A very few policies require annuitization to receive the premium bonus. There are also a few policies that apply what amounts to a persistency bonus, by crediting a retroactive premium bonus if the policy stays in force after the surrender period ends.

Annual reset structures may offer an enhanced first year participation rate, or reduced yield spread, that essentially represents a better rate than the index-linked pricing would permit. One point to be aware of is unlike a fixed rate annuity wherein the base rate is priced according to the insurer's current portfolio, the base fixed index participation rate relies on the price of options down the road at time of renewal.

Participation Floor

Many annual reset structures offer some crediting factor guarantees. These guarantees may say that the renewal participation rate can never go below X percent, or a cap may never be lower than Y, or a yield spread may never be greater than Z. These floors offer a degree of protection against uncompetitive renewal rates. However, most floors are so weak they offer little true renewal protection, but too strong a floor could cause losses for the insurer if future costs went too high.

Other Methods

The above methodologies are used in most of the available index annuities. Over 75% of the annuities sold use some degree of averaging, whether it is averaging the final year's index values in a term end point, or averaging the daily or monthly index values for annual reset calculations. A significant number of annuities apply ceilings or caps on maximum interest credited. And it's a pretty even split between structures that multiply index gains times a participation rate or deduct a yield spread.

Elements are often combined. Several annual reset structures use averaging of index values, have a cap, and either use a participation rate or a yield spread. One product uses both a participation rate and a yield spread and then deducts an administrative fee. There are several other crediting methods used.

Binary, Non-Negative Annual Reset

The index annuity will pay a stated interest rate if the index does not go down. That's it. If the index isn't lower at the end of the contract year the index will credit the declared rate.

Low Point Term (Low Water Mark)

A High Point Term method takes the highest anniversary index value and pushes it to the end of the period. A Low Point Term takes the lowest anniversary index value and pulls it to the start of the period. The Federal Stock index is at 100. One year later it has dropped to 90. A Low Point Term structure would change the starting index value from 100 to 90, because it is a lower value. The ideal scenario for this method would be on the eve of a bear market.

Term High Average Anniversary

This structure calculates a rolling annual average of monthly index values and uses the highest averaged anniversary value as an end point. It is <u>not</u> a high water mark methodology.

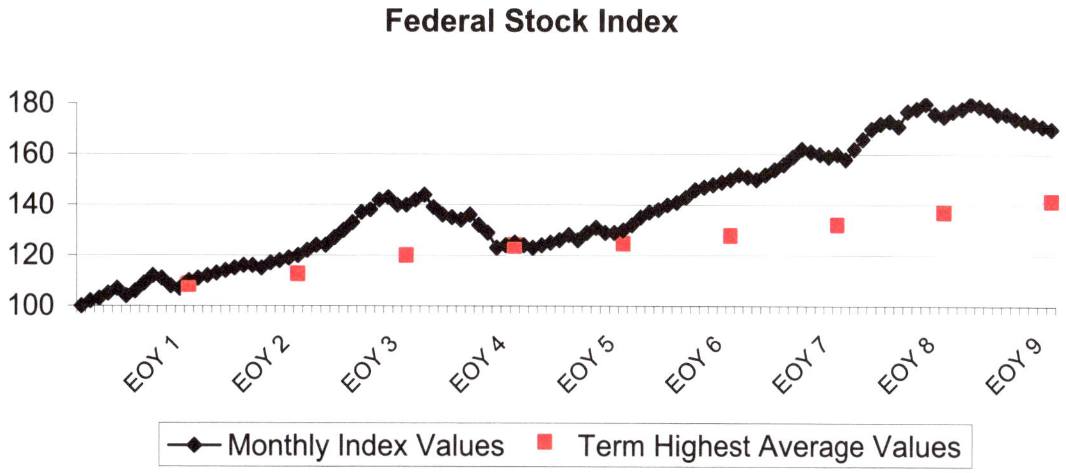

This method adds up the monthly index values, divides them by the cumulative months and uses the highest averaged value. If you tally up the monthly index values for year 1 the total is 1284; 1284 is divided by 12, producing a cumulative average value of 107. If you tally the monthly values for years 1 and 2 the total is 2670; 2670 divided by 24 months (2 Years) is 111.25. Since the cumulative averaged second year value is higher than the first, it becomes the new high value.

This calculation is done each year with the final averaged value compared against previous values to determine the highest. This example winds up with an end point value of 140.16 resulting in a realized index gain of 40.16% for the nine-year period (140.16/100-1). A participation rate would then be applied.

Annual Reset Fixed Rate with Equity Component (Equity Kicker)

There are a couple of variations to this theme currently in use. One method credits a fixed rate to a portion of the premium and the remainder participates in the index using an annual reset design. The other credits an annual fixed interest rate plus a percentage of term end point gains. For the second method the buyer typically selects a fixed rate ranging from 1% to 5% (the range of rates depends on the interest rate environment) and also participates in positive index movements over a four-year period. The higher the fixed interest rate selected the lower the participation rate applied to the index.

Each year the fixed rate is credited. At the end of the period any positive index gains are multiplied by the participation rate, and after some adjustments, the fixed index interest is added to the fixed rate interest.

Bond-Linked Interest With Base

Although there are a few annuities offering a bond index in addition to equity choices, that isn't what I mean. This crediting method links interest crediting to U.S. Treasury Notes. If the T-note rate is higher at policy anniversary, the annuity renewal rate is credited with a like increase. If the T-note rate is lower in subsequent years, the annuity rate goes down the same amount, but the annuity rate can never be less than the initial rate.

As an example say the initial annuity rate was 5.0%. One year from now the T-note yield had moved up 50 basis points. The second year annuity rate would be 5.5%. Let's say a year later T-note yields had fallen 1%. That would make the third year rate 4.5%, except the annuity rate can never be less than the initial rate, which was 5%.

Step Forward Step Back

How Interest Is Calculated
Step Forward Step Back

Beginning Value	100	2% Cap
Value Period 1	102	2.00%
Value Period 2	103	0.98%
Value Period 3	105	1.94%
Value Period 4	107	1.90%
Value Period 5	104	-2.80%
Value Period 6	106	1.92%
Value Period 7	109	2.00%
Value Period 8	112	2.00%
Value Period 9	111	-0.90%
Value Period 10	108	-2.70%
Value Period 11	107	-0.92%
Value Period 12	110	2.00%

2.00%+0.98%+1.94%+1.90%-2.80%+1.92%
+2.00%+2.00%-0.90%-2.70%-0.92%+2.00%

End 7.42% Interest Earned

One of the newest crediting methods is borrowed from a Wall Street principal protection security idea. It calculates gains and losses of the index on the monthly basis, adds up the monthly figures, and the final number is your interest for the period; the period's interest can never be less than zero. The maximum monthly gain recognized is subject to a cap, but losses are not subject to a cap.

If there was, say, a 2% cap a best scenario would be where the index increased 2% a month for twelve months and you received 24% interest for the year. A worst scenario would be a 2% cap on gains where the index increased, say, 40% in eleven months, and then fell back 22% in the 12th. The maximum possible gain for the eleven months is 22% (2% x 11), which would be offset by the 22% decline in the 12th, resulting in zero gain, even though the index was still up 18%.

Annual Resets – How It All Works

Here is a chart of the closing monthly index values for the nine-year period.

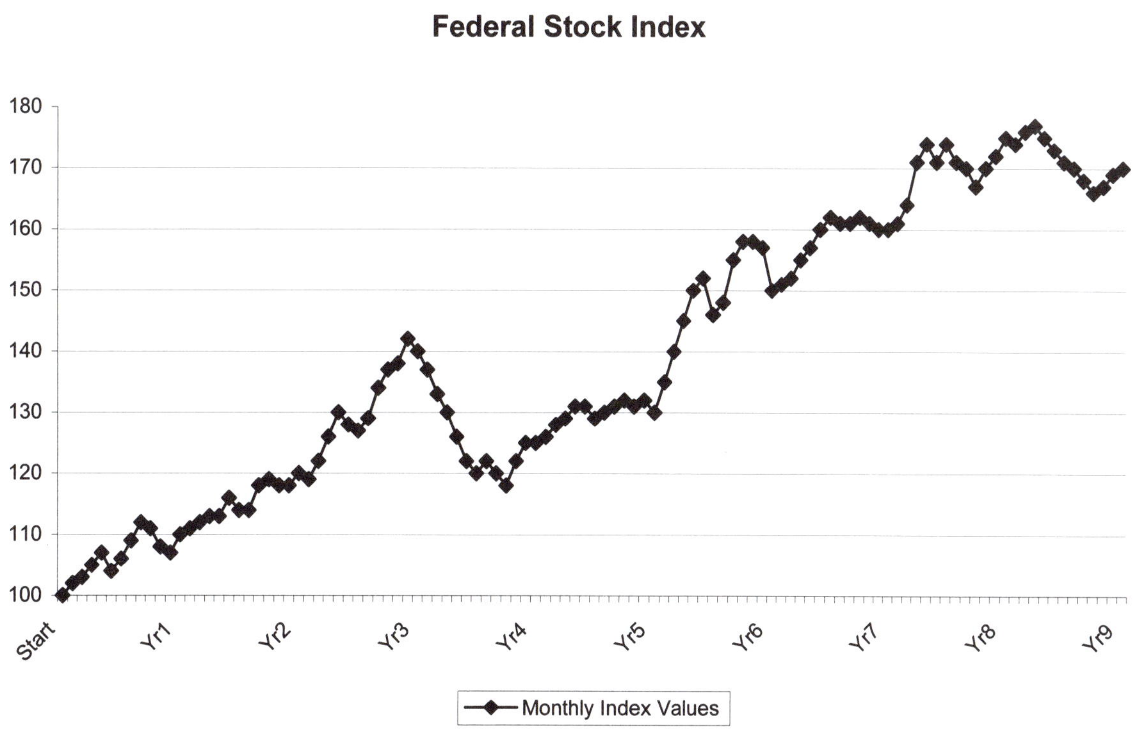

The yearly gains or losses of the index, and the annual closing index values, are these:

	Index Movement	Point-to-Point	Monthly Averaging
Yr 1	110	10.00%	7.00%
Yr 2	120	9.09%	5.00%
Yr 3	140	16.67%	9.17%
Yr 4	125	-10.71%	-10.71%
Yr 5	130	4.00%	4.00%
Yr 6	150	15.38%	15.00%
Yr 7	160	6.67%	5.67%
Yr 8	175	9.38%	6.25%
Yr 9	170	-2.86%	-2.10%

But since annual reset structures do not recognize negative years and begin calculating index movement using the previous year's closing value the chart becomes this:

	Index Movement	Point-to-Point	Monthly Averaging
Yr 1	110	10.00%	7.00%
Yr 2	120	9.09%	5.00%
Yr 3	140	16.67%	9.17%
Yr 4	125	0%	0%
Yr 5	130	4.00%	4.00%
Yr 6	150	15.38%	15.00%
Yr 7	160	6.67%	5.67%
Yr 8	175	9.38%	6.25%
Yr 9	170	0%	0%

And let's say we have the following methods and rates:

65% Annual Reset Point-to-Point, compounded
88% Annual Reset Monthly Averaged Values, compounded
100% Annual Reset Monthly Averaged Values less 1% Yield Spread, compounded
70% Annual Reset Point-to-Point with 13% Index (Gross) Cap, compounded
100% Annual Reset Point-to-Point with 7% Interest (Net) Cap, compounded

We would credit these yearly returns:

	65% P-to-P	88% Month Aver	Month Aver less 1% Spread	70% P-to-P w/13% Index Cap	100% P-to-P w/7% Interest Cap
Yr 1	6.50%	6.16%	6.00%	7.00%	7.00%
Yr 2	5.91%	4.40%	4.00%	6.36%	7.00%
Yr 3	10.84%	8.07%	8.17%	9.10%	7.00%
Yr 4	0%	0%	0%	0%	0%
Yr 5	2.60%	3.52%	3.00%	2.80%	4.00%
Yr 6	10.00%	13.20%	14.00%	9.10%	7.00%
Yr 7	4.34%	4.99%	4.67%	4.67%	6.67%
Yr 8	6.10%	5.50%	5.25%	6.57%	7.00%
Yr 9	0%	0%	0%	0%	0%

To determine the total return for the period we would compound the positive annual interest earned.

Pick The Best One

One usually selects an index annuity and knows the crediting method that will be used, at least the initial participation rate/yield spread/cap, and the only variable is how the index will move. Just for fun, I want you to select the index annuity you think will produce the highest return. But unlike the real world, we will leave nothing to chance

Here are nine index annuities and the crediting methods used. There are no moving parts, every crediting component is locked in and will not change, and we will even use the same rates for the five annuities from the previous section so you already know the interest credited. Which one produces the highest total return?

a. 80% Term End Point (Term Point-to-Point) period gain
b. 75% High Point Term (High Water Mark) period gain
c. 65% Annual Reset Point-to-Point, compounded
d. 88% Annual Reset Monthly Averaged Values, compounded
e. 100% Annual Reset Monthly Averaged Values less 1% Yield Spread, compounded
f. 70% Annual Reset Point-to-Point with 13% Index (Gross) Cap, compounded
g. 100% Annual Reset Point-to-Point with 7% Interest (Net) Cap, compounded
h.6.25% Binary, Non-Negative Annual Reset
i. 111% Term Average Highest Anniversary

And The Winner Is...

It is a trick question. Each index annuity earns a total return of 56% for the period.

Even though any index annuity crediting method could produce the highest return for a given period this example shows that you cannot choose an index annuity merely based on the highest rate, the highest cap, or the lowest spread. Different methodologies produce different results and react differently in different periods. The next chapter will help you in understanding how these crediting methods really work and help you select the index annuities that are right for the situation.

Summary

There are two main ways to credit index annuity interest. You either measure index movement over a year or two – an annual reset method, or you measure index movement over a period longer than a couple years – a term end point method.

Index movement may be calculated in dozens of different ways and any index methodology may result in the greatest return depending upon how the index moves and the degree of index participation. Because of all the variations you cannot simply pick the index annuity with the highest rate or lowest spread and assume you are getting the best one.

Addendum – Crediting Concepts

How many concepts need to be broached to explain the crediting methodology of a particular index annuity? If you understand how a fixed rate annuity works then the one new concept central to all index annuities is "This index annuity has a minimum guaranteed (or stated) interest rate of X% with the potential for excess interest based on the movements of an external index." The following is a list of all the variations of index annuity crediting concepts that might be needed to explain how the annuity credits interest. I found one needed to communicate five additional concepts, in addition to the central concept, to explain how the average index annuity works. A couple of annuities only required two variations to be mentioned; some required as many as eight variations be explained so one wouldn't be surprised by how the annuity performed.

A	Minimum or stated interest is not calculated and credited each year
B	Participates in less (or more) than 100% of index movement
C	Deducts a yield spread or asset fee
D	The maximum interest that can be earned is x% (cap)
E	Participation rate and/or spread and/or cap can be changed each year (or biennially)
F	Any gain is not fully credited until the end of the term (except death)
G	Annual index movement is based on daily or monthly averaged values
H	The minimum guaranteed interest rate is based on less than 100% of premium
I	End point of term is based on highest anniversary value
J	Index values for some part or all of the final year of the term are averaged
K	Must be annuitized to receive full index value
L	Annual interest is not compounded
M	Start point of term is based on lowest anniversary value
N	Deducts a spread from annualized term yield and recalculates interest
O	Averages all monthly values during term and uses highest anniversary as end point
P	Deducts an administrative fee
Q	Participation rate and/or spread and/or cap can be changed after five years
R	Gain is converted to annualized rate and a portion is deducted based on the result of multiplying the respective base rate by the participation rate
S	70% of account receives index-linked interest, 30% receives fixed rate
T	Participates in x% of index gain up to level y%, then participates in z%

Simply because one annuity's crediting method requires more explanation than another doesn't mean it is worse. As an example, the addition of a term high point variation to a term end point structure lowers the owner's risk of future market volatility harming returns. Or, the addition of a cap may reduce or eliminate the need for a yield spread and improve returns under certain market conditions.

Complexity is not a bad thing. My stereo system is much more complicated than the crystal radio I built as a boy, but the stereo does so much more. However, index annuities with fewer required concepts make it easier to at least begin listening to the music.

Basic Index Annuity Crediting Formulas

C = Cap
D = Declared Rate
E = Ending Index Value(s)
M = Index Movement
P = Participation Rate
Y = Yield Spread
S = Starting Index Value
R = Index Return
I = Interest Credited
n = number of periods
x = period

Simple (Binary, Non-Negative) Annual Reset

If $M \geq 0$ Then $I = D$

Term End Point

$(E - S)/S \times P = I$

Term Yield Spread

$(E/S)^{(1/n)} - 1 = R - Y = I$

Annual Reset Point-to-Point

$(E - S)/S \times P = I$ $\qquad$ $(E - S)/S - Y = I$

Annual Reset Point-to-Point with Interest (net) Cap

$(E - S)/S \times P = I$ $\qquad$ $I \leq C$ $\qquad$ $(E - S)/S - Y = I$ $\qquad$ $I \leq C$

Annual Reset Point-to-Point with Index (gross) Cap

$(E - S)/S = R \times P = I$ $\qquad$ If $R \geq C$ Then C

$(E - S)/S = R - Y = I$ $\qquad$ If $R \geq C$ Then C

Annual Reset, Monthly Average

$[(E^1+E^2+E^3...E^{12})/12 - S]/S \times P = I$ $\qquad$ $[(E^1+E^2+E^3...E^{12})/12 - S]/S - Y = I$

Annual Reset, Daily Average

$[\Sigma(E^n)/n - S]/S * P = I$

$[\Sigma(E^n)/n - S]/S - Y = I$

Cheat Sheet

- A typical term end point index annuity only credits interest realized from index movements at the end of the term. Interest is not calculated and credited annually.
- An index annuity asset fee or yield spread is in no way, shape, or form the same as a variable annuity asset fee or mutual fund asset fee. The index annuity "spread" is simply another way of saying participation rate. The insurance company does not receive the spread. And the "spread" can never result in a negative value because the lowest return an index annuity pays is zero.
- Averaging always drive numbers to the middle. In a generally rising market averaging usually produces a lower value than an actual end point, in a falling market averaging generally produces a higher ending value than an actual end point.
- If index movement is negative an annual reset structures treats it as zero positive interest.
- It's very important to note whether it is an interest cap or an index cap. An interest cap says this is the most interest that will be credited; an index cap says this is the most index gain that will be recognized. If you mistake an index (gross) cap for an interest (net) cap you could be negatively surprised
- An annuity using an annual reset design almost always has at least one crediting part that can be changed prior to the end of the surrender period. The carrier may guarantee a 100% participation rate, but the cap or spread can change.
- Even though any index annuity crediting method could produce the highest return for a given period this example shows that you cannot choose an index annuity merely based on the highest rate, the highest cap, or the lowest spread. Different methodologies produce different results and react differently in different periods.
- Annual reset methods reset. This means they use the index value at the end of the previous period. If the index fell during the previous period an annual reset structure would calculate future index movement from the lower starting value.

Discussion Questions

1. In what types of market is a yield spread method better than a participation rate method?

2. Is it better to have no moving parts when it comes to index crediting, or should the insurer have the flexibility to change? What are the pros and cons of each?

3. Is there a best overall index crediting method?

Chapter Quiz

1. An index has a starting value of 100 and an ending value of 152. The participation rate is 75% and the interest cap is 50%. What interest is credited to the annuity?

A. 37.5%
B. 39.0%
C. 50.0%
D. 137.5%

2. The index increases 20%. Annuity A has an 80% participation rate and an index cap of 12%. Annuity B has a 60% participation rate and an interest cap of 11%. Which annuity credits more interest?

A. Annuity A
B. Annuity B
C. The interest credited is the same
D. More information is needed

3. The crediting method that provides the least protection against index declines late in the surrender period is

A. Term End Point
B. Term High Point
C. Annual Reset
D. Binary Look Forward

4. An annual reset crediting method means

A. Interest calculated from positive index gains is credited annually
B. Credited interest cannot be lost
C. Years with negative index losses are treated as zero interest.
D. All of the above

5. If the index is going to be rising which crediting method would credit the most interest?

A. Annual Reset
B. Term High Point
C. Annual Reset
D. More information is needed

Chapter 4 – Evaluating Term End Point Methods

Building The Foundation

To compare different crediting methods you need to make certain basic assumptions. I do not declare that these assumptions are true, only that if they are false then all evaluation is a waste of time.

The first assumption is that at least the broad patterns of past stock market returns repeat. We can not predict how the stock market will perform in the next year, or the next five to fifteen years, but we will assume that long term general market trends hold true, which are that stock markets move in cycles – that is, they go up and down, but that the bias of the domestic stock market over the long term is up.

The second assumption is that pricing permits index annuities to participate in a meaningful percentage of index growth. For most of their existence the majority of index annuities have been able to offer policyowners 50% to near 100% of effective index performance, and this level of participation provided the potential for competitive returns. However, what if future pricing meant that index annuities were only able to offer 10%, 20% or 30% of actual index performance? At these rates even if the index grew 12% or 15% a year the annuities wouldn't be competitive. We have had periods where index annuity participation was not competitive, but to date these periods have been relatively brief. Over the long term index annuities need effective participation in at least 50% of index growth to provide meaningful interest.

The third assumption is that the insurance company will make an effort to ensure that index annuity participation rates at renewal reflect real market pricing most of the time. In other words, if pricing forces an insurer to cut index participation in a given year, that is the breaks, but if the carrier arbitrarily dropped a policy's participation rate below what the market would allow, then all of the hypothetical analysis in the world will not help in determining future returns because the insurer would be rigging the game.

Term End Point

Here is a simple concept. Start with the index value today. At the end of five, seven, ten, twelve years see how much the index has gone up, and credit as interest a predetermined percentage of the increase. You get the higher of the minimum guarantee or the index-linked interest. That is how a term end point participation rate crediting method works.

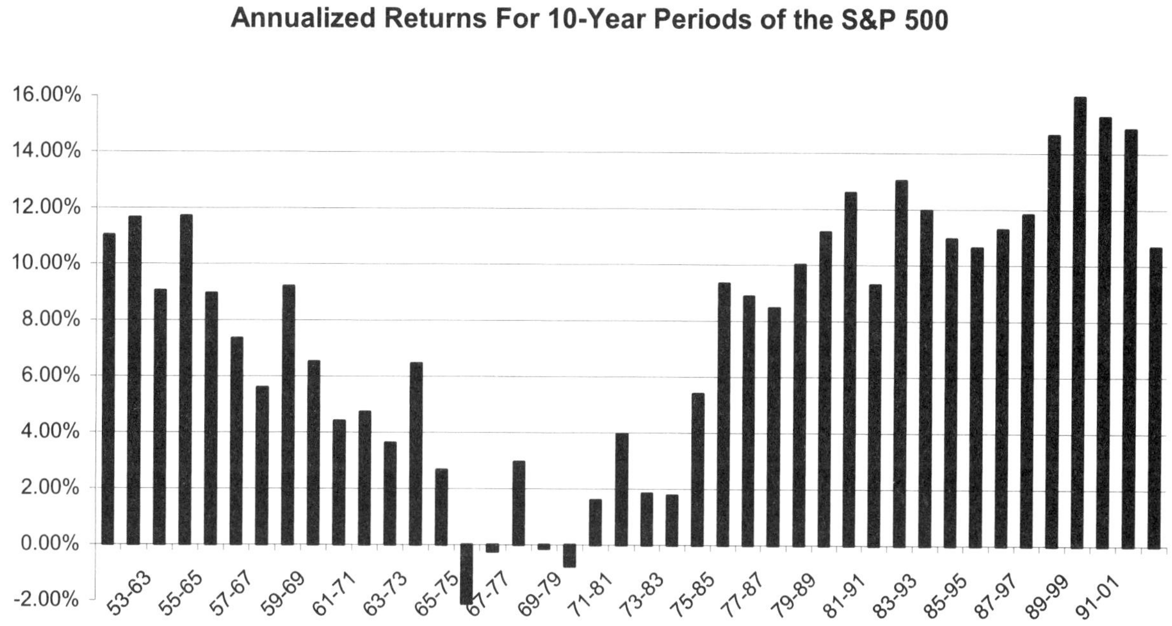

This chart shows the annualized returns for ten-year periods of the S&P 500 for the last 50 years (the S&P 500 was created March 1957, prior numbers are recreated with data from two prior indexes). Interest earned in a term end point designed index annuity would mimic the bars, except that returns would always be positive due to the minimum guarantee.

And the chart pretty much shows the good and bad of term end point designs. If index growth during the period is strong, the return can be strong. If the index is flat or declines during the period, the return stinks.

Averaging The Final Year

All but one term end point designed annuity averages the index values of at least a portion of the final year of the period. Generally, averaging the final year cuts the total return, with the effect less pronounced as the period gets longer. In a strongly rising market averaging could cut 10% off a typical total return if you are looking at five-year periods or 6% if you are looking at 12-year periods, when compared with a pure term end point. However, averaging allows the carrier to offer higher index participation, so if you could get, say, 55% index participation for a five-year period where the last year is averaged, versus 50% participation on a pure term end point, you should pick the averaging model. Averaging the final year also helps you avoid the scenario whereby you manage to end your period on the worst day of the year, although this possibility is more psychologically troubling than statistically valid.

The bottom line is averaging the final year of a term end point method has minimal negative impact on returns and is usually more than offset by higher index participation.

Which Term End Point Annuity?

Term end point methods apply a percentage of any gain as credited interest using a participation rate; or calculate the annualized index return, deduct a percentage or yield spread, and then recalculate interest credited; or take a two-step approach to calculating how index gains translate into index credited.

If you are looking at the same number of years in a period, and the annuities both use a participation rate, the highest rate wins. And if everything else is equal and the annuities use term yield spread designs, the lowest spread wins. If your choices are more involved, you're going to have to make some assumptions.

I show an annual reset *Participation Rate-Yield Spread Equivalency* chart in Chapter 3. Unfortunately, that type of math doesn't work nearly as well when comparing multiple year periods containing different numbers of years. However, using a rough rule of thumb – with an emphasis on rough – one can compare a term yield spread with a participation rate.

Comparing Term End Point Designs

A very rough rule of thumb is a 1% spread produces the same results as a 90% participation rate and a 2% spread is the equivalent of an 80% rate. But this ratio does not hold true as spreads approach and pass 3%.

If the term yield spread is 1%, and you multiply the spread by ten (1% x 10 = 10%), and you then subtract this total from 100% (100% - 10%), the resultant number will be roughly equal to an equivalent participation rate of 90%. Annuities with a 1% yield spread should produce returns that are close to those returns produced by a 90% participation rate over a rising index period.

A 1½% yield spread should approximate an 85% participation rate; a 2% spread will produce results close to those of an 80% participation rate. At 95% versus 0.5%, 90% versus 1%, 75% versus 2½%, the participation rate usually has a slight advantage in most period returns, but it is small. If you are looking at, say, a 1.9% spread versus an 82% participation rate, either method could produce a better return over time. But the bigger the spread, the farther apart the return gap becomes. If the yield spread increases to 3%, 4%, or 5% this comparison rule of thumb falls apart. Or if index growth is very low this rule of thumb begins to break down.

I like the Term Two-Step approach to term end point crediting because the design lowers hedging costs, which should provide more index participation in more market scenarios, while still providing additional upside if the index soars. What rule of thumb is there to compare a term end point participation rate with the Term Two-Step method? Darned if I can find one. The most effective way to compare this methodology with other term end point designs is to see how it might perform in different market climates.

Hypothetical Evaluation – Term End Point Methods

There are a few problems with using hypothetical back-testing in evaluating participation methods, not the least of which is all of the variables that can change future index participation rates. The good news is almost every index annuity using a term end point design locks in all of the crediting methods for the term, so the only variable is index movement. Hypothetical testing has the greatest validity when the only moving part is index movement.

Let's plug in different rates for term participation rate, term yield spread and term two-step structures to see the type of annual returns that are produced over ten-year periods within the last half-century. The assumptions are that the S&P 500 index without dividends is used (the S&P 500 index never includes the effects of reinvested dividends). The index annuities have a minimum 3% interest guarantee based on 90% of the principal (this translates into an effective annual return of 1.92% over the ten-year period). And that the rate cannot change, which would be true for almost every term end point designed index annuity.

Term End Point Hypo #1

Term end point participation rate is 90%, term yield spread is 1%, and term two-step credits 100% of the first 100% of index gain, 70% thereafter. Here is a chart of the annual returns within each of the ten-year periods over the last half century.

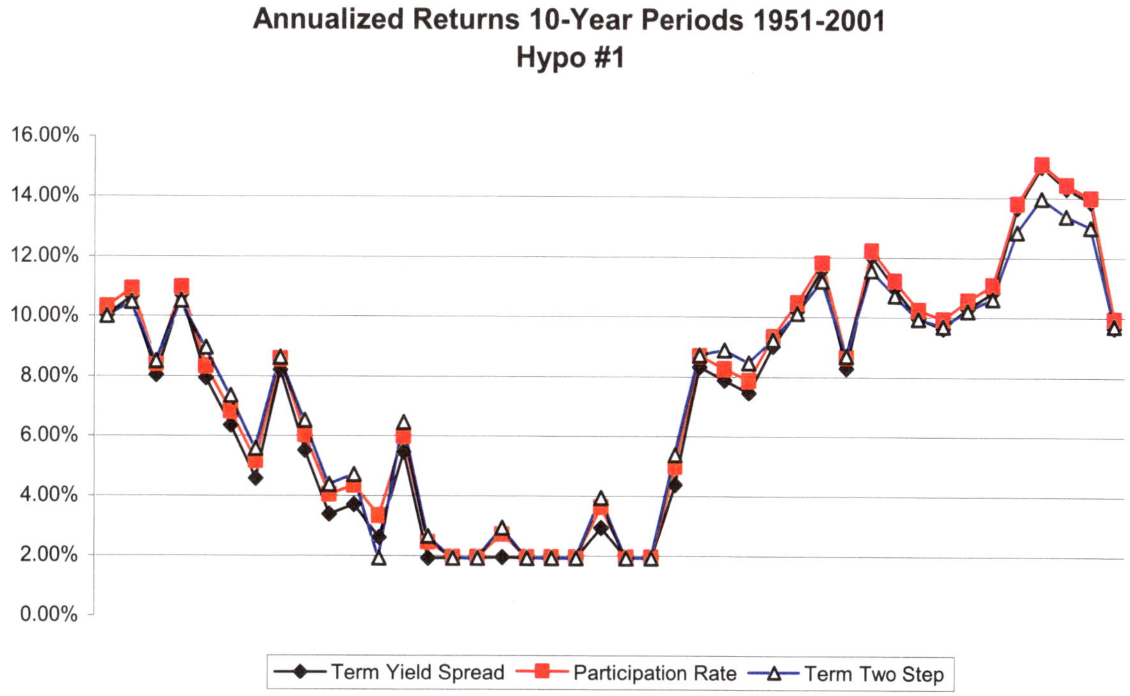

Which is the best index annuity? Even though the average long-term return of the participation rate method is a smidgen higher than the other two my interpretation is any of the three could produce the highest return for a given period. If possible outcomes are similar, you might make your decision based on product features or some other variable.

Term End Point Hypo #2

Let's be a little more dramatic. Term end point participation rate is 65%, term yield spread is 1½%, and term two-step credits 100% of the first 100% of index gain, 50% thereafter. Here is a chart of these annual returns for each of the ten-year periods over the last half century.

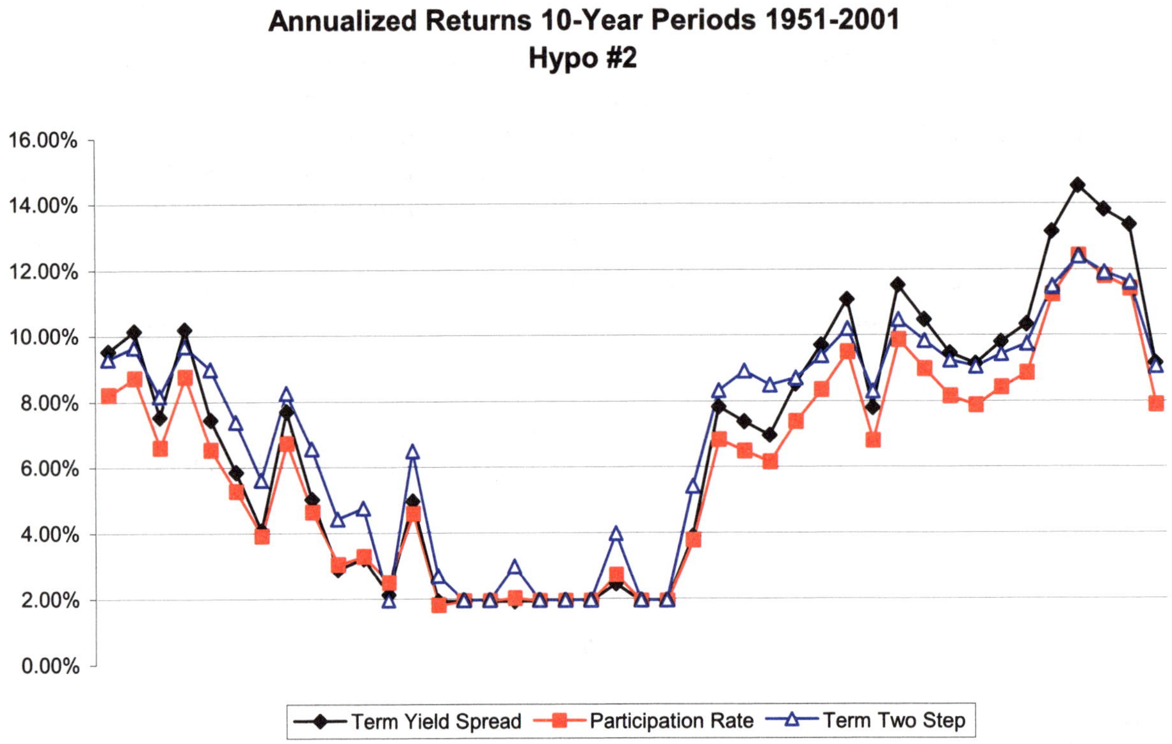

The best annuity may be easier to define, but it depends on what you think will happen. If the bull markets of the '80s and '90s repeat you would probably want the index annuity with the term yield spread method. If the future looks like the modest '50s and '60s you might want the term two-step design. But in any market scenario the term participation rate design would be your third choice.

Term End Point Hypo #3

And there are times when the decision is easy. Term end point participation rate is 90%, term yield spread is 5%, and term two-step credits 100% of the first 100% of index gain, 70% thereafter. Here is a chart of these annual returns for each of the ten-year periods over the last half century.

Annualized Returns 10-Year Periods 1951-2001
Hypo #3

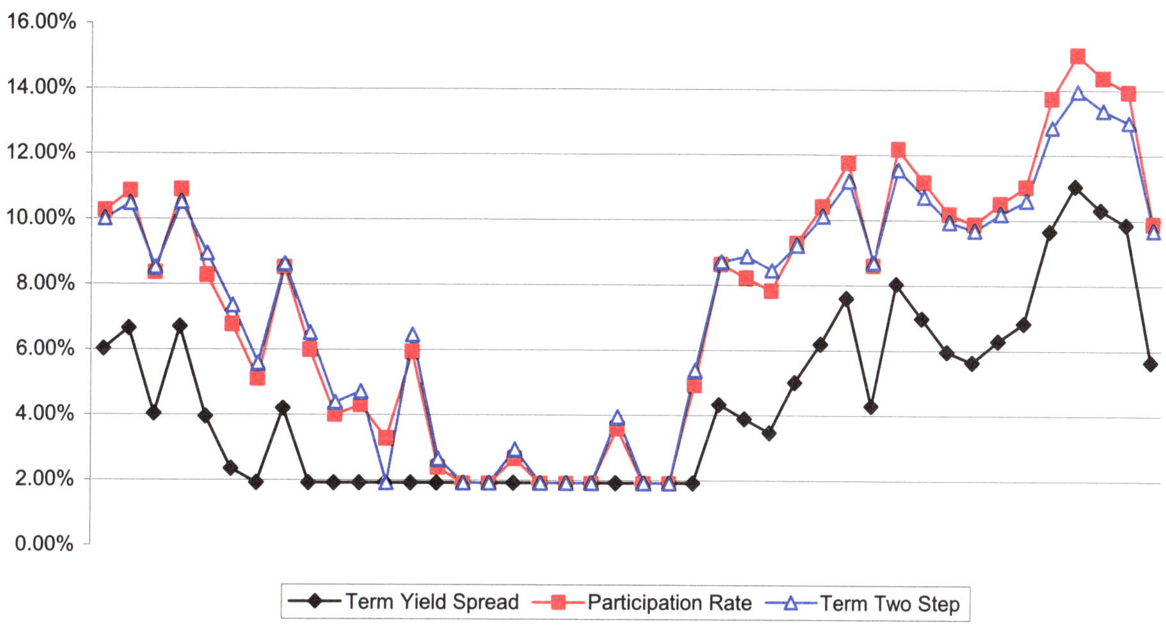

You may be undecided whether to choose the annuity with the term two-step or term participation rate structure, but at least you know you won't choose the term yield spread one. More often hypothetical testing will help you decide which index annuities you don't want to use, but not necessarily help you define the best one.

Key Points On Term End Points

- Term End Point designs can significantly beat annual reset returns in rising markets, but in a lousy market you're more likely to only get the minimum return
- No Moving Parts, no "trust me" at renewal times
- No potential gains are locked in until the end (unless you die)
- Hypothetical back-testing is useful in selecting which term end point

Key Points - Term End Point

Due to less expensive option hedging costs, term end point designs can provide significantly higher return potential than annual reset designs in rising markets. The tradeoff is that if the market period is flat or down term end point designs are more likely to only generate the minimum guaranteed return.

An advantage of almost every index annuity using a term end point method is that there are no moving parts for the entire crediting period, which is usually the same length as the surrender period. The risk of getting an uncompetitive renewal rate is eliminated. A possible disadvantage is that if the climate for index participation improves in the future the rate cannot be raised.

Term end point designs follow index movements. This means potential interest can be lost if the index falls back. In addition, interest is not credited until the end of the period. If a policy is surrendered any increases in the index from the beginning of the period are ignored and a charge may also be assessed. However, most index annuities treat death as the end of the cycle, credit any interest earned and waive surrender charges.

Term High Point (High Water Mark)

A variation of the term end point is the term high point. The first index annuity ever purchased used the high water mark method, and the high water mark method overcomes the biggest objection I hear voiced about regular term end point designs, which is that nothing is locked in until the end of the period. If you surrender the term end point contract early you get zero from any gains, and if the index dives late in the game you'll follow the index down (although averaging would help lessen the final year's slide).

An annuity with the term high point method typically vests any index gains, a bit each year, so you could get some or most of any gains if you surrender early. And this method locks in the highest anniversary level of the index, so you avoid late period index losses.

If you look back at, say, ten-year periods over the last 50 years the high point term method results in a higher total gain than a term end point method 40% of the time.

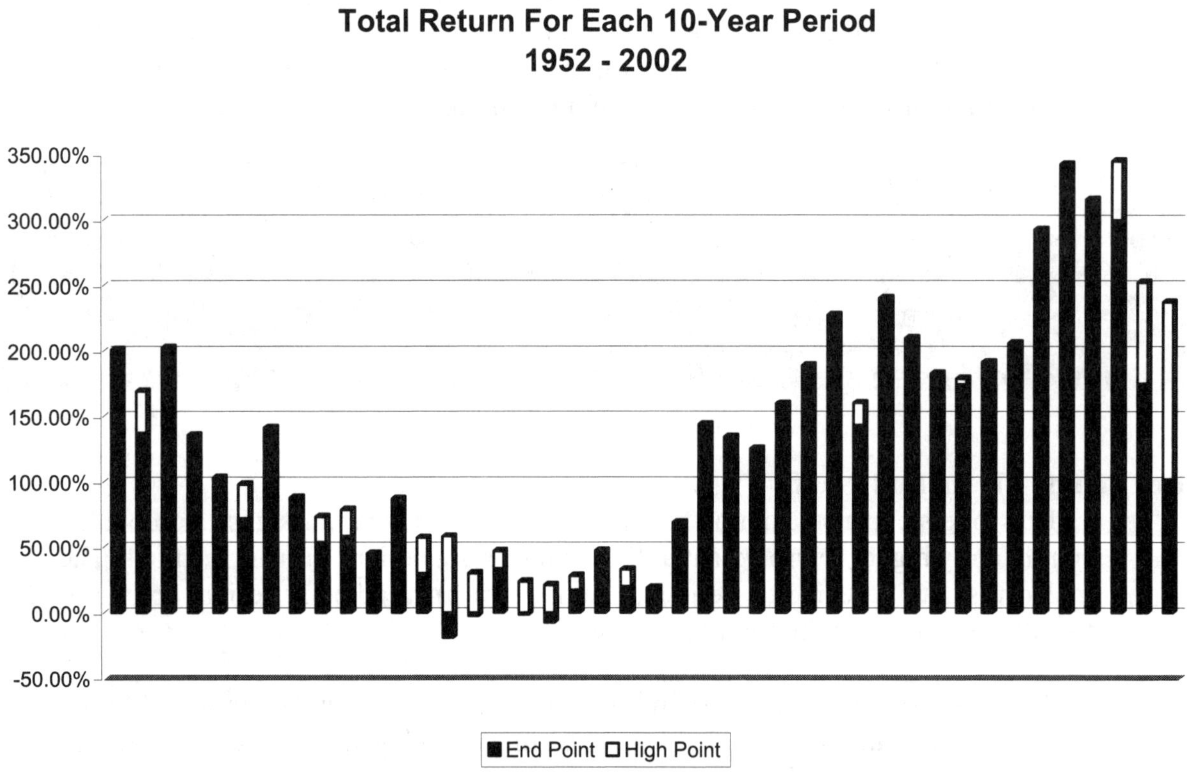

At the end of March 1997, the S&P 500 index stood at 757.12. One year later the index had risen to 1101.75. By March 31, 1999 the index hit 1286.37, and on March 31, 2000 the S&P 500 closed at 1498.92 – a 98% increase in only three years.

However, the millennium bear pounced and the index dropped to 1160.33 by the end of March 2001, and finished March 2002 at 1147.39 (the red line). The index gave back over 300 points of gain in two years.

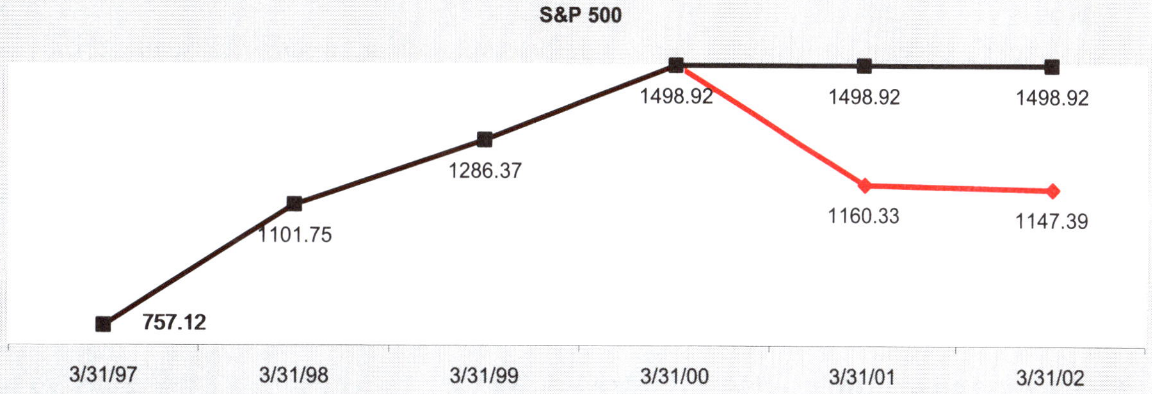

The index was still up 51% from five-years before, and that is still a respectable gain, but the Term High Point method would go back to 2000, using the highest anniversary value, thus basing the interest credited on the 98% increase.

Why Doesn't Everyone Use Term High Point?

It is more expensive for the insurance company to provide the protection of the high point term method and thus index participation is lower than it would be for term end point structures. Of course, if the index does decline at the end of the period the high point term benefit could more than offset the lower participation.

Key Points On Term High Point

- The term high point (high water mark) method provides the return potential of term end point designs in a rising market while still protecting any gains
- The term high point minimizes the risk and effects of a late period bear market.
- Index participation is lower for term high point designs because of the cost of protection, but the benefit could more than offset the cost.

Key Points - Term High Point

By locking in the highest anniversary level and providing vesting, term high point designs offer the potential of term end point returns without the negative of being at the mercy of the index until the end of the term. If two annuities have the same index participation and one annuity uses term high point and the other uses term end point, grab the term high point. However, because the protection is more expensive term high point designs usually offer lower index participation.

Term High Average Anniversary

This is not a high water mark methodology nor is it really an annual reset. This structure calculates a rolling annual average of monthly index values and uses the highest averaged anniversary value as an end point.

This method adds up the monthly index values, divides them by the cumulative months and uses the highest averaged value. This calculation is done each year with the final averaged value compared against previous values to determine the highest. A participation rate is then applied.

Under the Term End Point section I said that a participation rate of 90% or a term yield spread of 1% produced similar returns over 10-year periods going back to 1951. The term high average anniversary would need a participation rate of 160% to produce the same returns. If you compare it to an annual reset, the term average needs a 165% rate to compete with a 55% point-to-point. With a satisfactory participation rate the term high average anniversary can be just as competitive as any other index annuity, but it is in no way, shape or form a high water crediting design.

Required Annuitization

The dictionary definition of annuity is a regular income paid for a set period of time or as long as an individual lives. Annuitization provides several distinct benefits: a certainty of regular, predictable income, possible tax advantages, and peace of mind from investment volatility. The income you get is determined by the insurance company and tends to be a conservative estimate, and that is because the insurance company is taking the risk. When you annuitize you are saying that you are comfortable with the return from the insurance company, and in the case of life only annuitization, that you will live long enough to enjoy the return.

Fixed Annuitization

Good

- Income Guarantees
- Some Tax Advantages (Possible Relief From Income & Social Security Benefit Taxation)
- Portion Of Income Is Excluded From Taxes (Your Own Money Coming Back To You)
- Asset Protection Vehicle In Some Instances

Not So Good

- Insurer Credit Risk – Your continued income is dependent on the survival of the insurance company
- Perception Of Lousy Returns (The Higher The Exclusion Rate The Worse The Return)
- Rigid Inflation-Insensitive Income

Annuitization & Comparative Returns

I have looked at period certain annuity income factors from many companies over many past periods, and often a collection of bonds or certificates of deposits would have produced higher income than one would have received from a period certain annuitization payout at that time.

That's right. Over the years if you bought a collection of different CDs or bonds with varying maturities – in essence built an income ladder for a specific period – and compared that income with what you would have received from a period certain annuity payout purchased at the same time, the CDs or bonds often produced more income. What about the annuity's tax advantage from the exclusion factor? The CDs and bonds enjoy the same tax advantage because all an exclusion rate means is your own after-tax money paid back to you is not taxed twice.

Points in the annuity's favor are that it can be cumbersome to construct an income ladder, the transaction costs in buying individual bonds or brokered CDs could offset any income advantages when dealing with small amounts of money, and the income advantage of CDs or bonds often is not that great.

Life annuitization payouts are another matter. If you take a payout based on life expectancy, even with period certain guarantees, you're betting that not only are you going to outlive the insurance company's mortality tables, but you could not do as well investing on your own.

A couple of years ago when interest rates were higher the true annualized return for a 65 year old male taking a life-only annuitization payout from a typical annuity was 0% if he got hit by a bus the day after annuitizing the policy, in the 7% range if he lasted 20 more years, in the 8% to 9% range if he lived until age 95 or so, and if he took any period certain guarantees the annualized returns dropped a percent or two.

Deciding whether annuitization is good or bad depends on if you think you can beat the insurance company's returns and are willing to gamble your future income on your financial skills

Today, interest rates are lower. A life-only payout may only produce an annualized return of 5% to 7% even if the man lives 20 or 30 more years, and returns drop down to the 2% to 4% range if you throw in some long-term period guarantees. So, do you bet against the insurance company?

If you have good genes and healthy habits, you could very well outlive the tables and beat the insurance house. What if you are not a potential cover girl for *Modern Maturity*? Then you are talking about personally ensuring, but not insuring, that you do not outlast your money

In recent years matching the life only annuity income provided for 20 to 30 years would require an investor to earn a net investment return of 5% to 9%. Over the long term the broad stock market has averaged around a 10% return. But there were several 20 and 30-year periods where the stock market averaged much lower returns. Assuming you can beat a 9% return – or even a 5% return – over the next two or three decades could be an optimistic assumption. It really boils down to whether you want the certainty of guaranteed income or do you want to chance doing it yourself.

Annuitizing Index Annuities

Today 98% of the people do not convert the money they have built up in their annuity into a guaranteed income stream. And 98% of index annuities on the market do not require policy annuitization to receive the index-linked interest earned. The handful of annuities that do require annuitization to receive index-linked interest earned have a minimum payout period of usually 5-years, but the minimum may be as long as 10-years, and the minimum interest credited during payout can be as low as 2%.

If the intent is to annuitize the annuity and create a future guaranteed income stream, and you feel you can trust the insurance company to provide a fair annuitization return, then the forced annuitization will not be a detriment. But make sure you want to annuitize because the penalty for not annuitizing can be severe. One annuity on the market pays less than 1.5% annualized interest if you surrender instead of annuitize, regardless of how well the index does and regardless of when you surrender. Even if the index was up 20% each year for a decade and you surrendered their contract, the most you would be paid is less than 1.5% interest for every year you owned it. However, other required annuitization products may be less draconian.

What if your intent is not to turn the annuity into an income stream, but rather to reclaim the money for use someplace else. For example, your intention is get the money back for use in ten or 15 years and your hope is to get some higher index-linked returns in the meantime. My terribly vague answer is it depends on the interest you earn and the interest you might have earned.

For example, say that you averaged an 8% a year index-linked return for the first five years and then only received a 2% annual return when you annuitized it for the next five years? Your true overall return for the entire ten-years would be 4.92%. If you could have found a fixed rate annuity with a ten-year 5% rate guarantee you would be ahead. But if the best ten-year guaranteed rate you could find was 4%, then you were better off in the forced annuitization product.

Key Points On Annuitization

- Required annuitization may not be an issue if you intend to annuitize anyway
- 98% of index carriers don't require annuitization to receive index-linked interest
- Annuitization products amplify the "trust me" relationship with the insurance carrier
- Annuitization products usually severely limit any index-linked interest credited if the policy is surrendered and not annuitized
- Annuitization provides certainty of income and return

Premium Bonus

There is no such thing as a free bonus. Many index annuities offer a premium bonus ranging from 1% to 12% of premiums paid in. The money to pay for the bonus either reduces the agent commission, or it reduces future index (interest) participation, or both, when compared with a no bonus model.

Cheat Sheet

- For term end point methods a very rough rule of thumb is a 1% spread produces the same results as a 90% participation rate and a 2% spread is the equivalent of an 80% rate. But this ratio does not hold true as spreads approach and pass 3%.

- Hypothetical back-testing has the greatest validity when the only moving part is index movement, as with term end point designs. But, if crediting factors can be changed the hypothetical returns developed by testing of different annuity methods are of little use.

- An advantage of almost every index annuity using a term end point method is that there are no moving parts for the entire crediting period, which is usually the same length as the surrender period. The risk of getting an uncompetitive renewal rate is eliminated.

- Term end point designs follow index movements, which means potential interest can be lost if the index falls back. In addition, interest is not credited until the end of the period and is usually lost if a policy is surrendered early.

- Term high point (high water mark) designs offer the potential of term end point returns without being at the mercy of the index because the highest anniversary level of the term is used, but because the protection is more expensive, the rate is often lower

- Required annuitization isn't necessarily a bad thing if your intention is to annuitize the contract. However, 98% of people don't currently annuitize and 98% of index annuities do not require annuitization.

- A premium bonus is never free.

Discussion Questions

1. What are the pros and cons of annuitization?

2. Is it true that there's no such thing as a free premium bonus?

3. What other financial products are similar to index annuities?

Chapter Quiz

1. Which of the following are true about term end point crediting methods

A. It's a simple concept
B. No renewal rate risk
C. You can lose index gains during the period
D. All of the above

2. What is true about averaging the final year index values of a term end point crediting method?

A. In a strongly rising market averaging could cut 6%-10% off a typical total index return
B. Averaging the final year usually more than offset by higher index participation
C. Both A and B are true
D. Neither A nor B are true

3. Term high point crediting methods

A. Use the highest contract anniversary value of the index as the point for calculating gains
B. Are less expensive for the insurer to offer than a term end point method
C. Are also called term high average methods
D. All of the above

4. Annuitization of an index annuity to receive index-linked interest

A. Is almost never required
B. Provides a guaranteed income
C. Could have an annuitization interest rate as low as 2%
D. All of the above

5. A premium bonus

A. Can reduce future index participation
B. Is free for the insurer because of the decrease in morbidity cost
C. Does typically not affect commissions
D. None of the above

Chapter 5 – Evaluating Annual Reset Methods

Annual Reset

This chart shows the annual returns if you could have purchased the S&P 500 at the end of every month beginning January 1951(periods prior to March 1957 are recreated with data from two prior indexes). The first bar represents the annual return from January 1951 to January 1952. The last bar represents December 31, 2001 to December 31, 2002. The returns do not include reinvested dividends.

S&P 500 Annual Returns 1951 - 2002

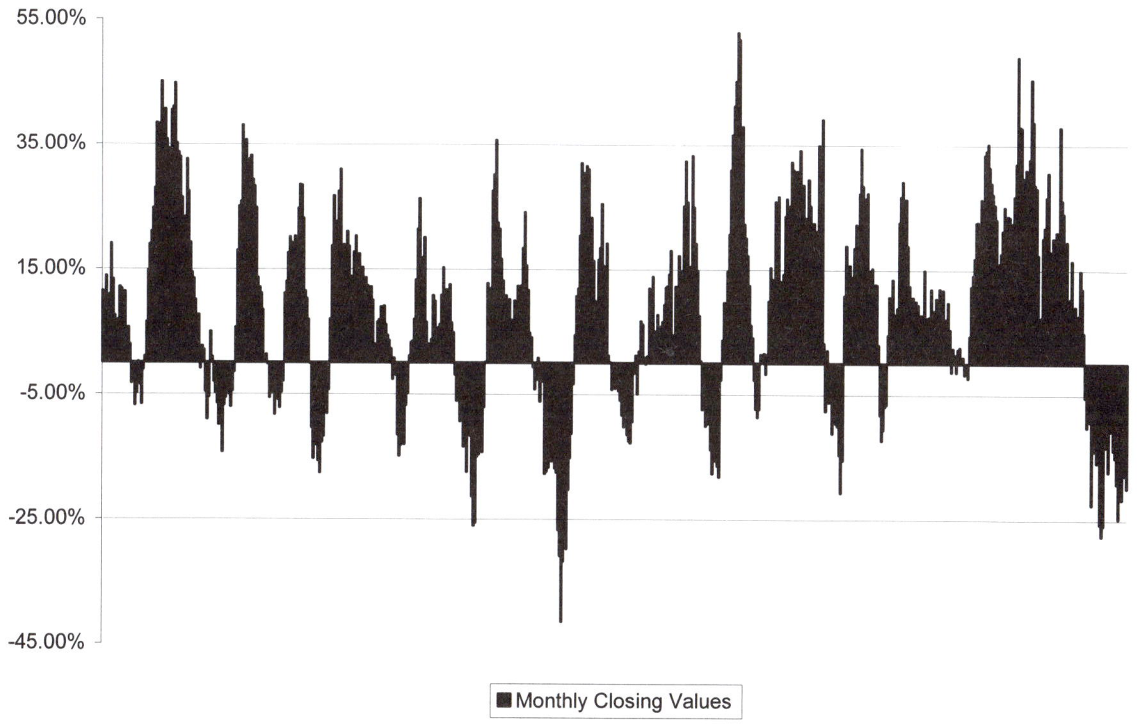

The best one-year period returned 52.94%. The worst period produced an annual loss of 41.40%. If you could have could have invested in every one of the periods, your annualized return was 8.90%.

Index annuities using annual reset crediting methods link interest earnings to movement of the index with three extraordinary differences from term end point designs:

- **Annual Credited interest cannot be lost if the index declines**
- **Years of negative index movement are treated as years of zero growth**
- **Index values are reset at the beginning of each year**

Take a look at the same chart if the index used an annual reset approach.

S&P 500 Annual Returns 1951 - 2002

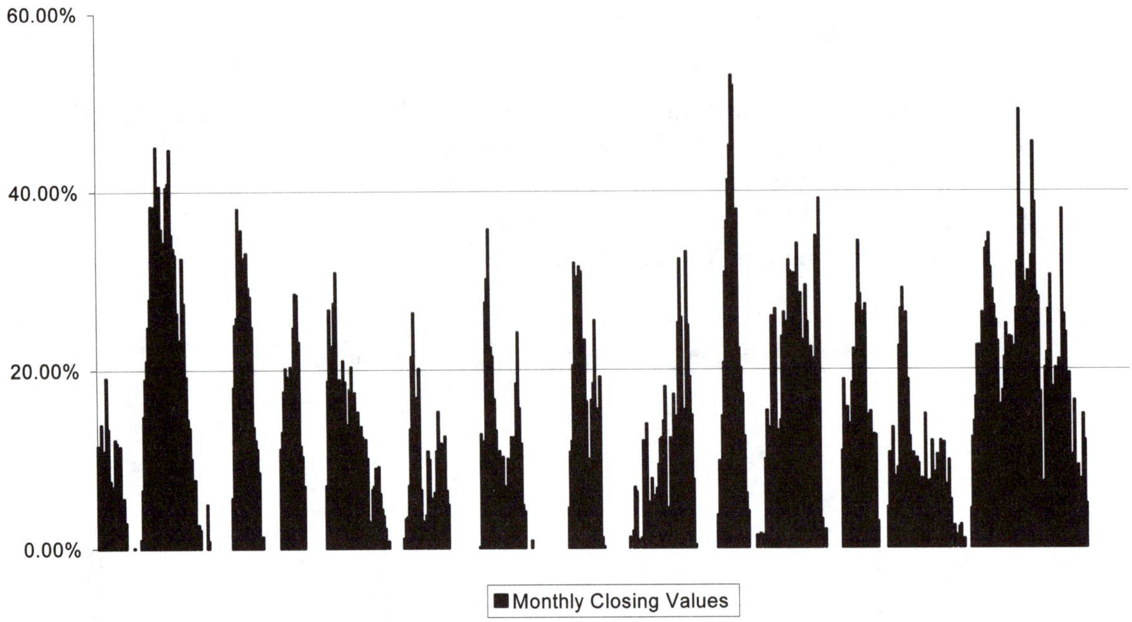

The best one-year period returned 52.94% a year. The worst period produced no loss, so no previous gains were lost. If you could have invested in every one of the periods, your annualized return was 11.89%.

Jump Up and Down and Spin Around
Annual Reset Methods Treat Negative Index Years As Zeros
This Means You Can't Lose Credited Interest
And You Begin Calculating New Movement From The Lower Index Value

Hypothetical Evaluation – Annual Reset Methods

Index annuities haven't been around for 50 years, so we don't know how the different crediting methods would have performed. And we do not know what participation rates would have been. However, the purpose of this section is not to "guestimate" what index annuity returns might have occurred, but to conceptually get an idea of how different annual reset structures perform in different markets.

While I do not know what rates might have been over the last 50 years, I do know that annual reset point-to-point structures within the last few years had actual participation rates of 55% for quite awhile. And I can plug a 55% participation rate into every up year during the last 50 years of S&P 500 returns (because index annuities treat down years as zeros), and determine the annualized return for all of the ten-year periods (because we used ten years for the term end point designs) is 6.40%. I can then use the Mean (average) return for this annual point-to-point (APP) design and see what index participation rates other designs would require to equal the return produced by the 55% APP method.

If I could have purchased an index annuity for every ten-year period since 1951, with this 55% APP annual reset structure, my annualized interest rate would have been 6.40%. Or, if I had purchased an annuity with a 100% APP and a 10.8% net interest cap (where I never would have earned more than 10.8% interest in a given year) my overall annualized return would have been 6.40%.

If I had purchased an index annuity using monthly averaging with a 91% participation rate I'd also have averaged a 6.40% annual return? And we can do the same analysis for other crediting methods. What I am trying to build is a level playing field using interest crediting factors that have actually been used, but I am adjusting them so that they all would have produced identical long term results. It does not matter which structure you picked, they all earned 6.4% on average.

Here are the rates needed by all of these different crediting methodologies to match the same 6.40% annualized returns.

Crediting Method Required To Produce The Same Annualized Return		
	Crediting Method	**Effective Rate**
Annual Point-to-Point	55%	82%
Monthly Averaging	91%	82%
Daily Averaging	96%	82%
Term High Average	165%	82%
Annual Point-to-Point	100% with 10.8% net cap	82%
Annual Point-to-Point	100% less 2.0% spread w/ 14% gross cap	82%
Annual Point-to-Point	100% less 8.4% yield spread	82%
Monthly Averaging	100% less 1.05% yield spread	82%
Biennial Daily Averaging	100% plus 2.9% positive yield spread	82%

If we could have put the same amount of money into annuities using each of these different index annuity crediting methods over the last 50 years our overall returns would be the same for each crediting method. I am not saying this is what index participation would have been, I am simply saying if you apply these crediting factors to the last 50 years you get the same returns.

Choosing The Highest Rate Won't Guarantee The Highest Return

The main conclusion this should point out is simply choosing the annuity with the lowest spread, or the highest rate, or the best cap will not ensure you of getting the highest return.

What Is This Effective Rate?

The annualized actual return of the S&P 500 was 7.80% for 10-year periods. The different crediting methods generate an annualized return of 6.40%, which means we are **effectively** getting 82% of what the entire index returned (6.40%/7.80% = 82%). The effective rate could also be called the real rate of index participation.

You could express participation in a particular crediting method as 55% of the annual point-to-point movement, 96% of the daily averaged movement, 100% of the monthly averaged movement less a 1.05% yield spread, but these numbers rarely represent the actual degree of index participation. Whether the stated or nominal rate is expressed as 55% or 96% or 100%, what we actually received was 82% of the index return for the period.

How can we get an effective real participation rate of 82% if our stated or nominal annual point-to-point participation rate is 55%? The reason why is unlike the actual index, index annuities with annual reset structures treat negative years as zeros instead of losses. If you eliminate years with negative returns, and only include years with positive or zero returns your average return goes up. This is why a lower participation rate can still provide competitive returns.

Annual Reset Returns In Different Markets

I adjusted crediting factors so that each method would have identical returns over a 50 year period. We are now going to plug in the same crediting factors in decidedly different stock market environments and see what happens to returns.

The '70s

The 1970s were a nasty decade for the stock market. In 1972 the S&P 500 closed at a new highest end of the year value and it didn't reach that level again until 1980. If you could have bought the index at the end of 1972 you were under water for the remainder of the '70s. For over seven years the S&P 500 closed at a loss from that 1972 value.

However, index annuities using an annual reset crediting method lock in the gain. A significant advantage of annual reset annuities in a choppy market is that they do just that, they reset. If the index drops 20% the annual reset annuity would record no growth for the year, but growth for the future would start at the lower level.

If you look at ten-year periods of S&P 500 performance ending in the 1970s the average annual return is 1.80%. What were the returns of our different crediting methods?

The highest returns were from the capped designs because caps permit the index annuity to offer higher index participation on initial gains; the lowest return came from the term average method, which acts a lot like term end point methods. Although stated participation rates are as low as 55%, the true effective index participation rate of these annuities for the decade is 200% to 300%.

Hypothetical Annualized Return For 10-Year Periods Ending In The '70s		
	Crediting Method	**Annual Return**
Annual Point-to-Point	55%	4.69%
Monthly Averaging	91%	4.94%
Daily Averaging	96%	4.96%
Term High Average	165%	2.68%
Annual Point-to-Point	100% with 10.8% net cap	5.58%
Annual Point-to-Point	100% less 2.0% spread w/ 14% gross cap	5.44%
Annual Point-to-Point	100% less 8.4% yield spread	3.97%
Monthly Averaging	100% less 1.05% yield spread	4.84%
Biennial Daily Averaging	100% plus 2.9% positive yield spread	4.80%

Even though over a long period of time every one of these crediting methods would produce the same return at the rates I've listed, if you look at shorter periods and different market situations the individual methods produce different returns. Even though the actual index return was 1.80% a year the annual reset structure produces returns of 2.68% to 5.58%.

The '80s

This was a transition decade. It began with a hard and long bear market, and ended with a short and mild bear market. In between it had six-years of double digit gains, and the addition of a new phrase to investor lexicon "Black October". If you look at ten-year periods of S&P 500 performance ending in the 1980s the average annual return is 7.88%. What were the returns of our different crediting methods?

Hypothetical Annualized Return For 10-Year Periods Ending In The '80s		
	Crediting Method	**Annual Return**
Annual Point-to-Point	55%	6.38%
Monthly Averaging	91%	6.49%
Daily Averaging	96%	6.45%
Term High Average	165%	5.70%
Annual Point-to-Point	100% with 10.8% net cap	6.62%
Annual Point-to-Point	100% less 2.0% spread w/ 14% gross cap	6.86%
Annual Point-to-Point	100% less 8.4% yield spread	6.35%
Monthly Averaging	100% less 1.05% yield spread	6.53%
Biennial Daily Averaging	100% plus 2.9% positive yield spread	6.74%

This is about as "normal" a period as you can find. The different crediting structures all produce about the same returns. The effective index participation rate of these annuities is around 80%.

The '90s

The 1990s represent the strongest bull market in American history. If you look at ten year periods of S&P 500 performance ending in the 1990s the average annual return is 12.98%. How did the index annuity structures do?

Hypothetical Annualized Return For 10-Year Periods Ending In The '90s		
	Crediting Method	**Annual Return**
Annual Point-to-Point	55%	7.65%
Monthly Averaging	91%	8.27%
Daily Averaging	96%	8.17%
Term High Average	165%	9.62%
Annual Point-to-Point	100% with 10.8% net cap	7.08%
Annual Point-to-Point	100% less 2.0% spread w/ 14% gross cap	7.10%
Annual Point-to-Point	100% less 8.4% yield spread	8.05%
Monthly Averaging	100% less 1.05% yield spread	8.35%
Biennial Daily Averaging	100% plus 2.9% positive yield spread	8.53%

The best performing method was the term high average anniversary, because it acts more like a term end point structure and term end point methods perform well in strong markets. The lowest returns resulted from cap structures. The effective index participation rate of these annuities for the decade, when compared with actual index returns, is from 55% to 65%.

Annual Reset Return Analysis

I chose an actual annual reset point-to-point participation rate available from the past, calculated the annualized return for the last 50 years using this rate, and then worked backwards to find the crediting criteria for other methods that matched my selected return. I rigged the results so that overall returns would be the same. The reason I did this was to highlight how different crediting structures can react in different markets, and to show that any crediting method can produce a competitive return.

The results indicate that crediting methods with caps seem to do better in choppy bearish periods and yield spread methods seem to provide slightly better returns in bullish markets. And after thousands of hours of return analysis I agree that cap structures work better when the market is middling or worse, and yield spreads take less off the top when the market is flying. But you can see that any method could produce the best return depending upon actual index movement and the degree of index participation.

My number crunching is not meant to imply that one index annuity rate will always correlate with another, although to a surprising extent they do. The reason you will find similar real world relationships between different crediting methods to my manufactured ones is because insurance companies all buy options in the same market from the same sellers and the sellers are not intentionally going to give one design a better shot at higher returns than another for the same money spent. Option sellers use the same pricing models as insurers and they will do their best to keep the playing field level for all crediting methods.

But this does not mean that index annuity crediting is an "efficient market" whereby the return produced by one crediting method will equal the return produced by another. The index annuity rate market isn't efficient either by accident or design. One needs to be aware of how crediting method variations affect returns.

Averaging

The vast majority of index annuity sales are in annual reset designs that average index values to determine index movement. There are two basic facts associated with averaging index values.

Averaging always drives numbers to the middle. In a steadily rising period, averaging produces roughly half of the gain of an unaveraged line. In a steadily falling period, averaging produces roughly half of the loss of an unaveraged line.

Second, the return of an annuity using averaging will not look like the index return that appears in the newspaper. The index does not average index values; the insurer does the calculation. This chart shows the annual returns of the S&P 500 measuring index movement from 1 January to 31 December, the average of the twelve-month end index values as the end point an insurer might use are also shown.

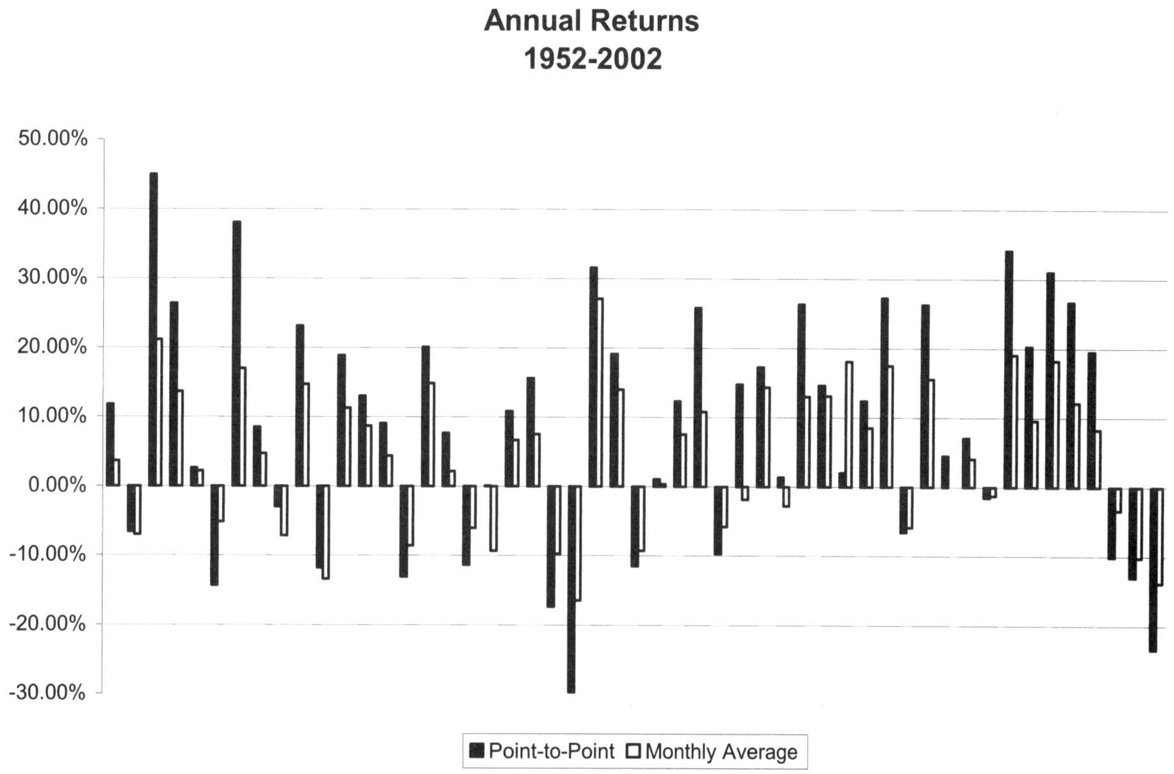

Averaging drives numbers to the middle. "Smoothing" index values means you will never finish a year locked in at the lowest index point of the year, but it also guarantees you will never hit the highest either. In fact, if you look at an entire half-century of returns, the overall monthly average index return is 54% of the point-to-point annual return; the overall daily average return is 52% of the point-to-point annual return. But this does not mean that index annuities using monthly averaged crediting methods will only do half as well as unaveraged ones, or that an averaged design needs double the index participation of an annual point-to-point structure to produce the same return.

If you do not use averaging in an index formula you will either have a lower participation rate and/or need to use a cap to limit gains.

Annual reset designs treat years of negative index performance as zero returns. If you substitute all of the negative index years with zeros, the effective monthly average return rises from 52% to 57% of the point-to-point return, so the averaging return is nearer to 60% than 50% of the point-to-point return. And the relationship between the two can vary depending on the how the market moves. For example, in the '80s the monthly averaged index return was 60% of the unaveraged return; in the '90s the averaged returned was almost two-thirds of the unaveraged returns.

The truth is over time if a point-to-point index annuity and an averaging index annuity have identical crediting criteria – the same rates, caps or spreads – then the returns of the index annuity using averaging would be 55% to 65% of the point-to-point annuity. However, index annuities using averaging offer higher rates or higher caps or lower spreads than point-to-point methods, so the highest return is dependent on the relative index crediting factors.

Using the last fifty years, the return of a monthly averaged structure is 57% of a point-to-point structure. Another way to say this is a monthly averaged structure needs 165% of a point-to-point's index participation to achieve the same return. In the previous section an annual point-to-point method with a participation rate of 55% was used. What participation rate does a monthly average method need to produce the same return? If you multiple 55% by 165% you get 91%, which just happens to be the rate we used to produce the same return in our examples.

The 165% factor might be a rough rule of thumb to judge whether participation rates of unaveraged and averaged index methods are comparable, but it's not a universal law. In the '90s the factor would have been 150%, meaning a 55% APP rate produced the same returns as an 84% monthly averaged rate, and the factor would vary for other market periods. In addition, only a relative handful of index annuities use only an unadorned participation rate. Both averaged and point-to-point structures add on caps or use spreads or a combination. I am unaware of any quick and dirty comparison rules of thumb than can be used between methodologies. The least bad way to determine whether an annual point-to-point or averaging methodology should produce better overall returns is to do some hypothetical historical testing.

There is absolutely nothing wrong with the averaging of index values. It can, under certain market conditions, provide significantly better results than unaveraged methods. The most interest ever credited in one year to a fixed annuity policy utilized averaging of index values. I do have some suggestions on presenting index annuities using averaging.

- Explain that the return printed on an annual statement from an annuity using averaging of index values will not reflect the same index annual returns quoted in the newspaper. If the index annuity has a 100% participation rate and uses averaging, and the index return for the year was 10%, the annuity statement might often say 6% interest was earned, it might say 4%, it might even say 17%, but it will never say 10%. Talk about index annuity concept, not rates or spreads. And

- Never use 1987 as an example of the benefits of averaging unless you also include 1982. Using 1987 as an example of how averaging honestly works is like saying the 114 degree record high temperature set on a day in 1936 is representative of all Minnesota weather.

Extreme Cherry Picking

For calendar year 1987 the S&P 500 finished up 2%. But if you use an average of the year's daily closing values for an end point the index finished up 18%! Why the huge disparity? Until the autumn, 1987 was a strong growing year for the market. On a single day in October – Black Monday – the index dropped 20.5%. Although the index drifted higher by New Years it wasn't enough to offset the wretched October freefall. But averaging also includes all the growth of the preceding nine months, so October's bad numbers are only a small part of the total. The result is an 18.5% increase for averaged values.

I have seen this used as an example of the benefits of averaging. I have even seen the year customized further so that the hypothetical index year ends on Black Monday resulting in a 22% gain for averaging and a 4.7% loss for the point-to-point real index. But you know, if you are going to cherry pick the best possible scenario for averaging it would be only fair to present the worst from the same decade.

For Calendar year 1982 the S&P 500 finished up 14.8%. But if you use an average of the year's daily closing values for an end point the index finished down 2.3%. Why? The year was really gnarly until August when the index finally took off.

Neither 1982 nor 1987 are representative of the overall effects of averaging. I personally wonder when someone tries to strengthen their case by presenting one of these extreme examples without the other, or without at least mentioning it is an extreme, what other facts they might be distorting.

Key Points On Averaging

- Averaging always drive values to the middle, but that does not mean index annuities using averaging will have half the return of an index annuity with a point-to-point design, because averaging structures typically have higher rates or higher caps or lower spreads than unaveraged ones.

- The use of averaging does mean you cannot figure out what your index annuity interest is by looking at the finance page in the newspaper.

Caps

A cap is a ceiling on interest earned – that is the negative. The cap allows you to get higher participation on index gains than you could if there was not a cap – that is the positive. An index annuity using a methodology with a reasonable cap can be very competitive with non-cap index annuities in most markets and provide the best returns in modest markets, but too a low a cap can hurt overall returns because market returns have a wide range.

When A Cap Is Seldom A Cap

There is an altitude cap on where I can walk. Once I get over 18,000 feet or so the air gets too thin for me to breathe and this limits my travels. But I do not normally climb Mount McKinley or hike in the Himalayas so this cap usually will not affect me.

Say that you had a choice between a structure that credited 55% of any annual index gains or one that credited 65%, but had a maximum interest cap of 14%. The cap design would credit more of any index gains until the index gain went beyond 25.5% (calculated by dividing the14% cap by the 55% rate). But what if the index rose 40%? Then the non-cap method would credit 22% while the cap version would credit 14%. However, if you look at actual calendar year S&P 500 movements over the last 50 years only eleven of those years had gains over 25.5%. In the vast majority of the years the cap design would have credited more interest.

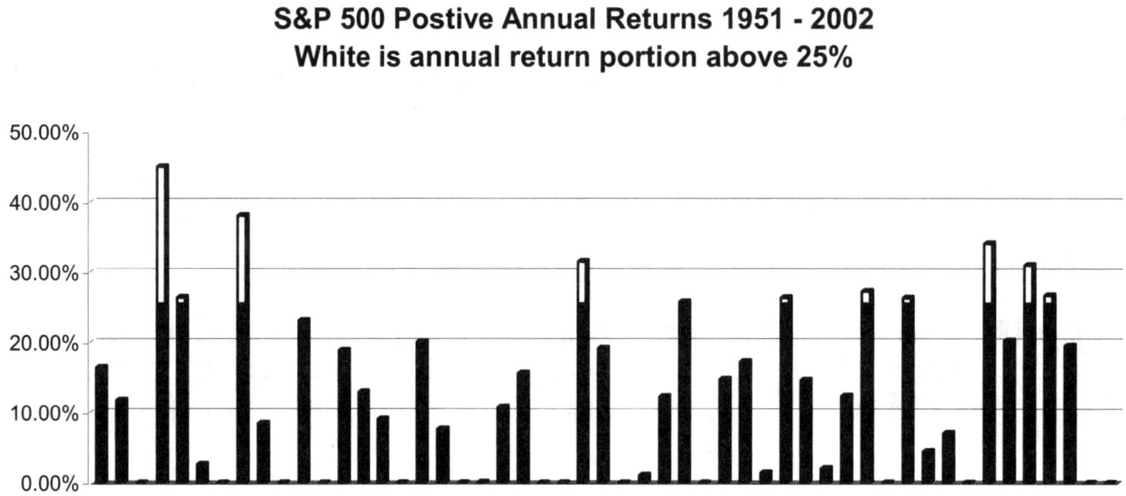

If the cap is high enough it will not limit gains because the index will not get up that high. I have analyzed annuities where the cap would never have been breached. Why bother with a cap then? Because it protects the insurance company from that one in a thousand scenario where the index goes up something like 70% in a year. In many cases a cap permits a higher interest rate to be credited and isn't a real limit.

And When A Cap Can Limit A Return

Or say that you had a choice between getting 100% of any index gains up to an 8% interest ceiling or 50% of any index gain. When the index gains 16% or less the cap version comes out better (8% cap divided by 50% rate). This cap means there were eighteen years when the non-cap version would credit more interest, and when you combine losing out on these high return years, with the years that returned zero, you kill the overall return.

S&P 500 Postive Annual Returns 1951 - 2002
White is annual return portion above 16%

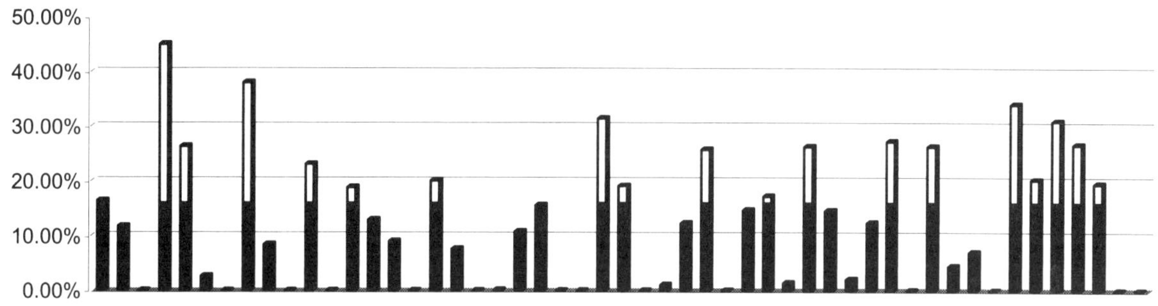

If the index always went up in stable increments, the capped version's return could average pretty close to the 8% ceiling, but it does not. In the last 50-years there would have been fourteen years where the index annuity would record zero.

If you get a bad year where the index goes down, but the following year the index goes up 32% the non-cap version would credit 16% interest. But with the capped version in the same scenario you'd earn 8%. A possible problem with a low cap is a string of flat index years and a year with a humongous gain. The non-cap still comes out okay because it offsets the zero years with one great year, but the cap gets too little of the great year upside.

Index Versus Interest Caps

There are two types of caps and you need to understand the difference. An interest or net cap means this is the most interest that will be credited. An index or gross cap means this is the most index gain that will be recognized.

Say that you are looking at two index annuities, both deduct a 2% yield spread, and both have a 12% cap. But one annuity has an interest cap and the other has an index cap. How will these caps affect returns?

►Index goes up 8%. Each annuity subtracts 2% from the 8% index gain and credit 6%.

►Index goes up 12%. Each annuity would subtract 2% from the 12% index gain and credit 10%.

►Index goes up 20%. The interest cap would subtract 2% from 20% resulting in 18%, and then ask is 18% higher then 12%? Since the answer is yes, this annuity would credit 12%.

►Index goes up 20%. The index cap asks is 20% higher than 12%? Since the answer is yes, this annuity uses the index cap of 12%, subtracts 2%, and credits 10% interest.

Another example: Two annuities, both have a 12% cap and both have a 70% participation rate. But one annuity has an interest cap and the other has an index cap. How are returns affected?

►Index goes up 12%. Each annuity would multiply 12% times 70% and credit 8.4%.

►Index goes up 20%. The interest cap would multiply 20% times 70% resulting in 14%, and then ask is 14% higher then 12%? Since the answer is yes, this annuity would credit 12%.

►Index goes up 20%. The index cap asks is 20% higher than 12%? Since the answer is yes, this annuity uses the index cap of 12%, multiples it by 70%, and credits 8.4% interest.

Because an index cap is a lower effective ceiling than an interest cap, an annuity using an index cap usually has a higher cap than another annuity with an interest cap. However, index and interest (or gross or net) are not the industry's definitions, but mine. You need to determine whether the cap is index or interest and sometimes you cannot tell from the marketing pieces.

Key Points On Caps

- Whether a cap is a real limit depends on what it is. A high cap may never come into play because most stock market years aren't blockbusters. However, too low a cap means you may never participate in enough good index gains to offset the bad years.
- If you do not know whether your annuity uses an interest or index cap you could be unpleasantly surprised. Use my examples and ask the carrier what interest would be credited under their cap method.

Cheat Sheet

- The jump up and down extraordinary points about annual reset crediting are credited interest cannot be lost if the index declines, years of negative index movement are treated as years of zero growth, and index values are reset at the beginning of each period.
- Simply choosing the annuity with the lowest spread, or the highest rate, or the best cap won't ensure you of getting the highest return.
- Any crediting method can produce the best return for a given period.
- It is not the nominal or stated rate, but the effective rate that is important. The nominal rate only tells you how much of the crediting method calculation you are participating in; the effective rate says how much of actual index performance you are getting.
- Because index annuities with annual reset structures treat negative years as zeros, instead of losses and only include years with positive or zero returns your effective return goes up. This is why a lower participation rate can still provide competitive returns.
- Averaging always drives values to the middle, but that does not mean index annuities using averaging will have half the return of an index annuity with a point-to-point design, because averaging structures typically have higher rates than unaveraged ones.
- Averaging needs to be explained because you ca not figure out what your index annuity interest is by looking at the finance page in the newspaper.
- Caps generally mean you get more of most instead of less than a lot, because an annuity with a cap has higher index participation than a similar annuity without a cap. A high cap may have minimal effect of returns because few stock market years are stratospheric, but too low a cap can kill returns because you cannot use higher years to offset zero years.

Discussion Questions

1. When would a term end point method be better than an annual reset method?

2. How could the insurer explain whether an interest or index cap is used?

3. Which crediting method is best?

Chapter Quiz

1. Annual reset crediting methods

A. Can take advantage of bad index markets
B. Limit losses to credited interest only
C. Work like index mutual funds
D. All of the above

2. The effective index participation of an index annuity using annual reset crediting is

A. Higher during periods that contain many years of negative index returns
B. Equal to the nominal participation
C. Equal to the stated participation
D. None of the above

3. Index Annuities using averaging crediting methods

A. Are often used
B. Smooth out low values while retaining high values
C. Generally produce higher index returns than point-to-point methods
D. B and C are correct

4. Caps

A. Can maximize credited interest in minimal markets
B. May be calculated in different ways
C. A and B are correct
D. None of the above

5. One absolute truth about index annuity crediting methods is

A. Term end point methods outperform annual reset methods
B. Any crediting method can produce the best return for a given period.
C. "No cap" methods are better than cap methods
D. Yield spread methods are better than participation rate methods

Chapter 6 – Evaluating Part III

Annual Reset Annuities Reset Annually

Unlike term end point designs that don't lock in index movement until the end of a multiple year period, annual reset index annuities calculate index movement for a one year period and then credit interest to the index annuity contract, applying a crediting formula to any recognized gain. If there is no gain the contract simply credits zero for the year, but previous interest credited is unaffected. The process then begins again using the actual end of the year index value as the starting point for the coming year. This is the basic structure for annual and biennial reset index annuity products and it is easy to understand. However, the simplicity of the index annuity structure does not portray the real power of the index annuity story.

Lock In Credited Interest

The index annuity locks in index-linked interest. The credited interest cannot be lost even if the index subsequently goes down. This is a very important feature. Equity investments have produced significantly higher returns over time than fixed rate vehicles. So, based on the long-term performance of equity investments why doesn't everyone simply buy stocks? The reason is that stocks can go down and you can lose money. Index annuities are designed to give the potential for higher returns than other savings vehicles, but without the market risk to principal associated with stocks.

Since they've been around, annual reset index annuities have been crediting effective index participation that averages 50% to 70% of the actual index gain. At first glance, participating in only half to slightly over two-thirds of an index yearly gain seems low, especially when compared with pure equity investments. However, you need to remember that these annuities ignore the bad years.

	Index Gains
Year 1	+26%
Year 2	+16%
Year 3	+12%
Year 4	-26%
Year 5	+14%

Suppose we had a five-year period where the index acted like the table on the left, and during this same period the annual reset index annuity was only able to participate in 50% of the index gains. The credited annuity gains would look like those on the right.

Index Participation	Annuity Gains
x 50%	13%
x 50%	8%
x 50%	6%
x 50%	0%
x 50%	7%

If we placed $10,000 in the index and $10,000 in the index annuity, here is what the accumulated values would be at the end of five-years:

	Index Value	Annuity Value
Year 1	$12,600	$11,300
Year 2	$14,616	$12,204
Year 3	$16,370	$12,936
Year 4	$12,114	$12,936
Year 5	$13,810	$13,842

Even though the annuity only participated in half of the index gains it still outperformed the index. The reason is while the index investment fully participated in the fourth year loss, previous index annuity gains were unaffected.

My example was rigged to show comparable results. Based on the actual index annuity participation rates we've seen equity investments should produce higher returns over time than index annuities with an annual reset design because in today's markets an annual reset index annuity cannot provide full index participation, but the difference in performance between the two might be closer than one would think.

Reset Annually

Another amazing feature is they reset. The index annuity begins each crediting period using the index value at the beginning of the period. What if the index dropped the previous period? The annuity would record zero index-linked interest earned for the last period and begin calculating the next period's interest beginning at today's lower level.

On October 9, 2001 the S&P 500 closed at 1056.75. One year later on October 9, 2002 the index closed at 776.76. If you had purchased the index at that higher level you needed the S&P 500 to increase 36% before you were back to even. However, if you had purchased an annual reset index annuity you simply record zero index-linked interest earned, and begin calculating future interest from the new lower level.

Key Points On Annual Reset

- Simply choosing the annuity with the lowest spread, or the highest rate, or the best cap won't ensure you of getting the highest return.
- There's no such thing as a free premium bonus
- Returns will differ in the short term depending on crediting method and index movement, but no one crediting method is best over the long haul
- Since almost every index annuity with an annual or biennial reset can adjust some aspect of index participation prior to the end of the surrender period, the integrity of the carrier at time of renewal is more important than the crediting methods

Key Points

Returns from different annual reset index annuities will not be identical over time for the same reasons that traditional fixed annuity returns differ from carrier to carrier and product to product. Products have different loads and different cost structures. Carriers have diverse Return-On-Equity requirements or internal costs. Some investment teams will do a better job of managing their portfolios than others, and some actuaries will use more aggressive or less aggressive assumptions than their peers.

But returns from different crediting methods will be closer than differences in rates or spreads might indicate because everybody is buying options in the same market and option sellers won't intentionally give one crediting style an advantage over another.

Moving Parts vs. No Moving Parts

Almost every index annuity crediting interest every year or two may change the participation rate and/or the yield spread and/or a cap on maximum credited gains at sometime during the surrender period and usually each year. This flexibility means that agents must select carriers whom they feel will treat their customers fairly when renewal time comes around. Why doesn't a carrier simply lock in all the moving parts? Because it can be very expensive. You can either trust me on this explanation for now, or move ahead to the section in Chapter 6 on options.

Renewal Rates

Almost every annual or biennial reset index annuity has the ability to change some aspect of their index crediting formula before the surrender period ends. They may say that the participation rate is guaranteed for the life of the contract, but they will still be able to change the cap. Or the cap is locked in, but they can change the yield spread. The reality is the insurance company needs the flexibility to change index participation on reset crediting structures because financial markets change.

And we have also talked about how all the different annual reset crediting methods should produce similar results over the long term because option sellers will do their best to keep the playing field level for all crediting methods. Since the basic return modeling for all of these different annual reset methodologies produces similar returns over time, the integrity of the carrier is far more important than selection of a crediting style.

Integrity Not Methodology

These are the criteria I look at in evaluating the renewal history of a carrier:

Available & Comprehensive - The carrier must show renewal rate factors (participation rate, cap, spread) on at least a monthly basis and this renewal rate data must be freely available. If they will not share their renewal history, do not do business with them.

Track Record - The carrier's index annuity renewal history must have a minimum track record of twelve months. What if they do not have a renewal history on their index annuities? That is not uncommon; index annuities have not been around that long. If the carrier does not have an index annuity renewal track record, look at the renewal history of their fixed rate annuities. If the carrier has treated fixed rate customers fairly at renewal, they will hopefully be fair to their index annuity customers.

Market Responsive - Index annuity crediting factors should reflect changes in the pricing environment. This means if a carrier worsened renewal factors in response to negative pricing pressures, subsequent positive pressure should improve these renewal factors. And if a carrier supported rates when pressures justified cutting rates, the carrier will be forgiven for not immediately raising rates when financial conditions improve.

Promises Kept - The carrier will keep real and implied promises of renewal rate integrity.

I firmly believe in the index annuity concept, and am optimistic about the future of the stock market and the ability of index annuities to competitively participate. The only thing that could really screw this up is if carriers are not fair at renewal time.

To help me get a handle on who has good or bad renewal rates I concocted something called IPRI, which stands for *Index Participation Rate Indicator*. I have included an example of how it works in the next chapter.

Hypothetical Returns – Which Past Do You Use

Depending on the actual movements of the index, the crediting structure utilized and the participation rate applied, any methodology may result in the highest return for any given period. Generally in rising markets the term end point and high point term structures should result in higher returns than other structures. In choppy markets annual reset structures should perform better. In a prolonged bear market no index annuity will produce a high return.

In my annuity back-testing I use the last fifty calendar year period as a basis for examination. Would the specific hypothetical returns change if I used different days of the year or shorter timeframes? Absolutely. However, given a sufficient timeframe the relative returns and distribution of those returns should remain similar. The purpose of this section is to see how selecting certain periods may provide false view of how the annuities might perform.

Answers derived by "cherry picking" past periods of hypothetical performance may give a distorted view of the actual return probabilities.

Let's examine three index annuity methodologies. We will look at seven-year periods, base crediting on calendar year movements of the S&P 500, base the minimum guaranteed return on 3% interest compounding on 90% of premium, and set the participation rates so that each methodology produces the same Mean return for the entire fifty year period. This requires the term end point structure to use a 75% rate, the annual reset point-to-point to have a 75% rate with a 12% interest cap, and the annual reset monthly average to have a 90% rate.

I am not saying these are necessarily realistic rates. As I did in the previous chapter I've purposely set this up so each method would have produced identical returns over the entire period to provide a level playing field.

First, we will look at hypothetical distributions based on seven-year periods for the last 50 years.

1951 – 2002	Over 10%	8.00%-9.99%	7.00%-7.99%	5.00%-6.99%	Under 5.00%
Term End Point	13.3%	26.7%	13.3%	8.9%	37.8%
Pt-to-Pt w/Cap	-0-	17.8%	8.9%	60.0%	13.3%
Monthly Average	4.4%	17.8%	17.8%	37.8%	22.2%

There are 45 seven-year periods within the last 50 calendar years (1951-1958, 1952-1960...1995-2002). When we apply the term end point 75% participation rate to the periods we produce a 10% or higher annual return for 6 or 13.3% of the periods.

What we are doing is plugging in the index crediting factors for each seven-year period, calculating the annualized return for each period, separating the annual returns we get into different groups, and seeing what percentage of the overall return pie of 45 periods each group contains. The raw numbers would look like this:

1951 – 2002	Over 10%	8.00%-9.99%	7.00%-7.99%	5.00%-6.99%	Under 5.00%
Term End Point	6	12	6	4	17
Pt-to-Pt w/Cap	-0-	8	4	27	6
Monthly Average	2	8	8	17	10

In other words, for 13.3% of the periods (45/6 = 13.3%) the annual returns were 10% or higher. In twelve of the periods (45/12 = 26.7%) the term end point produced annual returns between 8% and 9.99%. A return of 7% was earned 13.3% of the time(45/6 = 13.3%). Four times (or 8.9%) a return of 5% to 6.99% resulted, and 37.8% (45/17 = 37.8%) of the returns were under 5%. The same calculations were then done for the other two crediting methods.

Now let's look apply the same participation rates and do the same exercise to a 35-year snapshot of seven-year periods.

1966 – 2002	Over 10%	8.00%-9.99%	7.00%-7.99%	5.00%-6.99%	Under 5.00%
Term End Point	20.0%	23.3%	16.7%	3.3%	36.7%
Pt-to-Pt w/Cap	-0-	26.7%	6.7%	56.7%	10.0%
Monthly Average	6.7%	26.7%	13.3%	33.3%	20.0%

While the specific percentages changed, the overall distribution pattern of the returns for the 35-year period was similar to the 50-year period. The point-to-point with cap still had the fewest periods producing a return under 5% a year; the term end point still generated more periods with returns over 10% a year. Even though the individual percentages changed, the overall relationships were relatively constant. Although these graphs only look at calendar year periods the same patterns hold true even if you use different days, weeks or months of the year.

"Customized" periods with shorter time frames may not reflect realistic hypothetical performance. These are the distributions if you plug in the rates over a recent fifteen-year period.

1986 – 2002	*Over 10%*	*8.00%-9.99%*	*7.00%-7.99%*	*5.00%-6.99%*	*Under 5.00%*
Term End Point	50.0%	20.0%	30.0%	-0-	-0-
Pt-to-Pt w/Cap	-0-	30.0%	20.0%	50.0%	-0-
Monthly Average	-0-	60.0%	10.0%	30.0%	-0-

Based on only this example, you would probably conclude the term end point structure is the best one. However, let's look at a different fifteen-year period.

1965 – 1980	*Over 10%*	*8.00%-9.99%*	*7.00%-7.99%*	*5.00%-6.99%*	*Under 5.00%*
Term End Point	-0-	-0-	-0-	-0-	100.0%
Pt-to-Pt w/Cap	-0-	-0-	-0-	60.0%	40.0%
Monthly Average	-0-	-0-	10.0%	50.0%	40.0%

If you assume this timeframe will be representative of the future you'd probably select the annual reset methods. However, the data derived by "cherry picking" your periods may give a distorted view of the actual return parameters and probabilities. If you look at hypothetical returns it is important to use a timeframe that's long enough to include a variety of market conditions.

Evaluation Problems

This analysis applies participation rates to past index movements and does not reflect actual returns. It cannot be used to predict future movements nor can it be used to state exact returns in the past. Past index participation would have been higher for some past periods and lower for others. Due to all of the variables involved, I do not believe you can say what historical participation rates might have been.

Any hypothetical modeling has a bias. The returns for the periods are not truly independent because one period will include returns from years of a previous or subsequent period. Because there have been more rising periods than falling periods in the last 50-years, this analysis has higher hypothetical returns for structures that perform better in rising markets. Finally, the evaluation assumes the level of index participation remains constant; many structures may change at least one crediting factor yearly.

What you are really looking for are returns that fall way outside the group. If one annuity produces 10% returns 20% of the time and another produces 10% returns 75% of the time, you need to determine why there is a big difference. Is the hypothetical return too good to be true, then maybe the insurer's offering a first-year teaser participation rate that will be slashed next year? Or do the hypothetical returns reflect different crediting methods? Hypothetical testing is really used to uncover questions, not answers.

Key Points On Evaluation

- Although we do not know how the stock market will perform tomorrow, for any evaluation method to have validity we need to believe that long term trends hold true.
- Be wary of index annuity hypothetical illustrations that "cherry pick" certain periods. Any index annuity can be made to look good if you carefully select the right time frame.

Comparison Between Annual Reset and Term End Point Returns

One can graph the hypothetical returns of index annuities by looking at their distribution patterns. There are several ways to do this, but for this example let's simply see how often returns occur within certain ranges.

We will use the same participation rates we used in the last section. When we plug the return numbers from the three methods into the last 50 years we get this chart.

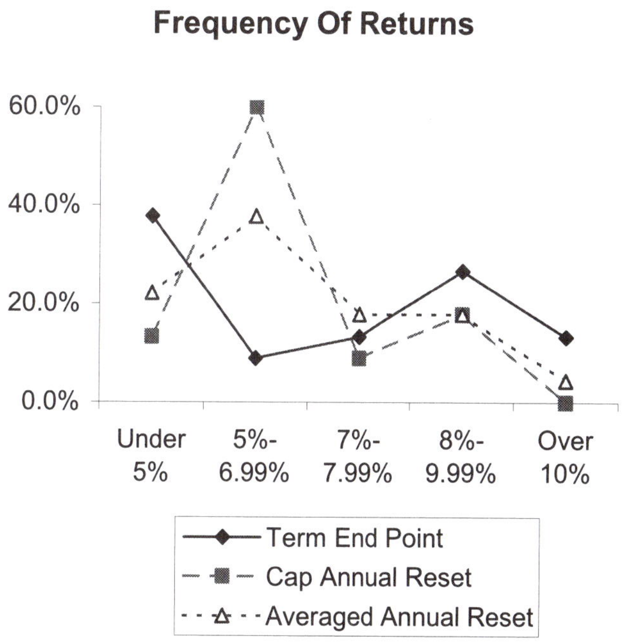

The frequency of the annual reset returns shows a small percentage of very low returns, a small percentage of very high returns, and a lot of returns in the middle. The term end point method shows more very low returns, more very high returns, and fewer returns in the middle. The distribution patterns are dissimilar even though the overall returns over the entire period are identical.

Why is there a difference in annual return distributions? Term end point designs, and other methods that measure index movement over long periods of time, tend to follow the actual performance of the index. A stock index often has a large number of years of very high returns and very low returns with relatively few returns in the middle.

Annual reset returns look more like a bell curve. Annual reset annuities ignore years with negative returns. This limits the periods with very low index returns, but annual reset structures tend to have higher total pricing costs than term end point structures, which means the annual reset methods usually have a lower effective participation rate than term end point designs. This means annual reset structures do not tend to produce extended periods of very high returns.

The shape of the graph lines depends upon the methodology and the rate applied. If the term end point and annual reset rates slipped to 70%, the lines would shift to the left. If rates had increased, the lines would shift to the right meaning higher returns.

Annual Reset Returns Are A Matter Of Degree

The following charts show the average annual return for each decade after applying different annual reset crediting methodologies and rates to each year. The Black lines reflect 100% participation in an annual point-to-point structure with a net interest cap. The White lines reflect varying participation in monthly averaging of index values. The Red Lines reflect 100% of the daily average of yearly index values plus or minus a yield spread. Years with negative returns are treated as zeros.

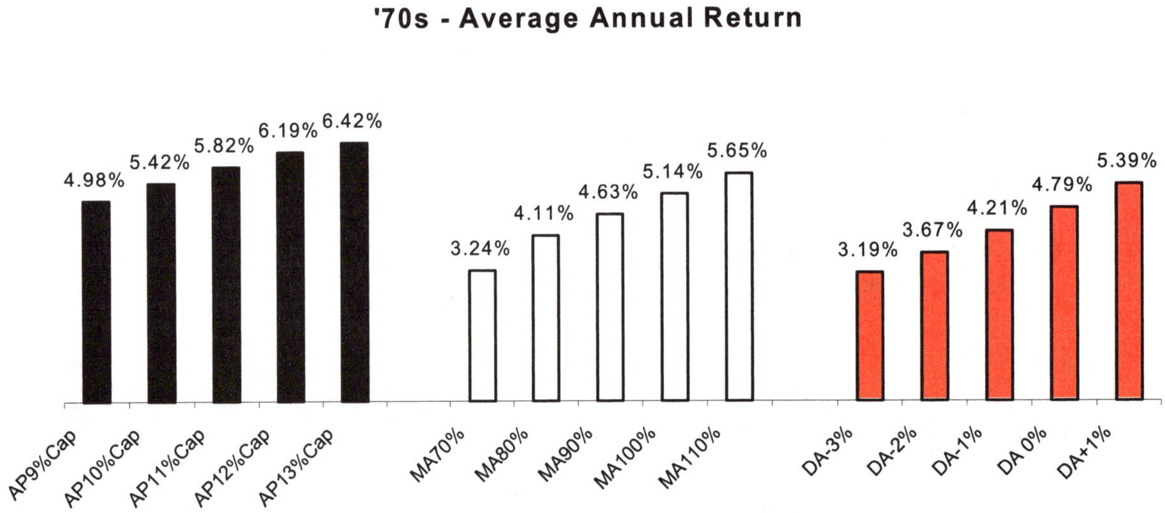

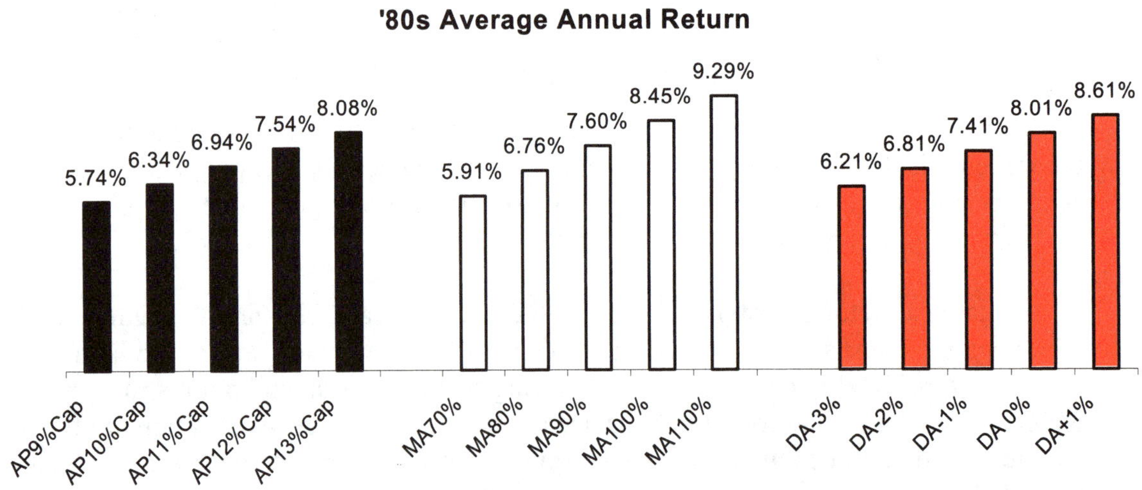

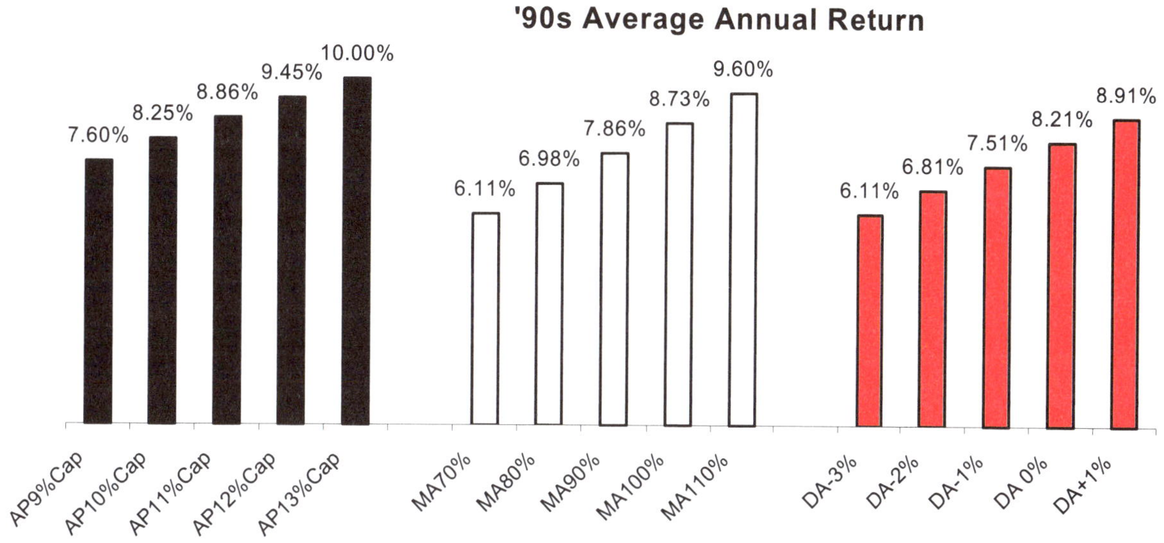

The purpose of the charts is not to illustrate the returns you will get from an index annuity, but to show that it doesn't take much change in index annuity crediting rates to dramatically change returns. A 2% higher cap or a 10% decrease in participation rate or a thinner yield spread can significantly change the amount of interest earned.

What Return Should I Expect?

Although the above charts reflect the hypothetical results of actual participation rates from previous years they may not reflect future returns. Part of the reason is the old and true adage that past performance does not predict future results. But an equally important reason is that the annuity interest is index-linked and not a result of direct index performance.

Index annuity interest is based on the movements of the index, the crediting method used, and the index participation of that method; index participation is based on the amount of money available to buy the option and the cost of the option. This means that there's no reason why in some year an index annuity couldn't wind up crediting 1% interest in a period when the index rose 10%, or credit 15% interest in a period when the index fell 5%.

Since index annuities have been available they have credited double digit interest rates when the stock market was soaring, modest rates when the market was uncertain, and protected credited interest when the stock market went down and others lost money. No one knows where the market will head in the future, but the goal of index annuities are to provide the potential for a higher rate than one might earn from other savings vehicles that don't subject the principal to market risk.

Some Truths I Think I Know

John and Mary live in St. Louis. If it takes John's car one half tank of gas to commute back and forth to work each week, and it takes Mary's car one full tank of gas to commute to work each week, which car gets better gas mileage?

I asked a number of people this question and several answered that John's car gets better mileage. However, this ignores the possibility that John's car may have a 25-gallon gas tank while Mary's car has a 10-gallon tank. Or, that John's office is three miles from his house while Mary commutes from St. Louis to Detroit and back every day. Or, that John turns his car off while going down hills and coasts until the car stops before restarting it, while Mary travels at 80-miles per hour with the air conditioning on, the tires under inflated, and towing a boat.

Attempting to compare the performance of different vehicles, without knowing and being able to adjust for all of the different variables involved, often results in wrong conclusions. And yet many people try to determine how different index annuities will perform solely based on a comparison of participation rates or other interest crediting mechanisms. The problem is unless the crediting structures of the index annuities are identical, any attempt to select the best performing annuity based on respective rates or caps or spreads will be flawed. This is not only because the various methods produce different answers when applied to the same set of index values, but also that the composition of any given set of index variables is made up of totally random numbers that cannot be predicted. Furthermore, in most cases, the respective rates or caps or spreads of the different crediting methods applied to these random, independent, index numbers can be arbitrarily changed by the carrier.

So, besides the primary difficulty of predicting how stock market indexes will move in the future, index annuities use crediting structures that not only produce different answers when given the same set of index values, but for the most part these crediting structures operate without the direct correlation or causality that would produce consistent answers if index values change, and for the most part insurers can arbitrarily modify the degree to which the crediting structures reflect the index value change.

The most common question I get from consumers and agents is "Which index annuity is best?" The preceding paragraphs show the difficulty I have in answering that question. However, based on many hours spent examining different index annuity crediting methods, different stock market scenarios, and tens of thousands of calculations, I have found out a few truths that I think I know, until proved otherwise.

If the stock market of the '80s or '90s repeats, index annuities could produce very respectable returns.

The last twenty years were a wonderful time for the market. At the rates I've seen, index annuities would produce average annual returns ranging from 7% to 12%. In general, term end point structures would produce the highest returns.

An annual reset (ratchet) structure treats negative years as zeros, which offsets the reinvested dividend benefit of direct equity investments.

A point often used to try to disparage index annuities is that index funds, or returns of similar investments, include the effects of reinvested dividends while index annuities do not. However, index annuities with annual reset structures treat negative index years as years with zero gain and do not give up credited interest based on previous gains. Over the last 50 years, the index annuity zero gain approach increases the return of an average index year by 2.5%, essentially offsetting the current benefit produced by the reinvested dividends of index funds.

If the stock market of the '70s repeats, index annuities could produce poor to fair returns.

An average stock market year between 1961 and 1981 returned less than 5%. Even if you substitute zeros for losses, at rates and spreads we have seen, the average index annuity year would credit 3% to 6% interest. The best performing structure in this period is an annual point-to-point with cap method.

But not necessarily.

This assumes that the index annuity participation rates we have seen to date represent the upper and lower limits, and this assumption is probably wrong. Crediting method, general interest rates and option prices drive index participation. There were market conditions in the past that would have permitted index annuities to credit two or three times actual index gains, and there's nothing to say that an index annuity wouldn't offer an effective 200% participation rate in the future, making it very competitive even with 5% stock market returns.

If you wait long enough, it doesn't matter what day of the year you buy a term end point index annuity, but annual reset structures make the day of the year you buy a little more important.

This is the reverse of what I first believed, but if you look at 50-years worth of index data the annual return difference between buying a term end point structure, on what turns out to be the best day of the year, is less than a half percent better than if you somehow had picked the worst day of the year.

However, annual reset structures purchased in the last half of the year hypothetically perform a bit better if markets represent the '60s and '70s, but if markets look like the '80s and '90s the middle of the year is the best time to buy for annual point-to-point structures and the last half of the year is the best time to start an averaging structures. I find this bit of analysis interesting, but I do not know what you can do with it or if it would hold up in the future.

If everything is equal, monthly averaging produces a slightly higher return than daily averaging.

On average, an annual return using the average of twelve monthly index values as an end point will be 107% of the annual return determined by using the daily average of a year's index value as an end point. Or conversely, a daily averaging return will be 93% of a monthly averaging return if other variables are identical. In others words, if a daily averaging return is 5% the monthly averaging return would be 5.35%.

The two key phrases are "slightly higher" and "variables are identical". The difference between returns in the previous paragraph is only 35 basis points. And if the monthly averaging had a 2% spread and the daily averaging showed a 1.5% spread, then daily averaging would credit more interest. Or, if the daily averaging model had a higher participation rate the results could be different, or if one had a net cap of 15% and the other had a gross cap of 17%, the results would also vary.

Index annuity renewal rates are the biggest performance variable.

Index annuity renewal rates are dependent upon the general level of interest rates — because bond yields determine how much of the premium dollar is needed to provide the minimum guaranteed return; the price of options — because cheaper options enable you to participate in more of the index movement whilst expensive options do the opposite; and the final decision of the insurer — because interest rates and option prices do not set renewal rates, people do.

I had hoped to find some kind of broad relationship between different crediting methods, whereby I could say that if index annuity A had a rate of *x* then index annuity B would need a rate of *y* to produce the same returns. I did find that certain correlations between methods did exist, but only under certain market conditions. For example, if you knew markets were going to rise, an annual point-to-point with a cap of *x* would produce the same return as a monthly averaged method with a spread of *y*. But if markets zigzagged instead of rising, the correlation fell apart. Instead, I found a few very limited relationships that worked in all market scenarios.

What all of this means is a tenet I discovered a few years ago still holds true, and that is the integrity of the insurer is far more important than the crediting method in receiving the highest index annuity return.

Cheat Sheet

- Equity investments should produce higher returns over time than index annuities, but the difference in performance between the two might be closer than one would think.
- Although locking in all the crediting factors eliminates renewal rate risk it is very expensive to do so with an annual or biennial design.
- The integrity of the carrier is far more important than selection of a crediting style.

Discussion Questions

1. Is hypothetical back-testing worth the effort?

2. What are some problems with hypothetical testing?

3. What returns should one expect from index annuities?

Chapter Quiz

1. Annual Reset Crediting Methods

A. Lock in credited interest
B. Protect credited interest from index declines
C. Reset each year to start fresh when calculating index movement
D. All of the above

2. Giving the insurer the flexibility to change crediting factors

A. Lowers the hedging costs which should mean higher index participation
B. Eliminates renewal rate concerns
C. Is against insurance department regulations
D. Is seldom done

3. The chapter says what is more important than the crediting method in receiving competitive index annuity returns

A. Commissions
B. Option costs
C. Integrity of the carrier
D. Interest rates

4. Which statements are generally true

A. In rising markets term end point methods should result in higher returns than other methods.
B. In choppy markets annual reset structures should perform better than term end point ones.
C. In a prolonged bear market no index annuity will produce a high return.
D. All of the above

5. The goal of index annuities

A. Is to provide mutual fund style returns and protect principal
B. Is to be an insurance version of an index fund
C. Is to be very competitive with other savings vehicles
D. None of the above

Why Indexing?

The intent of indexing is to match the performance of a certain group of investments. The idea is not to try to "beat the market" but to be the market. Indexing benefits from diversification that reduces the volatility and risk associated with owning only one or a few securities.

Relative Growth of Stock Value From Jan 1982 To Jan 2002

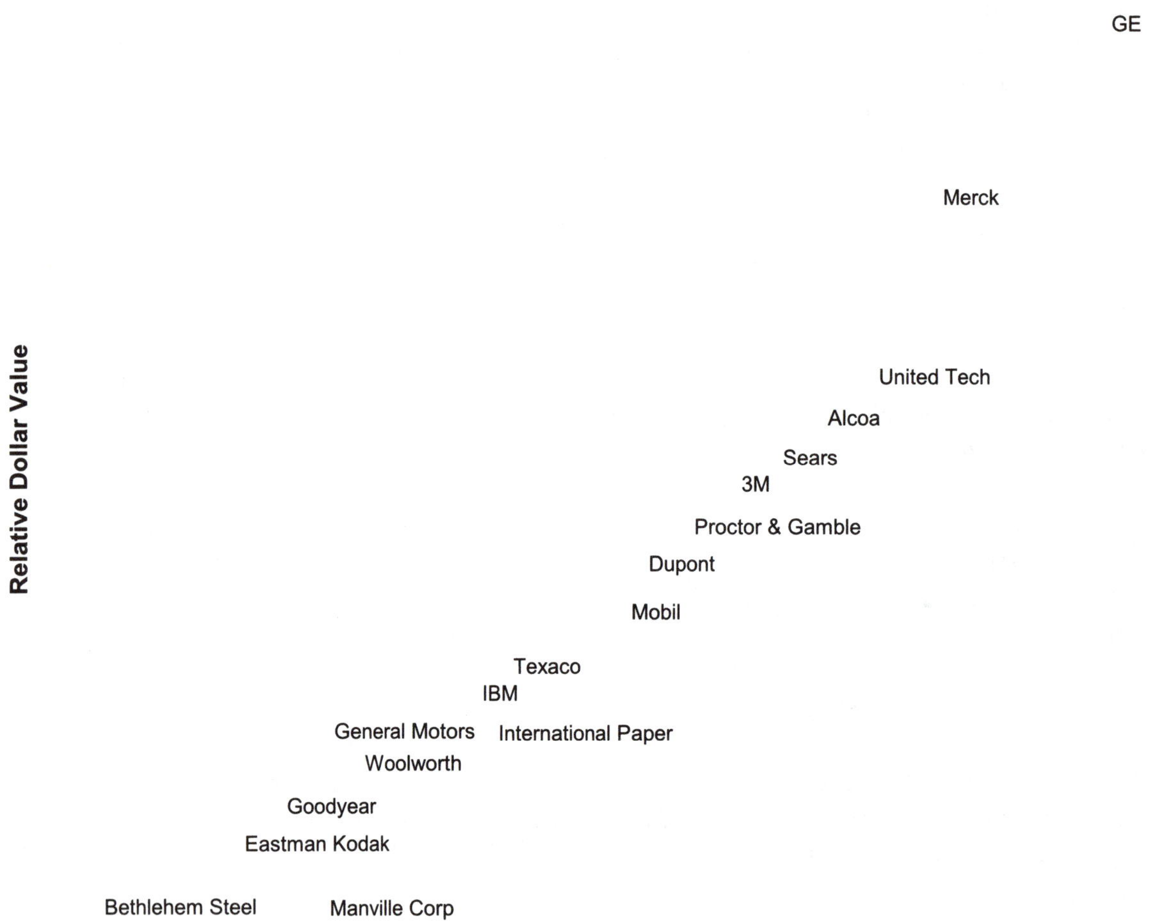

Data Source: Yahoo.finance.com

This chart shows the relative growth in the value of a share of stock – adjusted for dividends and splits – in eighteen of the largest corporations in America that were around at the start of 1982, and sees how they would have compared with S&P 500 performance – without dividends – for the twenty-years ending at the start of 2002.

If you had been wise enough to buy shares of General Electric or Merck a score of years ago, you have done very well. In fact, investing in nine of the eighteen companies would have made you more money than if you could have simply bought the S&P 500 index. But nine of the companies did worse than the index. Indeed, Bethlehem Steel and Johns Manville declared bankruptcy during this period. Indexing eliminates the possibility of placing all your eggs in the wrong basket.

Indices

The Standard & Poor's 500 Index is the external equity-linked index used in over 95% of the index annuities purchased today. The S&P 500 Index includes a representative sample of 500 common stocks from companies trading on the New York Stock Exchange, American Stock Exchange and Nasdaq National Market System. The objective of the index is to be a benchmark for U.S. stock market performance and represents approximately 80% of the domestic equity market capitalization.

S&P 500 Monthly Closing Values 1957 through 2002

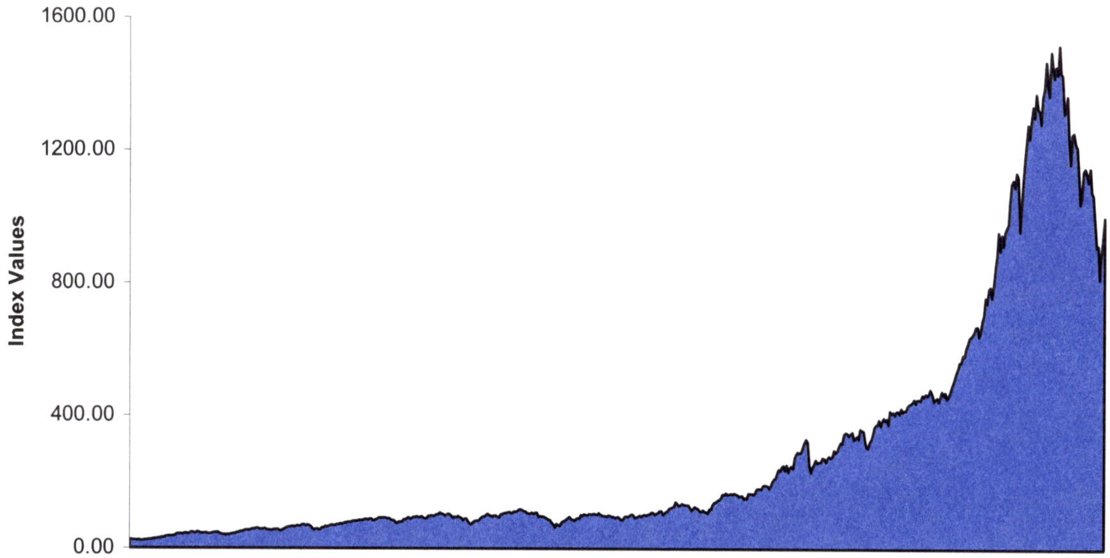

Date Source: Used with permission of Standard & Poor's

In 1996 Jackson National Life introduced an annuity with four index alternatives and a fixed account. The multiple index design was not initially copied, but a number of carriers began offering a fixed account option within an index product. American Equity introduced the first Dow Jones Industrial Average based index in the summer of 1999.

Although the S&P 500 index is the dominant external index utilized, carriers offer other indices. These other indices include the Dow Jones Industrial Average, S&P MidCap 400, Nasdaq 100, Russell 2000, U.S. 5-Year Treasury Rate, Lehman Brothers Aggregate Bond Index, Lehman Brothers Treasury Index and an international index. No respective index provider sponsors, endorses, sells or promotes any index annuity.

Ways to calculate the earning of linked-interest in an index annuity are limited only by imagination, and available linkage options. There would be nothing to preclude an index annuity that based excess interest earnings on the movement of a utility index or a gold index or even a specific stock.

Indexed Funds contrasted with Indexed Annuities

The benefits of indexing - diversification and simplicity, apply to both index mutual funds and index annuities, but they are different animals. Indexed mutual funds include reinvested dividends in their return calculations, but they charge management fees and offer no protection to principal or previous returns from market drops. Index annuity interest calculations do not include reinvested dividends, but principal and credited interest are protected from market risk.

Although Index Mutual Funds & Index Annuities both enjoy the diversification and simplicity of indexing they are totally separate animals. Index funds are investment vehicles; index annuities are a savings instruments.

Options

Insurance companies typically buy options to provide the potential index-linked annuity interest. When you purchase an option you have a right to either buy or sell something at a particular price within a particular time. A ***Call*** option gives you the right to buy something. A ***Put*** option gives you the right to sell something. Options are available on individual stocks, government debts, foreign currencies and indexes. The price the option buyer pays to the option seller (option holder) is called a ***Premium***. To ***Exercise*** an option means to ask to receive the cash settlement amount. This is the amount by which the settlement value exceeds the exercise price.

Say that you could buy a share of XYZ stock for $50. Instead of buying the actual stock we could buy a *call* option that gives us the right to buy the stock for $50 at anytime over the next year. The *premium* cost of the option is $2. If the stock price rose to $60 we would *exercise* our option and receive the cash settlement amount, which is the current market price or *settlement value* of $60, less the Exercise Price of $50, leaving us $10.

An ***American-style*** option may be exercised at any time before it expires. A ***European-style*** option may only be exercised on its expiration date. An option can be ***In The Money***, which means the market value of the optioned interest is above the exercise price of the option; ***Out Of The Money***, meaning the interest value is below the exercise price; or ***At The Money***, where the interest value is at the exercise price.

The exercise price of our XYZ Call option is 50. If XYZ stock is selling for more than $50 a share we could exercise our option to buy it cheaper because we're *in the money*. If XYZ were under $50 a share we'd be *out of the money* spent on the option. One-year from now the option expires. If you could only exercise the option on the expiration date you'd own a *European-style* option. If you exercise the option at any time you'd own an *American-style* option.

What is an option worth? An option's value consists of two elements. An option has an ***Intrinsic Value***, which is the degree the option is in the money. An option also has ***Time Value*** meaning any value above intrinsic value. An option that is out of the money only has time value. The more volatile the underlying interest behind the security the higher the time value of the option.

The exercise price of our XYZ call option is 50. If XYZ stock is selling for $55 a share the option has an intrinsic value of $5. Any option premium above $5 reflects *time value*. Time Value is influenced by the amount of time remaining on the option – more time until expiration gives the underlying security more time to go where you want it to, and the volatility of the security – if the value of the security bounces all over the place you have a better chance of winding up in the money. American-style options have higher time value than European-style options because there are more windows to exercise the option.

This Time In English

The two parts of an option's value are it's ***Intrinsic Value***, which is the degree the option is "in the money" and its ***Time Value*** meaning the period left in which you may exercise the option. The greater the amount of time left until the option expires, the greater its time value.

Let's talk about the "in the money", "at the money", and "out of the money" rigmarole first. We said we could buy an option that would let us buy XYZ stock at $50 a share. Suppose today XYZ stock was selling for $55 a share, what would you pay for the option?

If we could get an option that would let us buy the stock for $5 less than we could sell it for, the option would have an intrinsic value of $5. This option would be "in the money" – the amount we would gain by exercising it – by $5. What if the current market price of the stock was $50? An option permitting us to buy the stock at $50 would be "at the money" meaning there is no intrinsic value (we could not make any money by using the option instead of buying the stock; we wouldn't gain a benefit from using the option). What if the market price of the stock was $45 a share and we had an option to buy the stock at $50. The option again would have no intrinsic value because we would gain nothing by using it.

The intrinsic value component of an option is simply arithmetic. How much do I gain by exercising the option instead of directly using the underlying security? Any gain greater than zero is the option's intrinsic value. Time value is a more cosmic, transcendental element.

Say we could buy an option that would let us buy a share of XYZ stock for $50 and XYZ stock is currently selling for $45. What would we pay for the option?

Because the "*strike price*" of the option (the stock price at which the option can be exercised) is higher than the current market price of the stock, the option has no intrinsic value, and if the option expires and becomes worthless in 10-minutes we wouldn't pay anything for it, we would buy the stock instead. But what if the option would give us the right to buy XYZ stock for $50 at anytime in the next year. Even though the option isn't worth exercising today, perhaps it might be in six months? The price you would pay for that option would be its time value.

The longer an option has until it expires the greater its time value. You would pay more for an option that expires in three months and not two months, and you'd pay more for an option that could be exercised for three years instead of two. The reason why is because more time increases the possibility that the stock price will go up and thereby increase the option's value.

There are two primary risks associated with buying options. An option buyer could lose the premium paid for the option – if an option is out of the money on the expiration date the option has no value. The other risk is that the option writer is unable to exercise the option due to market conditions – if trading is halted in the option the buyer may not be able to exercise the option.

Option Multiplier Effect

How can an option's value increase more than the underlying security or index itself? The answer is the multiplier or leverage effect of options.

You could a buy share of XYZ stock for $50 today. Six months from now XYZ has a market price of $60. If you sold the stock you'd receive $60, $10 more than you paid, and you'd have a 20% profit ($10/$50 = 20%).

Instead of buying XYZ stock we buy an option from the seller that gives us the right to buy XYZ for $50 a share at anytime within the next year. For this right we pay the seller $2. At the end of six-months the price of the stock is $60 - a 20% increase from $50, but our option has increased in value fivefold. How can this be?

Our option gives us the right to buy the stock at $50 a share even though it's now worth $60 a share. Our option is now $10 – the difference between current price and exercise price. We would simply sell the option for $10. We've earned $10 on a $2 investment – a 500% increase ($10/$2 = 500%). The stock gained 20%; the stock option gained 500%.

This is how options work and it is why an index annuity can provide participation in an index even though only a few pennies out of each premium dollar are spent on the option. Of course, the leverage effect works both ways to a certain extent. If the price of the XYZ stock fell to $48 a share, and we owned the stock, we'd still have almost all of our money remaining, but if we owned that option we'd lose 100% of the option's value if the price of XYZ stayed at $50 and below. However, this is why most of the money from a dollar of index annuity premium is instead placed in bonds and similar vehicles.

Index options are a bit more complicated because there aren't specific stocks backing the option, but the basic concepts are the same. Options provide a leverage or multiplier effect when values rise.

Getting Back To Why No Moving Parts Is Expensive

We said the price of the option to buy a share of XYZ stock for $50 during the next twelve months was $2. What if we also wanted the ability to buy XYZ stock at $50 share during the second year? The seller of the option would charge more than $2 because the seller's exposure to the risk of a higher stock price has increased. If we wanted an option to buy XYZ stock in year three the price would be higher yet. The option buyer has rights and the longer he can use these rights the more they are worth, and corresponding the longer the obligation of the option seller the more he will charge.

If the market stayed the same, the option buyer might buy a new option on XYZ stock each year for $2 – if he bought options five years in a row the total cost would be $10. But if the option buyer wanted to buy all the options for all five years at once the seller is going to charge more because of the time value. The sellers might charge $2 for the first one, $3 for the one that could be exercised in year 2, $4 for the year 3 option, $5 for the year 4 option and $6 for the year 5 option. Instead of spending $10 for five years of options the option buyer might spend $20.

An index annuity buying options one year at a time is not paying for all that extra time value, so the cost is much cheaper and index participation is higher. Therefore, the index participation can be much higher than it would be for a different index annuity that locked in the future cost and guaranteed all moving parts.

If future option costs are the same or lower, then buying options one-year at a time permits the carriers to offer higher overall index participation. However, if option prices are higher in the future, then it might be better to lock in everything today.

But Term End Point Designs Are Usually Cheapest

I have repeatedly said that the longer the exercise period, the greater the time value, so the higher the option cost. I have also stated that term end point crediting methodologies using options that may not be exercised for five to twelve years are able to provide higher index participation than annual reset designs because their option cost is lower. It sounds like a contradiction, but it is not. The option cost of the term end point method is less expensive because you are buying fewer options.

This chart shows the relative option cost of buying a "full" option (100% index participation) that may be exercised within a specific time period at an assumed level of index volatility. The cost is expressed as the number of pennies out of each premium dollar. If you bought an option that had a one-year life (an annual reset), the cost would be 9 cents. If you bought an option with a two-year life (biennial reset), the cost would be 13 cents, and so on.

Option Cost (¢ out of a Premium $)

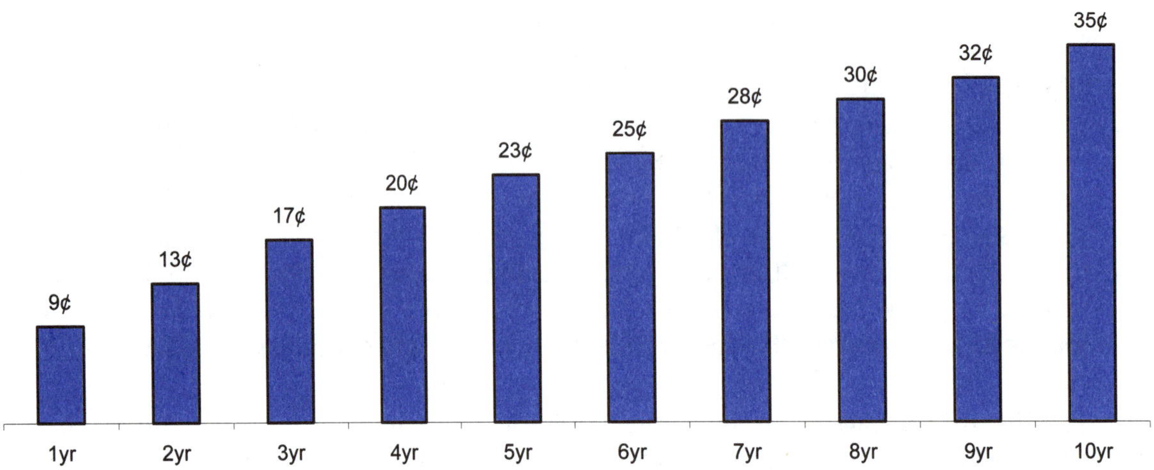

As you can see, the cost of the option increases as the life or exercise period increases, and this is due to the time value component. An option with a life of ten years costs 35 cents while the one-year option costs 9 cents. However, a term end point design with a ten-year period would only be buying one 35 cents option. An annual reset designed annuity would be buying an option each year, or ten separate options for a ten-year timeframe. Even though the individual option cost is cheaper for the annual reset method the total option cost is higher – 9 cents time 10 years versus 35 cents once. This is why effective index participation for term end point designs is higher than for annual resets designs, and why biennial resets usually have higher index participation than annual resets (one two-year option instead of two one-year options).

The bottom line effect on overall participation rates between different periods is not quite as vast as it might look. Even though the total option cost of the annual reset method in this example is 90 cents and the term end point's option cost is 35 cents, this does not mean the term end point rate is two and half times the annual reset participation rate. This is because the money not spent on options by the annual reset annuity is in bonds earning interest and this extra interest provides more money to buy annual reset options down the road and helps offset the additional cost.

Can You Buy An Option With A 12-Year Life?

Yes. Ordinary stock exchange traded options typically expire within eight months and many expire within a month or two. But there are also Long-term Equity Anticipation Securities (LEAPS®) options that can have up to a three-year life. And option sellers and buyers can design their own custom periods that could be for five, ten or even twenty years.

You Don't Have To Buy Options

The majority of carriers provide the index link by buying an assortment of generic options, but that is not the only way it can be done. As previously mentioned, sellers and buyers can create custom options to cover special needs or time periods. The negatives for a custom option are they tend to be more expensive than exchange options and more illiquid.

Carriers can avoid the whole option issue by having the index-linked portion essentially reinsured by a third party in which the writing carrier keeps the minimum guarantee exposure and hands off the index risk to another, but this can be costly and it can be difficult or impossible to find a reinsurer at times. Another approach is to use portfolio replication whereby an insurer uses a collection of stocks, futures, and specific stock options to duplicate movement of the index, and provide index-linked interest, at a lower cost than simply buying index options. This can work very well, the only concern is if the insurer screws up, the replication could not only wind up without money to cover the index-link interest, but with additional losses on the replication portfolio. A final method is to go naked by self-insuring and not do any hedging at all.

Going naked is not necessarily crazy. Perhaps a carrier wants to test the index annuity water and see if any sales result. If the product does not sell, the insurer has not wasted the money it takes to set up the option buying, and if sales are slight, the potential exposure is limited.

Markets

The next sections talk about past stock markets, investment topics, problems with correlation and the risks of forecasting. The good news is you do not have to read any of it to understand index annuities. It is a selfish section in that it contains many of my personal views of what I see as some problems in the whole investment planning arena, and it also shows the reason I like the safety features of the index annuity. There's a lot of personal opinion on the following pages, and if you disagree with some or all of my statements and concerns I won't say you're wrong.

Predicting The Past

#1 Monte Carlo simulations are designed to reflect the probability of achieving a desired result by randomly generating the outcomes of many periods given certain assumptions. The idea is the quantity of outcomes provides a better basis for decision making than merely looking at the average returns over a period, and the idea is true within this context. However, it seems that people are granting Monte Carlo testing a degree of accuracy that would challenge Nostradamus.

I have talked to financial counselors that base the allocation of assets on the results of Monte Carlo modeling and the perceived risk tolerance and goals of the consumer. As an example, a financial counselor will input a minimum desired return and a combination of assets, and the simulation might say that 80% of the time this mix of assets would have produced the return. And the counselor might tweak the asset mix, resulting in a simulation producing the desired return 90% of the time. These results accurately depict how these allocations would have performed in the past. The problem is with interpretation of the data.

I have had financial counselors tell me that the way they present the data to the consumers is by saying things like "Allocation A gives an 80% confidence level in hitting this return and Allocation B gives a 90% confidence level, therefore we should select Allocation B". Unfortunately, the consumer may think you are saying there is a 9 out of 10 chance that you will hit your desired return if you select Allocation B. The reality is you are taking a 100% gamble that the past will repeat and your confidence level for any particular period is an illusion. Historical data does a wonderful job of predicting the past, but a poor one at predicting the future.

I am not saying Monte Carlo simulation is a poor analytical aid. On the contrary, it is an excellent tool to show the wide variety of outcomes that can result from a given assumption. I have used a variation of this tool for years in my index annuity studies by showing the percentage of times different hypothetical returns result using differing index participation and crediting methods. But neither my hypothetical results nor Monte Carlo outcomes should be taken literally because the financial past does not mirror the future.

My data might show, at current rates, Index Annuity X would have generated 10% or better annual returns in 33% of the periods over the last 50 years, and that Index Annuity Y would never have generated 10% or better annual returns.

Does this mean that Index Annuity X has a 1 in 3 shot at producing a double digit return in the next period or that Index Annuity Y has zero chance? No, I think it means over time *X* should produce more periods of 10% or higher returns than *Y*. But I do not know when those periods will occur nor how many of them there will be. A Monte Carlo simulation that says one assumption produces a desired result 90% of the time and the other assumption hits the mark 80% of the time merely means the two assumptions are darn near equal, not that the desired return will be hit.

Coincidence Not Causality

#2 I bought my first car in 1969 and the S&P 500 finished that calendar year down 11.36%. I bought a Chevy in 1972 and the index went up 15.63%. I bought another car in 1973 and the index went down 17.37%. In 1977 I bought an Oldsmobile and the index declined 11.50%. In 1984 I purchased a car and the index rose 1.4%. In 1990 I bought a Ford and the index dropped 6.56%. In 2000 I bought my daughter a Hyundai Accent for her graduation and the index fell 10.14%. And in 2001 I bought another car for myself, and the S&P 500 again declined.

Over this period I bought 8 cars and the market went down 6 times. Therefore, the *Marrion Car Predictor Law of Market Performance* was correct 75% of the time (and in 1984 the market almost finished down which would have made it 7 out of 8). There have been 9 down years for the S&P 500 since 1969 and my car-buying indicator accurately predicted 6 of those 9 years.

Marrion Car Predictor Law

Bought Car	S&P 500 Ended Year
1969	–11.4%
1972	+15.6%
1973	–17.4%
1977	–11.5%
1984	+ 1.4%
1990	– 6.6%
2000	–10.1%
2001	–13.0%

If you compare the results of the *Marrion Car Predictor* with forecasts of economists, market analysts and Louie the bookie over the same period, the *Marrion Car Predictor* had a significantly higher accuracy rate. This could mean one of two things – either it is a good thing I quit buying cars as often as I used to because we would have been in a 30-year global depression, or the fact that the market usually dropped in the same year I purchased a car is coincidence.

#3 The Holy Grail in investment planning is finding assets with inverse or negative correlation. What I mean is if Investment A rose 10% whenever Investment B fell 10% you might attempt to reduce the risk of overall loss by adding Investment A to a portfolio containing Investment B.

Daily Closing Values January 00 to October 02

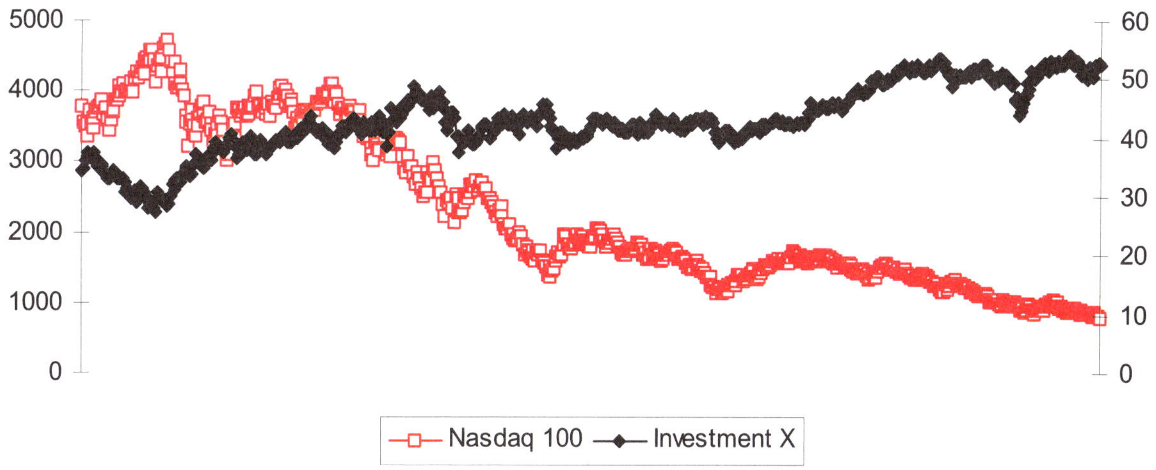

The chart shows in January 2000 the Nasdaq 100 Index was near the 3800 level. The Nasdaq 100 rose to over 4700 by early spring, took a hit in late spring 2000, and spent the next 2½ years sliding down. By the fall of 2002 the index was off almost 80%.

By contrast, take a gander at the squiggles of Investment X. In the spring of 2000 as Nasdaq levels began to drop Investment X values began to rise. In fact, over the next 2½ years the rise in Investment X values was almost the exact opposite of the fall in Nasdaq 100 values.

Back in January 2000 if you'd taken half your money out of the Nasdaq 100 and put it in Investment X your total combined return for this entire period would be close to zero. Now, zero may not be great, but it beats the heck out of an 80% loss.

What is Investment X? Is it a dynamic pricing model using linear regression? Does it involve put options, call options and butterfly straddles? No, it's Budweiser. The chart shows the daily closing price of Anheuser-Busch stock for the period, and if unlike me you had purchased the stock instead of the product, your portfolio and waistline would probably be in better shape.

Why did the stock perform well during the bear market? I am sure analysts would conclude that investors drifted to the certainty of defensive consumer stocks and away from high technology companies, that during recessions investors like companies that lead their industries, and that people drink more beer and less champagne when unemployment rates go up. Or, it could merely be coincidence.

Causality is what investors are really looking for in the market. Causality means if this happens then that happens. But in the market causality producing beneficial results is usually either coincidence or a fluke. My car buying does not affect the stock market, nor is October automatically a bad month for the market. There is no relationship; it is pure coincidence.

Although Anheuser-Busch stock would have offset certain risks in the last bear market, I would be willing to bet that it will not happen again because people are now prepared for the possibility.

#4 VAR, a risk management tool fully lettered as value-at-risk, emerged in the mid '90s as a way to determine the maximum possible losses in a portfolio, with a determined confidence of how right one was, within a specific time period. VAR was embraced by investment bankers and hedge funds, which would state that based on VAR models they were 96% or 98% or 99% sure that certain outcomes would occur. However, VAR modeling to a large part assumes the investment world is like the graph in your old high school algebra book and that risk can be plotted on a bell-shaped curve. The reality is financial events, especially negative ones, can sometimes be extreme and bell curves do not work well with data that is way outside the norm.

With the names and facts distorted to hide the guilty, here is the tale of an index annuity carrier that established a guaranteed minimum level of future index participation based on VAR modeling using past index volatility to determine confidence. When they issued their policies, their minimum guaranteed participation rate assumed long term implied volatility would remain under a value of, say, 30 as it had almost all of the preceding decade. In 2000 this implied volatility measure closed above a level of 30 on 42-days; the average level for the year was 25.9. In 2001 levels above 30 were recorded on 73-days and the year's average value was 28.4. Although 2002 began mildly, levels above 30 were recorded on 120-days and the year's average value was 30.4.

The VAR model, and the insurer, will be proven correct if volatility simmers down in the future. If not, the insurer will be giving the annuity owner too good a rate, and both the VAR model and the insurer will be losers. As I once said, you want your insurance company to pay a competitive return, but you also want it to stay in business.

What's the answer?

Does this mean you should ignore the past in investment planning? Except in very broad terms the answer may be yes. It is possible that creating complex investment algorithms gives us no more certainty about predicting future market events than the last fifty spins of the roulette wheel foretells the outcome of the next spin.

If the past does not aid us in developing diversified portfolios that avoid or minimize market loss, then perhaps we need to use vehicles or methods that offer greater protection from market loss and still offer the potential for gain. This would include greater direct hedging in equity portfolios, utilizing the death and living benefits of variable annuities, and using the protection of principal and credited interest features of indexed annuities.

Equity Correlation During Market Stress

A key principle of portfolio theory says that market risk can be reduced if equity investment portfolios are sufficiently diversified. Academic studies have developed formulas that attempt to determine the correct portfolio mixture to optimize returns at the lowest level of risk. These studies look at the correlation, or performance relationship, between different financial instruments and how they performed in the past. The goal is to put together a clump of investments that generate the greatest returns at the lowest risk over all periods.

Even when returns aren't highly correlated they can still move in the same direction at times

A fundamental problem with the whole concept is that correlation does not mean causality and the past does not exactly repeat in the future. By that I mean if historically one investment has always gone down when the other goes up every time, say, dividend yields reached "x" percent, there is no guarantee that the same thing will happen the next time "x" is reached. Unfortunately, the market is not an actuarial table.

The ultimate flaw in the diversification tale is that it fails to sufficiently protect portfolios during times of severe market stress. When the stock markets are trudging along diversification may increase returns, but diversification is often sold as a way to reduce losses if the market tanks. However, the reality is that diversification across equity sectors may not offer the protection desired if the market plummets.

October 1987 was a particularly nasty month for the stock market. If you had owned the S&P 500 index at the start of October you were down 23.1% on All Saint's Eve. During a period of severe market stress this common market benchmark plunged; how were other indices affected?

For the same period the Dow Jones Industrial Average dropped 24.5%. Well, similar drops for the Dow and S&P 500 may not be surprising because both are broad market indicators, but how were other equity sectors affected? In October 1987 the Nasdaq fell 28.4%; the Russell 2000 plummeted 31.0% and even the London FTSE slid 26.3%. During this time of severe market stress all of these sectors were similarly affected. There were sectors that responded a little differently – the Tokyo Nikkei 225 only dropped 9.3% and the drop in precious metal stocks was also down less than the broad markets. However, if you had then determined that the stocks of Japan and gold shares were the place to put your money, your returns for the next fifteen-years would have been abysmal.

For many investors 1987 is ancient history. An argument could be made that advances in portfolio theory make lessons of past declines less relevant. After all, weren't the '90s a new paradigm in investing in which the old rules didn't apply?

In 1998 the stock market was hit with several shocks. The first shock was a concern that growth in corporate earnings might be slowing. This was followed by a banking crisis in Asia, a president on the verge of impeachment, and a Russian government that said, "You want us to actually pay off on our bonds?" The resultant uncertainty caused the S&P 500 to drop 11.3% in the month of August. During the same period the Dow fell 11.3%, the London FTSE fell 11.4%, the NASDAQ dropped 11.8%, the Tokyo Nikkei 225 slid 12.3%, and the Russell 2000 declined 17.5%.

Correlation During Market Stress

	10/01/87 – 10/30/87	8/01/98 – 9/01/98	3/23/00 – 10/09/02
DJIA	(24.5%)	(11.9%)	(37.8%)
S&P 500	(23.1%)	(11.3%)	(49.1%)
Nasdaq	(28.4%)	(11.8%)	(77.9%)
Russell 2000	(31.0%)	(17.5%)	(46.0%)
London FTSE 100	(26.3%)	(11.4%)	(43.9%)
Tokyo Nikkei 225	(9.3%)	(12.3%)	(56.7%)

Let's examine a more recent period. Spring 2000 saw the Dow flirt with 11000, the S&P 500 tarry near 1500, and the Nasdaq close above 5000. On October 9, 2002 the Dow closed at 7286, the S&P 500 finished at 776 and the Nasdaq ended at 1114. The following thirty months produced declines of 38%, 49% and 78% respectively.

In these periods of severe market stress the indices were almost perfectly correlated - they ALL went down. Stock diversification did not protect the portfolio from loss. Although I do not believe equity diversification will protect portfolios during severe stress, hedging can. Various hedging strategies using puts and calls, or short selling can protect portfolios against loss; however, hedging is a direct cost against returns in rising markets and is not a diversification tool to maximize returns. Diversification can increase returns over the long haul, because history does not repeat and diversification may mean we accidentally benefit from unforeseen growth in some neglected sector.

Index Annuities & Equity Correlation

A stock investor has only two choices if the market declines. He can sell and take his losses, or he can wait and hope the market quits falling and heads back up before he needs the money. An index annuity owner has sell and hold choices, but with more positive outcomes and without the uncertainty.

The annuity owner could cash in the annuity and receive a specified amount known in advance – the net surrender value, or hold the annuity with the knowledge that a minimum interest guarantee will continue to increase the annuity's value regardless of what the market does. If the annuity uses an annual reset crediting methodology the annuity owner knows that the annuity will not share in any losses, but that any future market gains will be based on current market levels. The index annuity is positively correlated for market increases, but has zero correlation if the market declines. These attributes give the index annuity owner a great deal of power.

The Risk of Forecasting Models

Predictions of future market performance involve using historical data and then extrapolating this data through techniques like linear regression. This is the basis for modern portfolio theory.

If you examine past annual returns of, say the S&P 500, you can determine how often returns occurred. You find that the S&P 500, like most general market indexes, produces a few very low returns, a few very high returns and many returns in the middle. When you graph the frequency of these returns your picture looks like a bell curve.

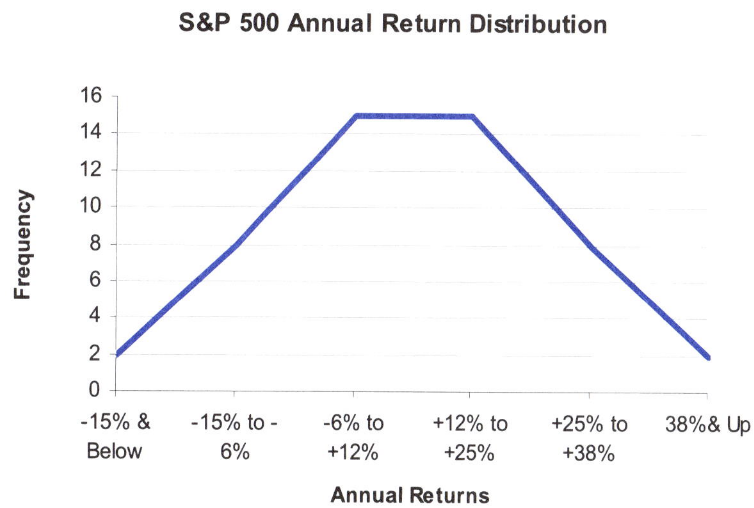

Modern portfolio theory says you use this history and attempt to determine the probability of these returns occurring in the future and develop appropriate hedging strategies.

As an example, based on the fifty year period from 1950 through 1999 there had only been two-calendar years when the S&P 500 index lost more than 15% in any given year. So, over 96% of the time the index has posted a better return than a 15% loss. On a probability basis, you would then develop a general hedging strategy that took into account these parameters.

However, while historical data is helpful, the past doesn't exactly repeat in the future. Portfolio theory to a large part ignores the possibility of extreme events, which can devastate expectations. Extraordinary events are not truly covered by portfolio theory and it's the main reason that hedge funds lost millions in 1998 and market timing did not provide protection from the ravages of the millennium bear market.

Bond Correlation

Corporate bonds are often proposed as a counterweight to stocks; however, bond values can also plummet when stocks go down. One environment that is nasty for both stocks and bonds are rising interest rates. Higher interest rates make bonds more attractive than stocks, which means stocks sell for less in order to provide higher competitive returns at the same earnings level. At the same time higher rates mean existing bonds issued at lower rates sell at a discount to new bonds with higher coupon rates. A prime example of this double dirty scenario is the 1970s in which both stocks and bonds had a rocky time.

In a recession stock values fall because the expectation of corporate earnings declines. During this time bond values often increase providing the desired counterweight, but a severe recession can move both stock and bond values down. A sagging economy puts downward pressure on earnings per share, but it also decreases corporate profits. If a corporation's credit worthiness declines, the value of their bonds declines. If a corporation is smote by economic troubles their bonds could be worthless.

The collapse of the telecom bubble in 2002 left many people holding worthless stock and it also left bonds that could only be sold for pennies on the dollar. A portfolio of telecom stocks and bonds were almost perfectly correlated – the value of both sank like a rock. In bad economic times corporate bonds can move in tandem with stocks and not provide the positive zig to a bear market's zag.

Natural Laws

Two of the most intellectually dishonest ploys used in the investment world are expressing generalizations as facts and beginning comparisons with "in a perfect world". As an example, you have probably read time and time again that a mutual fund with lower fees will produce better returns than one with higher fees. This is often stated with the certainty of a natural law and is used to promote the purchase of mutual funds with the lowest fees with the smugness that they must be inherently superior. But the generalization is not necessarily true.

A few years ago I analyzed the most recent five year results of growth mutual funds. The funds were than ranked according to annual expenses and five year performance. What I discovered was the quartile of funds with the highest annual expenses returned 4% more each year than the quartile of funds with the lowest annual expenses. If you want specifics, the highest expense funds averaged 19.6% a year for this period while the lowest expense funds averaged 15.6%.

I did the same study a year later for the next five-year period and the highest expense funds once again beat the lowest expense funds, but by a narrower margin. Does all this mean we now have a new natural law – that higher fees mean higher returns? No, it merely means in these two real world examples the low fees generalization stated as fact was wrong, and may not be an indisputable natural law at all. In a perfect world lower fees would mean higher returns, but the world ain't perfect and other factors come into play.

In the index annuity world one bromide in particular is often expressed as an unconditional fact, "index annuities don't include reinvested dividends so their returns will be worse than stock mutual funds". I'm not going to take the easy road and dismiss this statement by simply repeating another statement I've often read that says that most stock mutual funds under perform the indexes the annuities use, and the fund's lower returns could more than offset the reinvested dividends received, because I do not have actual performance data handy. What I will examine are other factors affecting comparative returns.

If you look at the last 50 calendar years (1952-2002) the average annual return of the S&P 500 was 9.5%. If you include dividends the annual return is close to 12%. On the surface it looks like the unconditional statement is correct. Even if an index annuity had 100% index participation it appears that funds with reinvested dividends would still win.

But even no-load mutual funds have management fees and other expenses, which range from as little as 0.12% for index funds to over 2.0% for some managed funds. In addition, asset sales within the fund's portfolio (portfolio turnover) can generate taxable income resulting in taxes paid resulting in a reduced return for the investor. The SEC said [SEC Final Rule 33-7941 Disclosure of Mutual Fund After-Tax Returns] that anywhere from a few basis points to as much as 5.6% of a stock mutual fund's return is lost to taxes and the average stock fund loses 2.5% of its return due to taxes.

So maybe the reality is if you factor in expenses and taxes the net average long-term stock fund return would have been around, maybe 8% to 9%, with a high of 11.0% to 11.5% for an index fund (or for a low-expense, tax-efficient managed fund). Index annuities with term end point structures have recently offered participation rates of 100% to 105%, and they do not charge management fees and they are 100% tax-efficient. So in theory, term end point index annuities might have delivered average returns in this macro example of 9.5% to 10.0% beating many stock mutual funds and disproving the unconditional fact, at least as it relates to saying <u>all</u> stock mutual funds win.

Index annuities with annual reset crediting methods offer a unique feature; they treat years of negative returns as years of zero interest. If you plug in reinvested dividends the average annualized S&P 500 index return is around 12.0%. But if you omit the dividends and swap years with index losses for zeros, the average annualized index return jumps from 9.5% to 12.6%.

This means that an annual reset structured annuity, with net index participation of 55%, would have beat many stock funds, and 90% net participation would have beat index funds. Now, unlike annuities with term end point structures, in the real world index annuities with annual reset crediting methods have not yet provided periods of 90% net index participation, but almost all have repeatedly been over 55% effective participation.

If you want to go even further to defrock the "mutual funds with reinvested dividends will always do better" criers, consider that the degree to which index annuities participate in the index is largely determined by the interest rate environment and option prices. Today, and throughout most of the relatively brief history of index annuities, index option prices have been above their historic average and interest rates have been below those of the preceding quarter century. If you haul out your index annuity interest crediting formula, and plug in some of the interest rates and option prices from the past, your model will throw out participation rates of 200%, 300% and 400%. ...Your mutual fund earned an additional 2% in reinvested dividends on that 10% market gain? ...Fine, we just credited 30% interest to the index annuity on that 10% market gain without the dividends!

The point of all this is not to say you should replace mutual funds with index annuities. Index annuities aren't designed to be replacements for index and managed funds, because these are investments and index annuities are saving vehicles. And the point is not that index annuities will someday offer 200% participation. The point is index annuities shouldn't simply be dismissed with the generalization "index annuities don't include reinvested dividends so their return will be bad" because it's not always true and may not even be important depending on your goals.

There will be times when index annuities do better than index funds and managed investments, and some index annuities could conceivably beat some stock funds much of the time. In fact, because of their risk-adverse design the returns from index annuities just might be a lot closer to managed stock and index funds over the long haul than one would think. But the role of index annuities is to provide the potential for a higher return than other savings vehicles that offer the same principal protection from market risk. Index annuities are viable solutions for many financial situations and are not easily dismissed or generalized.

Bear Markets

"When hamburgers go down in price we sing 'Hallelujah'...When they go up, we weep. For most of us, it's the same with everything we will be buying – except stocks."

– Warren Buffett [Fortune, 12/10/01 "Warren Buffett on the Stock Market"]

The problem with bear markets is they refuse to follow a script. The 1980-1982 Bear took three years to regain a top, as did the 1968-1970 Bear. The OPEC Bear of the '70s outlasted the terms of three presidents while going from peak to valley to peak. On another historical note, the last bear market to endure as long as the Millennium Bear market occurred when Hitler invaded Poland.

Future economists will probably shake their heads and wonder why the accompanying Millennium recession happened at all. Unlike the economic picture going into the 1990 recession, both the banking and housing industries were strong going into the 2001 recession. Unlike the 1981 recession scenario, there wasn't a tremendous amount of excess industrial capacity, nor were inventories at record highs (with the ample exception of routers and telecommunication lines). Unlike the 1973-1974 recession oil prices hadn't tripled. And, unlike any previous recession of the last thirty years, the economy had low interest rates and a very low rate of inflation. Hindsight might tell us that if interest rates had been raised in the late 1990s, thus slowing growth, both the bubble and resultant crash would have been avoided.

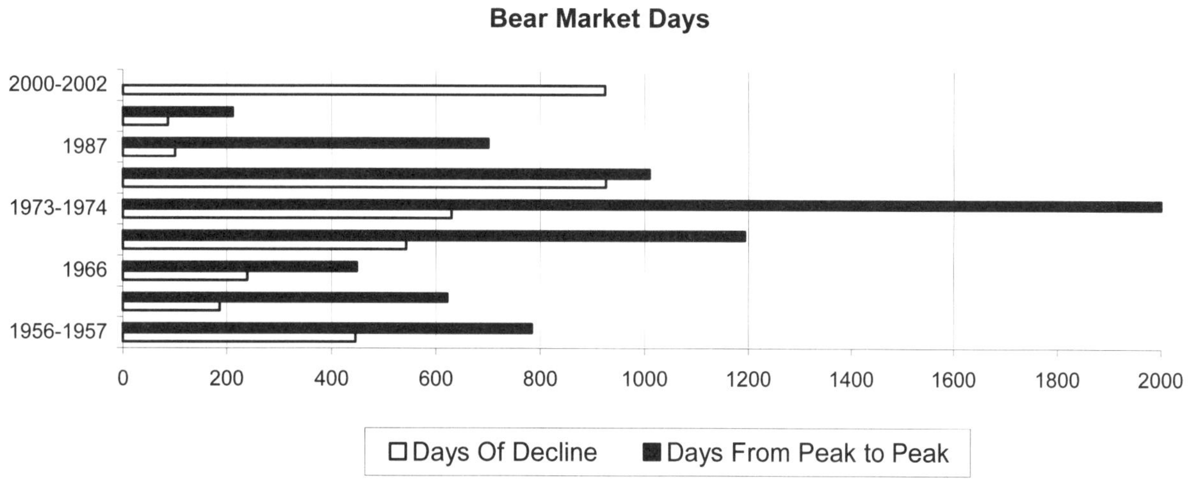

Interest in index annuities dramatically increased in the last bear market due to the protection from market risk benefit. Consumers realized that an index annuity provides at least a minimum guaranteed return. But minimizing loss is only one consideration in financial planning; the other half of the equation is maximizing gain.

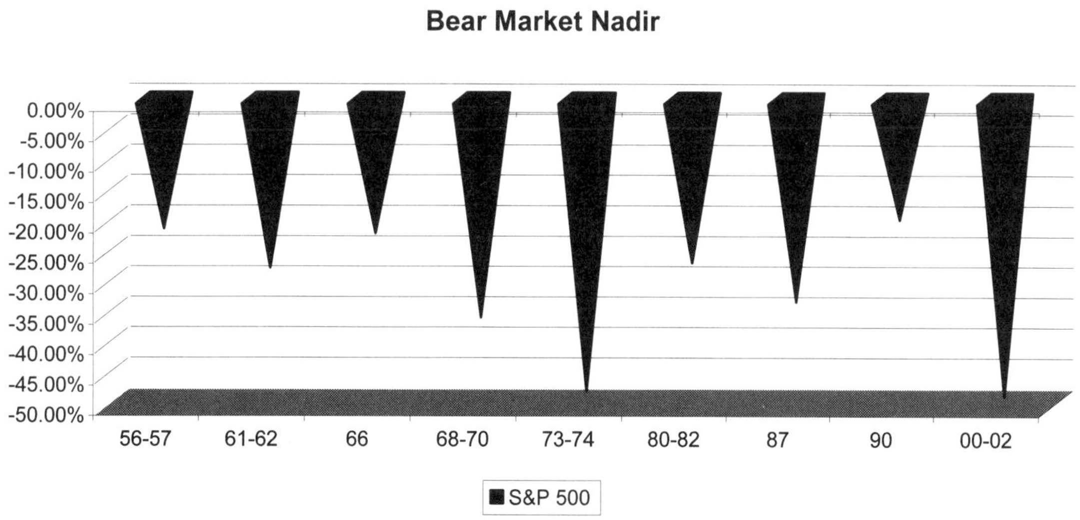

Unfortunately, the market doesn't announce its low point

In a bear market people tend to sit on the market sideline waiting until they are absolutely sure that the bottom has been reached before they buy. The problem is that the market doesn't announce when it has reached its low point, so you risk missing the bottom and missing potential profits by not diving in, or diving in and getting caught in a bear rally whereby the market sinks even further.

I went back and looked at the last nine bear markets. The question I asked was what would the ultimate gain be if we could have purchased the index on the day the S&P 500 first dropped 20% from its previous high, if we held the index until nine-years after that point. Or, what would have happened if we bought the index six-months after it reached the low point of that particular bear market and held it to the end of the same nine-year point.

S&P 500 Bear Markets - Buy or Wait?

Previous High Value	Low Value	Buy on 20% Decline	Wait 6 Months	Final End Point	Gain If Buy At 20%	Gain If Wait 6 m
08/02/56 49.64	*10/22/57* 38.98	*10/21/57* 39.15	*04/22/58* 42.80	*10/21/66* 78.19	99.7%	82.7%
12/21/61 72.64	*06/26/62* 52.32	*05/29/62* 58.08	*12/26/62* 63.02	*05/28/71* 99.63	71.5%	58.1%
02/09/66 94.06	*10/07/66* 73.20	*08/29/66* 74.53	*04/07/67* 89.36	*08/29/75* 86.88	16.6%	(2.8%)
11/29/68 108.37	*05/26/70* 69.29	*01/29/70* 85.69	*11/25/70* 85.09	*01/29/79* 101.55	18.5%	19.3%
01/11/73 120.24	*10/03/74* 62.28	*11/27/73* 95.70	*04/03/75* 81.51	*11/26/82* 134.88	40.9%	65.5%
09/21/76 107.83	*03/06/78* 86.90	*03/06/78* 86.90	*09/06/78* 105.38	*03/06/87* 290.66	234.5%	175.8%
11/28/80 140.52	*08/12/82* 102.42	*03/03/82* 110.92	*02/12/83* 147.76	*03/03/91* 370.47	234.0%	150.7%
08/25/87 336.77	*12/04/87* 223.92	*10/19/87* 224.84	*06/03/88* 266.45	*10/19/96* 700.66	211.6%	163.0%
07/16/90 368.95	*10/11/90* 295.46	*10/11/90* 295.46	*04/11/90* 377.63	*10/11/99* 1335.21	351.9%	253.6%

The *buy on the 20% decline* strategy versus *waiting six months* would have produced higher returns in seven of the nine markets. Even after including the horrendous 1973-1974 bear market, the buy on the decline method resulted in a 28% higher average return than if you waited six-months after the ultimate low to enter.

In all but one of the bear markets the *buy on the 20% decline* method means you would have watched the index sink further before it bottomed out, but in all but two corrections buying early generated higher gains than waiting until the next bull market had been formally announced.

In these instances you would have been far ahead if you had simply decided to ignore intuition, hunches and market experts and bought the index when it first closed 20% below the previous high. However, in the millennium bear market you would not have bought near the bottom by buying on the dip. The index first closed off 20% on March 12, 2001 at a level of 1180.16, and then proceeded down another 30%.

Extrapolation

Life is such a string of randomness and uncertainty that man is always attempting to find some way to predict the future. Extrapolation is where one infers unknown information by projecting known information. It is used with great accuracy in mathematics to estimate values of a function. It is also used in financial and economic forecasting; however, the accuracy in these areas is less than great.

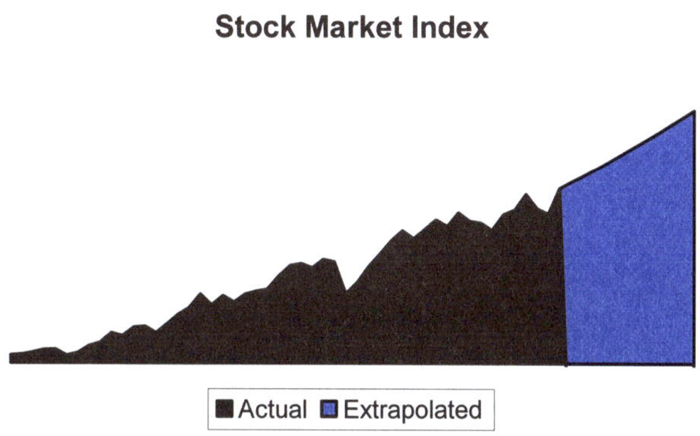

This chart reflects the values of a stock market index over a four year period. If you extrapolate the past values to predict movement in the fifth year you wind up with a projected fifth year gain of 24%. But reality was a little different

The first chart represents the monthly S&P 500 index values from March 1996 through March 2000. Unfortunately, as this chart shows the next 12 months weren't as kind as the prediction.

If extrapolation is not a surefire forecaster of continued growth, perhaps it does better in predicting declines.

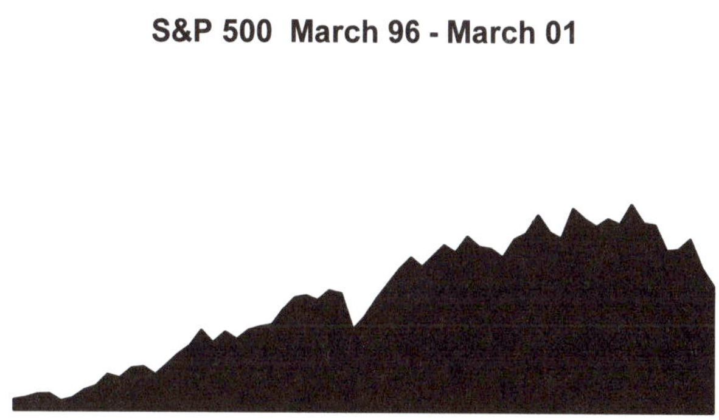

Stock Market Index

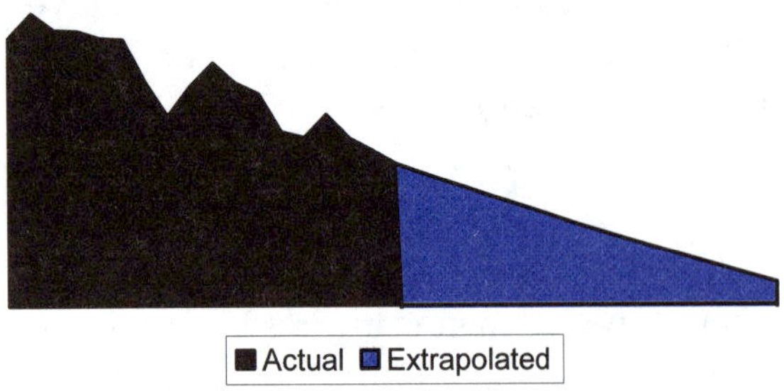

This chart reflects stock market values over an eighteen month period. As you can see, even though twice the index moved higher the general trend is down, and our extrapolation of past values follows this pattern.

But the previous chart shows the eighteen months between January 1981 and July 1982. The reality is this was not an omen because, as the next chart shows, the greatest bull market in history was about to begin.

The problem with extrapolating financial data is future values are not based on scientific or mathematical laws, but on human emotion and opinions of financial value, neither of which can be predicted. Using past "knowns" to predict future investment unknowns is sometimes accurate, but flipping a coin will also produce correct answers about half of the time.

S& P 500 January 81 - January 01

Defined Liquidity

As mentioned before, a stock investor has only two choices if the market declines. He can sell and take his losses, or he can wait and hope the market quits falling and heads back up before he needs the money. An index annuity owner has similar choices, but with greater certainty.

Many annuities have charges that may eat into the principal if the policy is surrendered early, but with the exception of market value adjustment products the cost of liquidity is known. A typical fixed annuity buyer knows the worst they could receive is 80 or 90 or 92 cents for every dollar of premium. And the annuity buyer knows if they hold their financial instrument long enough the interest buildup within the account will make them whole regardless of how the market performs. Unlike stocks or bonds, index annuities have defined liquidity. Regardless of how the market performs you usually know exactly what your surrender value is at any time.

Liquidity Cost

Say that a fixed annuity had a surrender charge of 7% for the first seven years and also an interest rate of 7%. If you had to liquidate the annuity at the end of the first year the interest earned would roughly offset the surrender charge and you would merely get back your original principal.

However, let's say that if you had not purchased the annuity you would have left it in a money market earning 3%. What is the surrender charge – or liquidity cost – of surrendering the annuity? Your true cost is not 7%, the amount of the surrender charge. Your true cost is 3%, the amount you could have earned in your alternative vehicle.

Let's say you did not surrender the annuity, but instead kept it for another year before surrendering, and in that second year the annuity again earned 7% and the money market paid 3%. What is your liquidity cost at the end of year two? Zero! You earned 14% in the annuity, paid back 7% in surrender charges, and had a net return of 7%. The money market earned 3% in year one and 3% in year two, for a total of 6%. Even after paying the surrender charge the annuity resulted in more money in your pocket.

How can there be a cost when you made more? If anything, there is a 1% liquidity cost associated with owning the money market.

The cost of liquidity - be it a surrender charge or an early withdrawal penalty or a "b-share" fee – isn't the nominal charge, but the net return after the cost when compared with the alternative instrument.

IPRI

Even though all index annuities use the same basic building blocks, with over 30 crediting methods in use it is difficult to determine if one annuity's index participation reflects the reality of the overall market, and direct comparisons are difficult. I developed IPRI to be a standard indicator of index participation that could be used to help see whether specific index annuities were, in fact, changing their rates to reflect markets costs and yields, and whether these product rate changes reflected the degree of change in the overall market.

The Index Participation Rate Indicator (IPRI) attempts to reflect changes in the portfolio yield of an insurance company combined with changes in the cost of index options. A higher indicator value reflects a more favorable environment for index annuities and thus, increased annuity participation should be observed. A falling indicator value should mean that product participation rates are declining as well.

IPRI uses the arithmetic average yield of Moody's Seasoned Corporate Bond Yield Aaa, Moody's Seasoned Corporate Bond Yield Baa, and 10 Year Treasury Constant Maturity Rate. The monthly yields are an average of monthly business days. Data on all of these vehicles are available at the Federal Reserve Board.

The resultant average yield of the three bond vehicles is multiplied by a factor of 10. From this yield variable the average monthly value of the Volatility Option Index (VIX) of the CBOE is subtracted (VIX values reflect option volatility of the S&P 100 Index and are widely available). The remaining product is the IPRI value for that specific month.

As an example, if the average monthly yield for the three bond instruments were 7%, 8%, 6% and the VIX monthly average value was 25, IPRI would be calculated as follows: The average yield of 7% [(7%+8%+6%)/3] is multiplied by 10 to produce a yield variable of 70, then the VIX value of 25 is deducted, leaving an IPRI value of 45.

Aaa Rated Yield	7%
Baa Rated Yield	8%
10-Year Treasury Rate	6%
Average Yield	7%
Multiplied By Factor	x 10
	70
Less VIX	- 25
Equals IPRI Value	45

This chart applies the formula to the period from 1995 to the close of 2002 – the product lifetime of index annuities. The chart says that index participation should have been at its highest levels in 1995 and 1996; would have fallen dramatically around September 1998 and taken approximately nine months to recover. Index participation then should have modestly risen, until beginning to decline in 2001, with big shock in 2002

Index Participation Rate Indicator

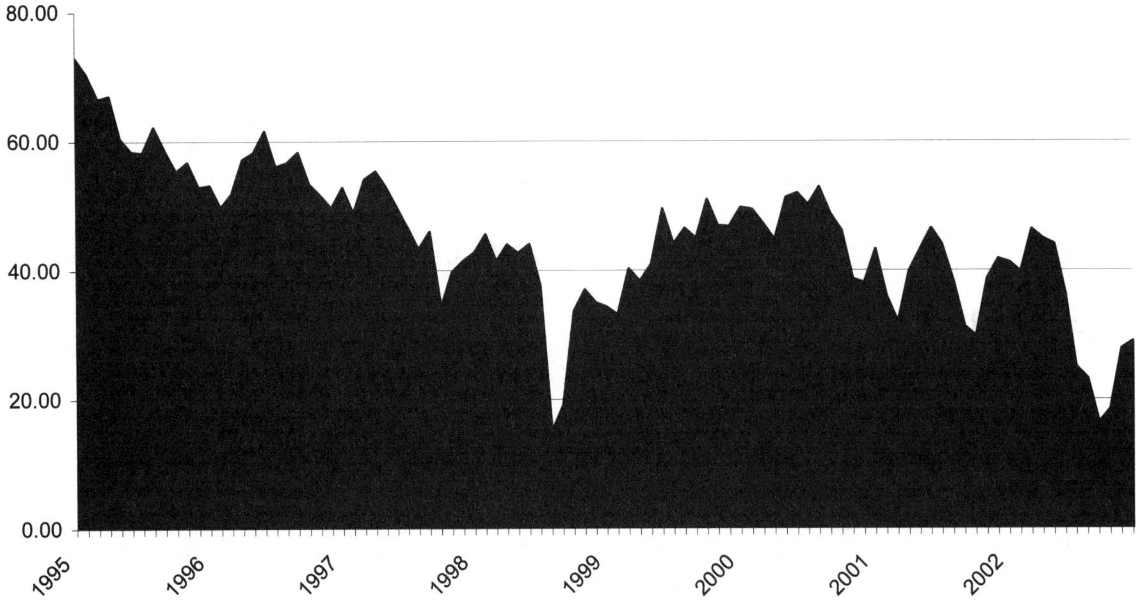

And index annuity participation generally did react as IPRI said they would.

IPRI may help identify index pricing models that do not reflect reality: If an index annuity is lowering rates when IPRI indicates more favorable conditions exist for index annuity pricing, other questions may need to be asked. Or, if a carrier raises rates when IPRI says they should be falling, perhaps the carrier is spending tomorrow's dollars today.

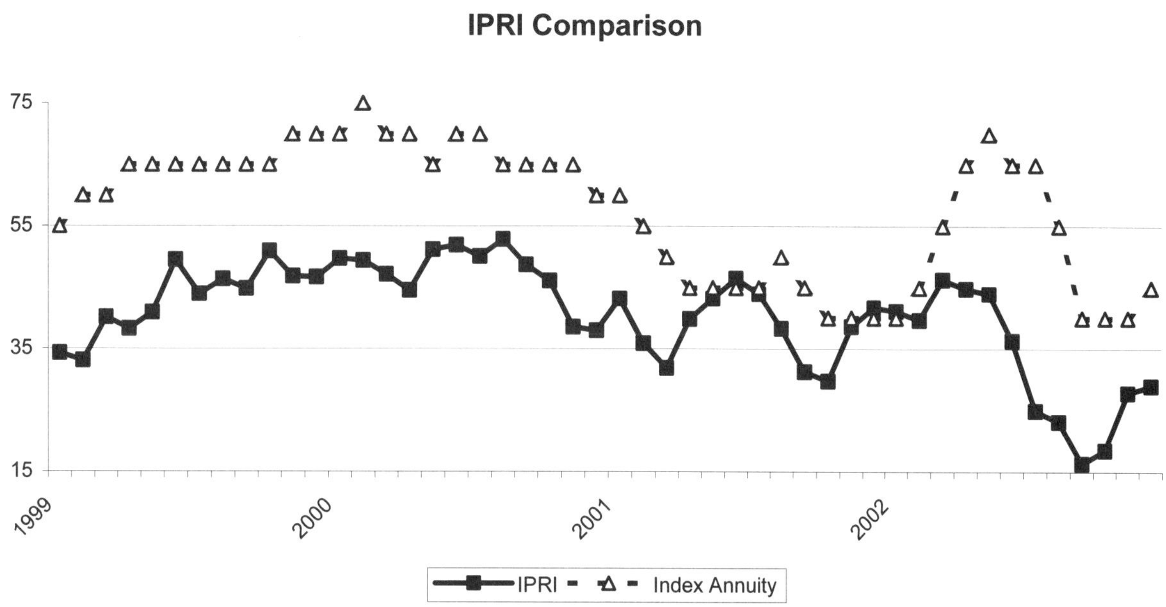

This chart reflects the actual average participation rate of a term end point styled index annuity, and the indicated IPRI values, from January 1999 through December 2002. Whether one line is higher than the other is immaterial, the purpose of the chart is to see if the index annuity rates adjusted to meet changing pricing conditions.

The answer is the index annuity did indeed raise the participation rate when pricing became more favorable and lowered the rate when prices worsened. The rate changes tended to follow actual market forces but weren't in perfect sync (the carrier probably supported rates a bit too long in mid 2002). All in all, I would say this index annuity's pricing does reflect market realities.

I have conducted numerous comparisons of IPRI with different index annuities and feel the indicator does reflect the overall effects of portfolio interest rates and option prices on index annuity rates. My conclusion is that a rising IPRI value reflects a more favorable index annuity environment whereby participation rate increases, or yield spread decreases, would be warranted, and that a falling IPRI value would indicate the reverse. However, the magnitude of the rise or fall in IPRI does not directly correspond to the degree of change in the index annuity rate.

Cheat Sheet

- Index Mutual Funds and Index Annuities are totally separate animals. Index funds are investment vehicles; index annuities are a savings instruments.

- Buying options leverages your power and enables a few cents of premium dollar to provide the potential for index-linked interest.

- An index annuity buying options one year at a time isn't paying for all that extra time value, so the cost is much cheaper and index participation is higher. Therefore, the index participation can be much higher than it would be for a different index annuity that locked in the future cost and guaranteed all moving parts. But, a term end point can usually offer a higher rate – even though the option is for a longer period – because fewer options are purchased.

- A ***Call*** option gives you the right to buy something. A ***Put*** option gives you the right to sell something. Options are available on individual stocks, government debts, foreign currencies and indexes

- The two parts of an option's value are it's ***Intrinsic Value***, which is the degree the option is "in the money" and its ***Time Value*** meaning the period left in which you may exercise the option. The greater the amount of time left until the option expires, the greater its time value.

- The two primary risks associated with buying option are losing your premium if the option expires and being unable to exercise the option due to market conditions.

- Carriers can avoid the whole option issue by being reinsured by a third party in which the writing carrier keeps the minimum guarantee exposure and hands off the index risk to another or using portfolio replication to duplicate movement of the index.

Discussion Questions

1. What other indices do you think index annuities will utilize in the future?

2. When would it make sense for an annual reset styled annuity to lock in all crediting parts?

3. Look at the financial section of the newspaper and find examples of options that are in, at, and out of the money. Can you determine the time value of the options?

Chapter Quiz

1. The Standard & Poor's 500 index

A. Is a government supported index
B. Includes reinvested dividends
C. Is used in over 95% of the index annuities purchased
D. All of the above

2. To provide the potential for index-linked interest the insurance company usually

A. Buys put options
B. Buys call options
C. Sells put options
D. Sells call options

3. The two parts of an option's value are

A. Time and intrinsic
B. Time and multiplier effect
C. Intrinsic and diversification
D. Diversification and simplicity

4. Methods used by insurers to provide the potential for index-linked interest include

A. Buying options
B. Portfolio Replication
C. Reinsurance
D. All of the above

5. The following statement is true

A. Indexed mutual fund returns include reinvested dividends
B. Index annuity returns include reinvested dividends
C. Indexed mutual fund credited returns are protected from market risk
D. Two primary benefits of indexing are simplicity and beating the market

Chapter 8 – Index Annuity Solutions

Who Buys This Stuff?

How do you identify an index annuity prospect? Index annuities are designed for people that are averse to risk. The type of person whom, if given a choice between an investment that has an equal chance of doubling in a year or losing 20% of its value, versus an investment that will make 6%, would choose the 6% low risk/low return alternative. Certificate of deposit and traditional fixed annuity buyers fit this profile. However, the message communicated to consumers about index annuities does not always reflect the consumers' aversion to risk.

The wrong message is to focus on using index annuities as an alternative to mutual funds and focus on the possibility of double-digit returns. The message this sends to consumers is that index annuities are growth vehicles offering protection of principal

But consumers say the reason they like index annuities is because they offer safety of principal from market risk. What consumers are saying is that they see index annuities as savings vehicles offering higher interest potential.

There can be a breakdown in communication. If a consumer says they want a car with ABS brakes, air bags and reinforced bumpers, the incorrect response is to emphasis the turbo-charged engine and the speedometer that tops out at 140. Agents miss prospects for index annuities if they stress performance over safety and target cautious investors instead of risk adverse savers.

Due to the volatility of the market there will be years when index annuities perform poorly and times of exceptional performance, but index annuities are designed to generate long term competitive returns that fall in the middle, between those of equity and fixed instruments. The good news is that consumers are satisfied with this potential because their key reason for buying an index annuity is protection of principal.

Index annuities are designed for risk averse people interested in safety over performance

The Wheel

There is an investor's cycle of hope, fear and greed. All markets revolve around a circle. Over time a market will rise in value then fall in value, then rise and fall again.

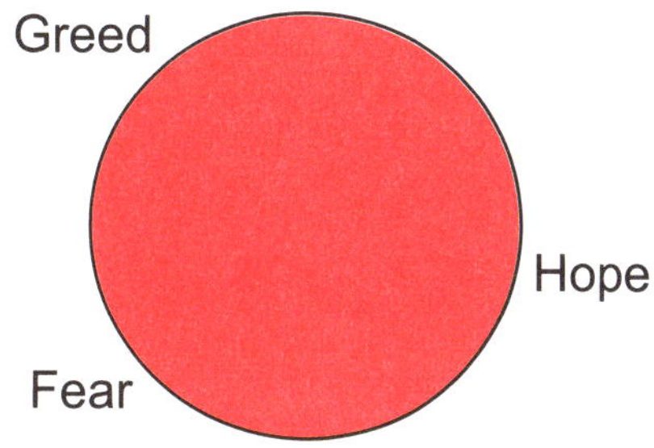

The only variable is the amount of time needed to complete the circle.

Ideally, one would buy at the bottom of the circle and sell at the top, but typical investors are guided by emotion and not facts when making investment decisions.

After the market has risen and is near the top, the greed emotion takes over and investors begin to buy. After the market has peaked and begins to decline, the investor continues to buy because they hope the market will rise again. After the market has bottomed out and started rising, the typical investor sells out and sits on the sidelines because of the fear that the market will again fall.

This pattern is repeated in market cycle after market cycle. Index annuities appeal to the fear part of the psyche. Index annuities can be used to overcome this aversion to risk by providing the potential for higher returns than traditional savings vehicles without market risk to principal.

Realistic Expectations

Back in 1994 when the concept of using movements of a stock index to determine the interest that would be credited to a fixed annuity was coming to fruition, the players decided that since this excess interest crediting was based on an equity index they would call these new critters Equity Indexed Annuities. People looked upon an equity index annuity, or EIA, as a whole new instrument that would give them upside potential while protecting their principal from market loss.

***"What's wrong with this Equity Index Annuity?
The equity market went up 20% but my Annuity only paid me 14%!"***

A problem that surfaced early was when one talked about Equity Indexed Annuities, regardless of how well the concept was expressed, and notwithstanding the caveats and return limitations contained within the presentation, many people heard the word "equity" and created unrealistic return expectations in their own minds. I had calls back in 1998 and 1999 from people that were incensed when their index annuity only returned 12% or 14%. Some people turned away from index annuities because the credited interest realized was "only" double that of traditional fixed annuities. In fact, index annuities were performing just like they were supposed to; the problem is that the word "equity" distorted return expectations.

"My son says I shouldn't invest in equities.
Please cash in my index annuity and put my money in a 2% money market account."

During the millennium bear market I heard from some people that said they couldn't sell equity index annuities because their prospects were burnt by the stock market and turned pale when the word "equity" is mentioned. The stock market did go through a nasty spell and many investors lost all of their paper gains and many lost principal, but no index annuity owner lost one dollar of premium or credited interest due to the bear market during this entire period. Once again, index annuities performed just like they were supposed to by protecting owners from market loss.

Index annuities have a wonderful story to tell, but realistic expectations need to be conveyed.

When you hear someone talking about equities what kind of returns spring to mind? In 1999 you might have thought of 12%, 20%, or even more. In 2001 or 2002 the word equity probably made you think of losses. When you hear the words "fixed annuity" what are your return expectations? I would imagine they are quite different.

Index annuities are long-term savings vehicles designed to provide an opportunity for returns higher than you would receive from fixed rate annuities. In a macro view of the world if stocks are earning 10% to 12% and banks are paying 4% to 6%, index annuities might come in at 6% to 9%. However, if you talk about EQUITY index annuities people subconsciously hear "Equity Returns...Market Risk...20%...Go to Tahiti". Instead, talk about fixed annuities linked to an index, because then people hear "Safety...Might Do Better Than The Bank...Sleep At Night".

No market risk to principal, interest already credited to the policy is protected, minimum guarantees...these features are all associated with annuities not equities.

An index annuity is a fixed annuity. Unlike equity investments, bonds, or index funds the annuity owner cannot lose principal even if the index declines - no stock market risk to principal is a feature of a fixed annuity. Unlike equity or bond vehicles the annuity owner cannot lose credited interest even if the index drops – protection of credited interest is a feature of a fixed annuity. Although stock markets over time have generally trended higher, there is no guarantee that an index will be higher than its starting point at the end of a specified period. Unlike any other equity vehicle out there the annuity owner will receive a guaranteed minimum return which will at the very least give back the premium at the end of an agreed upon period – guaranteed minimum returns are a feature of fixed annuities. In point of fact then, it is more accurate to call these saving vessels Fixed Index Annuities instead of Equity Index Annuities, an FIA instead of an EIA.

"Fixed Index Annuity" does a better job of telling a consumer how these instruments will perform.

The appellation Fixed Index Annuity creates realistic return expectation in both good and bad markets. No one should be surprised when the stock market jumps 20% and the fixed annuity linked to an index credits 9%, and no one should be concerned when the stock market drops because everyone knows a fixed annuity protects premium and credited interest. The marketing of fixed index annuities generates realistic return expectations in both bull and bear markets.

Index Annuities As A Bridge

Index annuities are an ideal bridge for someone that has never invested in the stock market because of the fear of loss, but wants the potential for a higher return than they're earning on other saving instruments.

Index annuities are also attractive for stock market investors that want to take their profits (or prevent further losses), don't want to lose principal, but want the potential for a higher return than they might get from a money market account. Index annuities can provide solutions for specific financial concerns.

- Say that an individual has taken early retirement and received a lump sum pension plan distribution. The person will start drawing on these funds to provide income in a few years. The money could be invested in mutual funds. Over time equity investments have produced high returns, but the stock market is fickle in the short term and could go down. An index annuity guards against risk to principal if the market goes down while providing higher upside potential than certificates of deposit.

- Or, a retired couple already owns fixed rate annuities and is planning to leave the money in the annuities to their children. An index annuity assures them of earning at least a minimum return while giving them the possibility of bequeathing an even greater legacy.

- Or, many people invest their retirement funds in fixed rate instruments. This may be prudent for a worker in their fifties, but it is a costly strategy for a thirty year old. An index annuity gives these younger workers guarantees and higher potential growth.

- Or, an individual may decide they like the concept of indexing, but does not want the risks of an index fund (because low fees do not mean low risk). An index annuity uses indexing and offers protection.

- Or, a person has seen their bond fund values fall as general interest rates rose. An index annuity offers the potential for competitive returns without losing credited returns.

- Or, a pensioner has seen his certificate of deposit interest decline over 75% between 2000 and 2002, and wants the potential for earning more interest without exposing principal to market risk.

Index annuities are an attractive tool for SEP, SIMPLE and 403(b) retirement plans. They are attractive to the no-load investor and they may be an alternative to bonds.

Index Annuities As Cash

The Wall Street universe consists of stocks and bonds; cash is where your money sits until you buy some more stocks or bonds. Cash typically sits in money market accounts, treasury bills, and occasionally short-term certificates of deposit or fixed rate annuities. The two main characteristics of cash are very low risk to principal and general liquidity.

A few carriers offer index annuities with surrender periods of one year. These annuities could be used as parking places for the cash portion of a client's portfolios. The index annuities have credited actual returns of 3% to 10% a year in the past, which compares very favorably to traditional cash alternatives. Of course, if the index doesn't cooperate most of the index annuities will simply give you your money back at the end of the year without interest.

Index Annuities Instead Of Bonds

Bonds are used as a portfolio's zigs to the stock markets' zags, and are usually offered as the lower risk complement to equities. However, bonds can be extremely volatile and bearish bond markets can occur in tandem with bear stock markets. Ultimately, whether bonds would lower overall portfolio losses depends upon whether interest rates are rising or falling.

The last twenty years were a period of generally falling interest rates and a very favorable environment for bonds. However, if you look at a general index of bonds using ten-year periods from 1945 through 1981, a period of rising interest rates, the principal value of the bonds was lower at the end of every period. I don't know whether interest rates will be rising or falling over the next score of years, but I do know current interest rates don't have a great deal of room to go down.

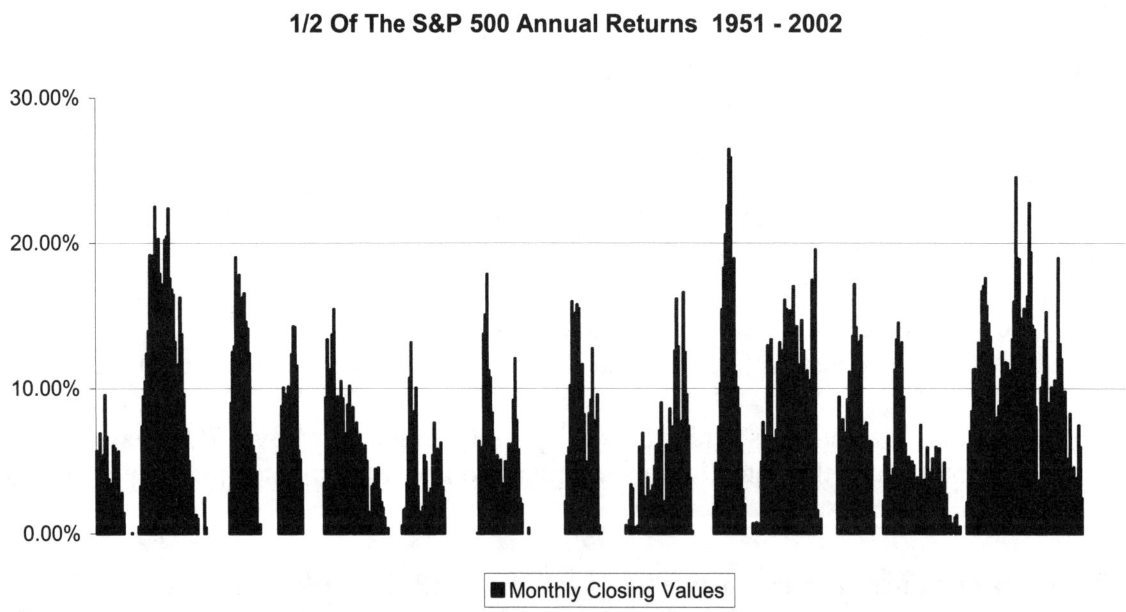

The chart shows one-half of any positive annual stock index returns over the last 50 years. To reflect index annuity annual reset methodology, any negative years have been replaced with zeros. Even at 50% participation, the hypothetical annual return over the last 50 years averages 6%. If index annuities average 60% participation in the index, the average annual return is 7%. A strong argument can be made that an index annuity model could outperform bonds, especially in a low interest rate environment.

Index annuities using annual reset methodologies may be used as the bond alternative in a portfolio. Even though the index annuity would mirror the movements of the index, the annuity's protection of principal and credited interest from market loss could result in higher returns than bonds.

Index Annuities For Nervous Investors

There are people that would like to be in the stock market, but simply do not have the temperament. There are people that just can't emotionally handle loss and need protection of principal. Certain index annuity interest crediting methodologies – like term end point and term yield spread designs – have credited 60% to 100% of the equity index movement over time. Even though no index annuity includes reinvested dividends, neither are there management fees. For nervous investors giving up a little upside potential may well be worth the peace of mind in knowing that they can never lose principal from a market decline.

Index Annuities Instead Of Variable Annuities

If you'd like to be in the stock market, but would like a little more protection from market risk than you get with the typical mutual fund, why not simply buy a variable annuity?

Variable annuities promise to at least return principal if the owner dies, even if the account is worth less, and many index annuities bump up the death benefit by a few percent each year. So, even if your investments decline in value the "death value" of your variable annuity would steadily increase. In addition, more variable annuities are offering some type of principal guarantee whereby if you maintain the account for a minimum number of years, and the ending account value is less than original principal, the variable annuity carrier will make up the difference. The carrier typically charges 0.25% a year for the principal protection feature, which would be added on to the 2% to 2½% charged for investment management, mortality and annuity expenses.

Why not buy a variable annuity instead of an index annuity? There is absolutely nothing wrong with variable annuities. Whether you select a variable annuity or an index annuity depends on what your goals are and respective index participation.

VAs versus Term End Point Index Annuities

Index annuities using term end point designs feel more like variable annuities because you're looking at a longer time horizons. The variable annuity return includes reinvested dividends and deducts two percent plus each year in charges. The index annuity interest does not include reinvested dividends, does not deduct charges, and participates in a degree of index movement. If you're looking at a variable annuity offering a pure guarantee of principal feature the ultimate decision may rest on index participation.

Variable annuity returns include reinvested dividends; dividend yields have been hanging around 2%. Total variable annuity costs are 2% to 2½%. It would seem to me, that at least today, VA charges offset the benefit of reinvested dividends. The implication would be that a term end point designed index annuity with around 100% index participation would deliver comparable returns to the variable annuity, and index annuities with term end point crediting have locked in participation rates as high as 105% in the past.

What if index annuity participation is 60%, 70% or 80%? Then the variable annuity would decidedly outperform the index annuity in a rising market. In a falling market the index annuity would provide a higher return than the VA due to the minimum guarantee, but if your desire is to maximize returns the VA makes more sense.

- Variable annuity fees offset the benefit of reinvested dividends
- Whether a higher return is produced by a variable annuity or an index annuity using a term end point method depends on index participation
- Depending on how they're structured variable annuity principal protection riders can offer a real benefit or provide diluted returns and poor protection
- You can't compare a variable annuity with an annual reset index annuity because they are designed to meet two different goals

If you're counting on a principal protection rider to cover your VA assets in a rough market, my only caution is to look how the variable annuity's principal protection is structured. Some carrier's charge a fixed percentage, like a quarter percent, and bear the risk of any potential loss – I'm sure the carrier's betting on the fact that markets don't usually lose money over long periods of time. However, some carriers protect principal by moving money from equity sub-accounts to bond or fixed sub-accounts and thereby lowering equity risk. But in a rising market this has the effect of diluting equity returns and effectively cuts the variable annuity's market participation and returns (perhaps below the index annuity).

VAs versus Annual Reset Index Annuities

Comparing variable annuities with index annuities that use annual reset methodologies is like trying to compare an airplane ride with a boat trip down the river. When they're both loaded with fuel the airplane goes faster and farther than the boat. If you're trying to go fast and maximize returns use the variable annuity.

But if the airplane runs out of gas, it'll go down. If the boat runs out of gas it'll still continue to move ahead with the current. If your desire is to never go backwards and have a chance at covering more ground than the financial currents, use an index annuity.

Index annuities using annual reset structures will probably not equal the performance of variable annuities in rising markets, but they're not supposed to. Annual reset designs attempt to be competitive with other fixed savings instruments. They protect both principal and credited interest from market loss. They treat years of negative index returns as years with zero positive interest. And even though an annual reset design does not include reinvested dividends, if you compare the performance of an equity index that includes reinvested dividends, with the performance of the same index without reinvested dividends but where the negative years are replaced with zeros, the two performances are relatively close.

Variable annuities are investments; gains can be lost. Index annuities are savings instruments; credited index-linked interest cannot be lost.

Index Annuities As The Ultimate Hedge

A popular method of getting the most upside equity potential while minimizing the downside is to marry an equity position with the purchase of a put option. If the market goes up you get the gain, less the cost of the put. If the market goes down, the value of the put option should grow offsetting losses from the equity position. A problem with this hedging strategy is that buying put options to cover your downside risk exposure can be expensive. An alternative strategy is buying index annuities that use term end point crediting methods.

Index annuities using term end point methods don't lock in gains until the end of the multiple year term (most annuities do lock in gains if the owner dies). Because gains aren't locked in each year, the costs of offering term end point designed index annuities are less than annual reset designs, and higher effective index participation is the result.

With the index annuity you probably won't get all of the upside, and index annuities do not share in the reinvested dividends that you might get with mutual funds, but index annuities do not have the portfolio commissions and transaction costs associated with mutual funds, do not charge management fees, and are more tax-efficient than any mutual fund on the planet. Longer-term end point annuities have in the past matched or nearly matched 100% of index gains.

What about the downside? All index annuities provide guaranteed returns promising at least a minimum amount of interest by the end of the term, even if the index tanks. But what happens if you're one year into the index annuity and the index drops 20%, 30%, 40%, and you don't want to wait ten-years just to see the market, and your principal, simply make it back to where it is today? Easy, surrender the annuity and start over.

Currently, the maximum first year surrender charge of any term end point designed annuity is 10%. If the unthinkable happens to the market and you surrender the policy, you'll have at least 90% of your original cash in your hand. Compare this maximum known liquidity benefit to the costs and uncertainty of buying put options.

Index Annuities For Insurance Agents

Many life insurance agents have been battling the world for twenty years selling fixed rate instruments, as equity investments ate their lunch from a return standpoint. In reality – and it doesn't matter who does the math – over time equity instruments do outperform fixed rate vehicles.

Consumers owning only fixed rate products weren't eviscerated by the millennium bear market, but it also means they missed out on significantly higher overall returns. A life insurance agent consistently offering only fixed rate annuities and non-variable life insurance may have a "fixed good - stocks bad" mindset, mentally overstating the effects of bad stock market years and underestimating the power of good years on final results. For these agents and their customers, index annuities can be viewed as "how the stock market would work if it were run by an insurance company".

Index products minimize bad year returns and eliminate market risk to principal. Most index products have both fixed and indexed elements, so that just a toe may be dipped into the index side of the market. Eventually, as interest is credited from both fixed and indexed sides and results compared, more of the account dollars will be moved to the index bucket.

Advantage IPRI Composite Bond Yield Index

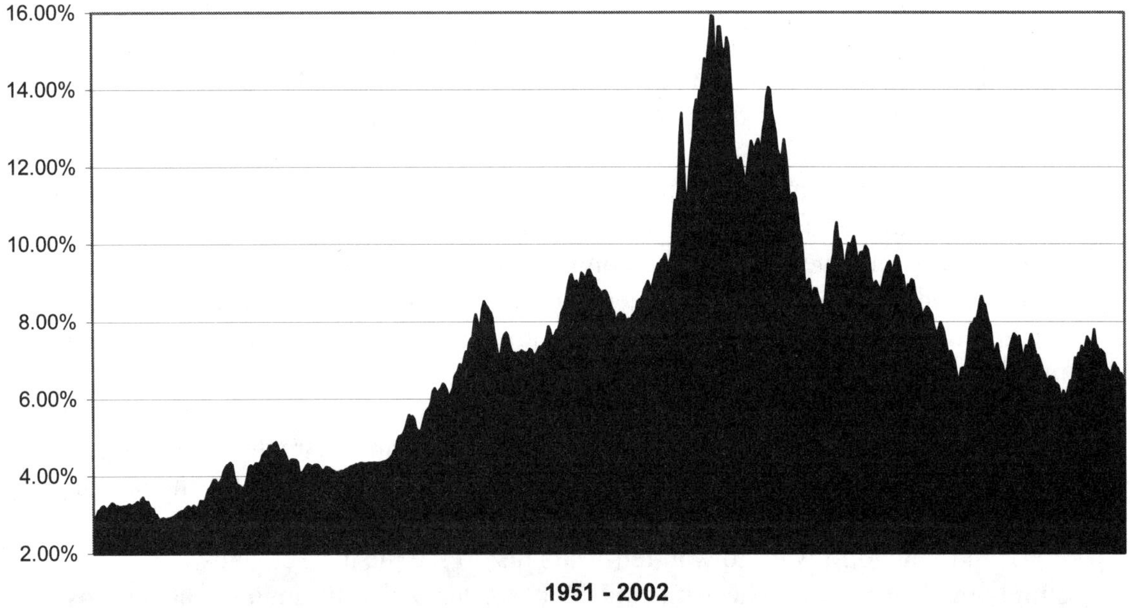

This chart uses the Advantage Group IPRI Composite Bond Index and shows annual yields on a portfolio of corporate and government bonds over the last fifty years (it could be viewed as a rough representation of the returns earned on an insurer's investment portfolio).

Although the '70's and '80s had average bond portfolio yields of 8.8% and 11.3%, the '60s averaged a 5.4% annual yield and today's bonds are around 6% to 7%. The average yield for the bond index is 7% over the last 50 years. Contrast this 7% return, representing 100% participation in the bond index, with the 7% average return one would have received representing only 60% of the positive stock index performance. An insurer's index approach to equities can produce higher returns than a net fixed rate.

Index Annuities In IRAs

There are a multitude of choices to use in planning for a secure retirement. Today's workers may invest in individual stocks, choose from thousands of different mutual funds and hundreds of variable annuities, or select bonds or certificates of deposit. However, most workers today may not have sufficient assets to permit them to maintain their lifestyle in retirement. These people will need to lower their standard of living or continue to work. The reasons are that many workers continue to believe in the myths of retirement planning.

Retirement Planning Facts & Myths	
Myth: Pensions and Social Security will provide the retirement income I need.	**Fact: Social Security and pensions replace 40% to 60% of the average retiree's pre-retirement income (*Your Best Money Moves Now*).**
Myth: My IRA and 401(k) contributions will make up any shortfall at retirement.	**Fact: The average worker is only saving a third of what they'll need at retirement (*Money*).**
Myth: Today, retired individuals are better off than ever before.	**Fact: While many retirees are enjoying a higher standard of living, 1 in 4 retired widows have an annual income below the poverty line (*AARP*).**
Myth: Fixed income investments are safer for my retirement than stocks.	**Fact: Over any 20 year holding period since 1926 stocks have never lost money and the average returns are more than double those of fixed income vehicles (*Ibbotson Associates*).**
Myth: Stock investments are too risky for a retirement plan.	**Fact: Professional pension plan managers invest over half of total pension assets in stocks (*Access Research*).**

The two main reasons for having inadequate funds at retirement are not saving enough and investing too conservatively

Not Saving Enough

As a rough rule of thumb you need to save 5% of your salary if you begin saving in your 20's, 10% if you begin in your 30's and 15% if you are in your 40's.

Investing Too Conservatively

Many people keep too many of their retirement dollars invested in cash and fixed interest accounts even though stock investments have averaged an annual return over the last four score years that is roughly double the return on bonds. Investing too conservatively translates into having inadequate funds at retirement. This chart shows the balance at age 65 if you invest $2,000 a year beginning at different ages at different rates of returns.

Even a 2% increase in your average annual return can mean hundreds of thousand of dollars more at retirement. It can mean the difference between spending your retirement years in comfort or asking many people a day "Do you want fries with that"

$2,000/year Invested To Age 65			
Age	*at 6%*	*at 8%*	*at 10%*
25	$309,524	$518,113	$885,185
35	$158,116	$226,566	$328,988
45	$73,571	$91,524	$114,550

Risk and Return

"Don't gamble. Take all of your savings and buy a good stock, and hold it till it goes up, then sell it. If it don't go up, don't buy it." **- Will Rogers**

Over time, stock investments have proven they provide higher returns than fixed interest vehicles. If we have a sufficient period of time before retirement to outlast any market downturns - usually defined as at least five years, retirement money should be invested in a diversified blend of equity investments. However, many people do not have the temperament to deal with the ups and downs of the market. They would like to earn a higher return than they're getting from fixed rate instruments, but they want their principal protected from market risk. A solution to this need is the index annuity.

Index annuities base the crediting of excess interest on the movements of an index. They are not mutual funds or variable annuities. Mutual fund returns include reinvested dividends. However, a mutual fund return is not realized until the fund is sold. Any fund gains are paper gains and can be lost if the market declines.

Index annuities returns do not include reinvested dividends, but the principal and credited interest is protected from market risk. Fixed index annuities offer the potential for higher returns than fixed rate annuities with the same principal protection from market risk.

Tax-Deferred Tax-Deferral

Some people try to dismiss putting fixed annuities inside an IRA because a qualified retirement account already provides tax-deferral. Their logic is that you're not getting the benefit of the annuity's tax-deferral, so why put a tax-deferred vehicle inside a tax-deferred vehicle. If tax-deferral was the only benefit fixed annuities provide the logic would be valid, but annuities provide other benefits.

The simplest reason to use a fixed annuity is when it has a higher return. Say you could buy a fixed annuity with a rate of 7% for your IRA or a certificate of deposit yielding 6%. Do you care about the tax-deferral benefit of the annuity going unused in an IRA? No. You'd choose the annuity to get the higher rate.

Index Annuities In IRAs

There are many vehicles to choose from in planning for retirement. However, even if a person is saving they can still have inadequate funds at retirement if they invest too conservatively. For the risk averse individual an index annuity can provide the potential for a higher return than fixed rate instruments with the principal protection that lets them sleep at night. Index annuities are excellent vehicle for retirement saving.

The type of crediting method used and liquidity features of an index annuity may become a factor in scenarios involving required minimum distributions. Index annuities using term end point methods tend to have constraints on withdrawals before the end of the period and this could pose a problem if most or all of your qualified money was placed therein. The simple solution is money that may be needed before the end of the period shouldn't be placed in a term end point designed index annuity.

Your Parents Never Told You

The Biggest Difference Between

Boys & Girls...

Girls Live Longer

This Means Women Need To Save More For Retirement Than Men,
Earn A Higher Return Than Men
Or Both

New IRA Minimum Distribution Guidelines

On January 11, 2001 the Internal Revenue Service issued new proposals that simplify mandatory retirement plan distributions. The regulations apply to distributions taken on or after January 1, 2002.

The Old Way

This area had been governed by the 1987 proposal that required the IRA owner to mandate a distribution pattern that could not be slowed after the owner became 70 1/2. The previous year's balance was used to determine the minimum required distribution based on the age of the owner and primary beneficiary, and different methods could be used to calculate life expectancy. When a surviving spouse beneficiary died before the owner it often caused an acceleration of the taxes owed at both deaths.

Current Proposal

Normally, your required minimum distribution calculation will be unaffected by the selection of beneficiary. With one exception, all calculations will be based on the account owner's age, less ten years, as published in the IRS tables. An exception is made for a spousal beneficiary that is more than ten years younger than the account owner - the couple can use a joint life expectancy table that uses the younger age. Beneficiary selection at the Required Beginning Date (RBD) is no longer irrevocable; you can change beneficiaries as often as you like.

Upon death of the account owner non-spousal beneficiaries will be required to take the required minimum distribution over their life expectancy. The new rules let the surviving spouse keep the proceeds and rollover the IRA to their own IRA or disclaim the IRA to their children or others.

Kind & Simple

No longer will most distribution amounts need to be calculated on the age of the account owner and beneficiary. The recalculation/no recalculation decision is eliminated. No longer can the death of a beneficiary after the RBD cause an acceleration of taxes. The need to satisfy the separate incidental death benefit rule is eliminated. The IRS predicts that minimum distributions for most people will be reduced.

Minimum Distribution Proposal Highlights

Required Minimum Distributions should be reduced.

The beneficiary's age is irrelevant. Minimum Distributions will be based on the account owner's age less 10-years.

No Recalculation decisions. No acceleration of taxes upon premature death of a beneficiary.

Beneficiaries may be named after death of the account owner providing opportunities for disclaimer and "stretching" IRAs.

Surviving spouses have much greater flexibility.

Beneficiary

The proposal allows the beneficiary to be determined as late as the end of the year following the year of the account owner's death. This permits after death estate planning and grants a high degree of flexibility. People will be able to use their own life expectancy to calculate distributions from inherited IRA's.

All in all, the proposals are a win for taxpayers and will enable people to pass along a greater portion of their qualified plans to family and others. The freedom to change beneficiaries at anytime is a great benefit.

Index Annuities In A 7% Index World

In the December 10, 2001 issue of *Fortune* Warren Buffett was interviewed and asked for his outlook on the stock market. As always, Mr. Buffett's comments and analysis were insightful and well reasoned. However, what made me sit up in my chair were his closing remarks where he said that the American public should *expect equity returns over the next decade or two of perhaps 7% - including dividends.*

Would Index Annuities Be Dead in a Warren Buffett Stock World?

My first thought was that if Mr. Buffett was right, index annuities were dead as a viable instrument. If you are expecting an average 7% annual return from the overall market — and an index by definition attempts to reflect the entire market — and this return includes dividends, then your index return without dividends would be in the range of, maybe, 5% to 6% a year. Currently, index annuity rates, after the effects of averaging, caps or spreads, reflect, at best, 60% of actual index movement. So, my initial calculations assumed that a Warren Buffett market would result in average index annuity returns of 3% to 3.5% in an arena that could still produce 5% traditional fixed annuity yields.

Environments of less than double digit annual stock market returns lasting for long periods of time, are much more common than one might realize after seeing the wild bull market of the '90s. Although the S&P 500 Index produced an average 15.22% a year return in the last decade, compounded ten-year period index returns never exceeded 10% in the years from 1955 through 1986. In fact, if you look at ten-year periods starting in 1960 and look at the entire decade (1960-1969, 1961-1970...1969-1978), the <u>best</u> ten-year period averaged a return of 6.46%.

But then it occurred to me, these average returns include the effects of negative years when the market goes down, and index annuities using annual or biannual reset structures treat negative years as zeros (although you will not usually earn interest if the index goes down, the previous credited interest is protected). The question this posed was "What happens when you swap the annual losses of an equity index investment for the no-less-than-zero element of index annuities?"

Replacing FIA Zeros for Stock Index Losses Increased Returns 30%

If you look at the calendar year returns of the S&P 500 from 1951 through 2001, the average annual return is 9.49%, without dividends. If you substitute zeros for any negative years, and then calculate the average anew, the return increases to 12.60% for the fifty-year period.

I went back and plugged in zeros and redid my ten-year period math. The average annual returns for the new ten year periods — in which down years were replaced with zero returns — increased from 1% to as much as 7%. In fact, the best ten-year period return of the '60s previously mentioned went from 6.46% to 9.28% when zeros were inserted.

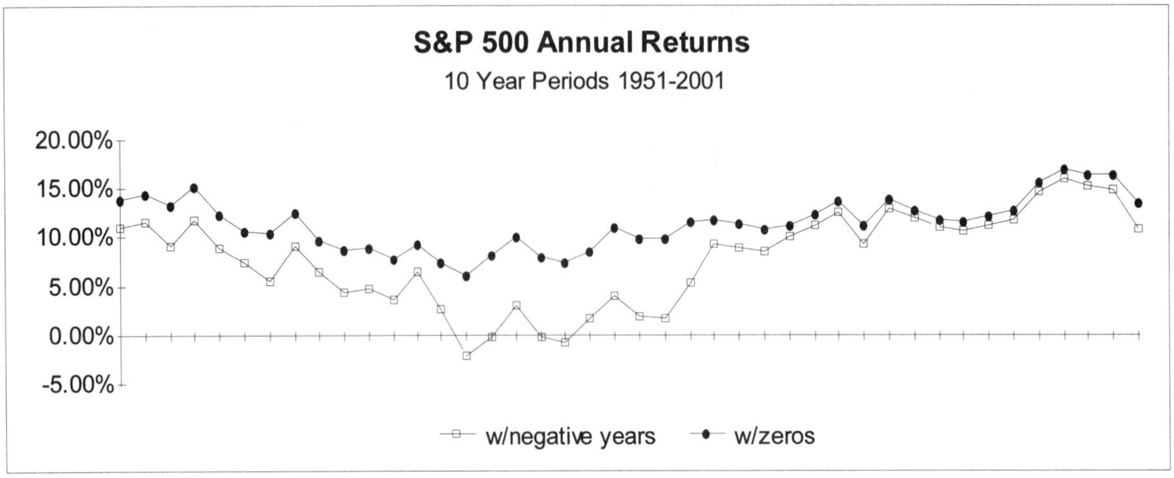

What does this mean? If Mr. Buffett is correct about a 7% world including dividends, which becomes a 5% to 6% index return world without dividends, an annual reset index annuity structure substituting zeros in down years means that over longer periods of time the average returns upon which the index annuity crediting is based would be 2% to 3% higher than the pure index values.

Unlike a stock market investment the index annuity doesn't lose ground when the index drops, so if a stock market index would average 5% to 6% over time the index annuity method would show an average return of 7% to 9% and base crediting on that number. The bottom line is even in a 7% stock return-with-dividends world the no-loss aspect of the index annuity crediting structure more than offsets the lack of reinvested dividends.

Okay. The good news is even if the stock market averages 7% returns over the next 20 years, the crediting element of annual reset index annuities should base interest calculations on index gains averaging better than 8%. The bad news is even at 8% gross annual gains, if effective index annuity participation rates are still at 60%, we're still only talking 4.8% index annuity returns in a 5% traditional fixed annuity scenario. However, a Warren Buffett stock market would lower the costs of providing the equity index linked interest.

In recent years, option prices have been higher than the historical average because market volatility has been very high. This volatility caused participation rates and caps to go down, and yield spreads to go up, because the price of options rose. Ever since index annuities were introduced they've existed in a market with high volatility, because the stock market has been nuts for the last few years — either very bullish or very bearish.

A Warren Buffett stock market would be, well, boring. There just would not be a lot of volatility and sellers of options would have less fear of extreme moves. Volatility could drop to levels not seen since the '80s, thus lowering option prices.

In a Warren Buffett market, option prices could drop so much that we could be looking at annual reset point-to-point designs with participation rates of 100% and 15% caps, or 120% with 12% caps. Annual reset models using daily or monthly averaging could honestly show 140% participation rates, or have positive yield spreads adding 3% to 4% on top of the actual index gain. Imagine telling an index annuity owner "The index only went up 5%, so you made 8% this year". What this all could mean, is a 7% stock market environment could readily produce index annuity returns which would be 40% to 50% higher than traditional fixed annuity returns or returns from bank instruments.

I don't know whether Mr. Buffett's forecast will come true. The stock market could well put forth another score of years that resemble the previous twenty, or muddle along as the Omaha sage predicts. However, in either scenario fixed index annuities should do the job they were designed for – providing the potential for paying higher interest rates than one would receive from other savings instruments without subjecting the principal to market risk.

Index Annuities To Avoid Social Security Benefit Taxation (SSBT)

The Social Security Administration web site says benefit taxation "affects only people who have substantial income in addition to their Social Security". However, if you're single and have total income over $25,000 a year, or married and have total income over $32,000 a year - and this includes taxable income, tax-free municipal bond interest, and one half of your social security benefits - you will pay taxes on your social security benefits. Currently one in five people collecting Social Security are taxed on their benefits. And because the threshold limits are not indexed for inflation, more and more people will float over the taxation threshold as time goes by.

The taxation formula is calculated as follows: We have a married couple with an adjusted gross income of $25,000. They receive $10,000 in social security benefits and $4,000 in tax-free municipal bond interest. What the IRS says to do is add on top of the normal taxable income of $25,000, one half of your social security income ($5,000), all of your tax-free municipal bond interest ($4,000), and total it. From the $34,000 total, subtract the threshold amount of $32,000 ($25,000 for single taxpayers, $0 for married filing separately). Any amount over this threshold the IRS considers "excess" income.

Adjusted Gross Income	$25,000
½ Social Security Benefit	+ 5,000
Tax-Free Bond Interest	+ 4,000
Total	$34,000
Threshold Amount	(32,000)
Excess Income	$ 2,000

Adjusted Gross Income	$25,000
½ Excess Income	+ 1,000
MAGI Income	$26,000

You then add on to your normal taxable income one half of your social security benefit or one half of the excess - whichever is less - to your normal taxable income. The bottom line is that this couple is now paying taxes on $1,000 of their social security income. They could be paying taxes on as much as one half of their social security income - and all the municipal bond interest in the world won't help.

SSBT Highlights:

If your total Social Security Benefit Taxable Income is ($32,000-joint, $25,000-single) or less you won't be taxed on your benefits.

If your total Social Security Benefit Taxable Income is ($44,000-joint, $34,000-single) or less you won't be taxed on more than one half of your benefits.

The amount taxable is limited to 85% of your benefit and is not retroactive. Tax planning may help you reduce or avoid taxation on your social security benefits.

There are a couple of things that you can do to get under the threshold. Tax deferred income is not included. If you have interest income that you are not spending but letting grow for future use – like the income produced inside an IRA or a tax-deferred annuity – that income is not taxed until received. Unless you have to take the income, it is probably better spending your taxable interest income and dividends first. Second, the cash value build-up, or tax-free loans, obtained from a qualified life insurance policy are not subject to social security benefit taxation.

Social Security Benefit Tax Planning

If the Social Security recipient is only a bit over the threshold amount tax planning may be successful in reducing or avoiding the taxation of benefits. For example, say that you have a couple with this situation.

Couple: $12,000 social security benefit, $4,000 tax-exempt income, $26,000 adjusted gross income consisting of $4,000 IRA distributions, $2,000 interest income, $12,000 pension, and $4,000 reinvested taxable interest and $4,000 reinvested capital gains.

Current Situation

$ 26,000	Adjusted Gross Income	$ 26,000	Adjusted Gross Income
+ 6,000	1/2 Social Security	+ 2,000	1/2 Excess Income
+ 4,000	Tax-Exempt Income	$ 28,000	Modified AGI
$ 36,000	Total Income		
- 32,000	Threshold	$ 42,000	Actual Income
$ 4,000	Excess Income		

This couple would have a taxable income of $26,000 if it weren't for SSBT; benefit taxation has increased taxable income by $2,000. But what if we work on reducing benefit taxation while still preserving the income from the assets. For example, what if this couple is under age 70½ and has been receiving $4,000 in distributions from their IRA, but at the same time they're getting a Form 1099 on $4,000 of interest compounding on their CDs. If we simply shift the character of the income by spending the interest income we're already paying taxes on from the certificate of deposit, and keep the IRA income growing tax-deferred, both current and future income is preserved (and we reduce our regular taxable income too).

Solution #1 Defer IRA payout, receive taxable interest

$ 22,000	Adjusted Gross Income	$ 22,000	Adjusted Gross Income
+ 6,000	1/2 Social Security	+ -0-	1/2 Excess Income
+ 4,000	Tax-Exempt Income	$ 22,000	Modified AGI
$ 32,000	Total Income		
- 32,000	Threshold	$ 42,000	Actual Income
$ -0-	Excess Income		

Or what if we continue to receive the IRA distribution but we transfer the money out of the taxable bank account into a tax-deferred annuity. Interest compounding within a fixed rate or fixed index annuity is not subject to income or Social Security taxation.

Solution #2 Transfer compounding interest principal to annuity

$ 22,000	Adjusted Gross Income	$ 22,000	Adjusted Gross Income
+ 6,000	1/2 Social Security	+ -0-	1/2 Excess Income
+ 4,000	Tax-Exempt Income	$ 22,000	Modified AGI
$ 32,000	Total Income		
- 32,000	Threshold	$ 42,000	Actual Income
$ -0-	Excess Income		

Or what if we eliminate the $4,000 of taxable reinvested capital gains generated by our mutual funds by moving these assets into a variable annuity. Growth within a variable annuity is free from current income and Social Security taxes.

Solution #3 Move capital gains principal to variable annuity

$ 22,000	Adjusted Gross Income	$ 22,000	Adjusted Gross Income
+ 6,000	1/2 Social Security	+ -0-	1/2 Excess Income
+ 4,000	Tax-Exempt Income	$ 22,000	Modified AGI
$ 32,000	Total Income		
- 32,000	Threshold	$ 42,000	Actual Income
$ -0-	Excess Income		

Of course, if we moved both the CD and mutual fund money to annuities not only would SSBT be avoided, but also our regular taxable income would be $8,000 less than we when we began.

Solution #4 Move bank and fund taxable sources to annuities

$ 18,000	Adjusted Gross Income	$ 18,000	Adjusted Gross Income
+ 6,000	1/2 Social Security	+ -0-	1/2 Excess Income
+ 4,000	Tax-Exempt Income	$ 18,000	Modified AGI
$ 28,000	Total Income		
- 32,000	Threshold	$ 42,000	Actual Income
$ -0-	Excess Income		

Annuities, whether fixed or variable, can be wonderful tools in reducing or avoiding taxation of benefits. And although annuity interest may be tax-deferred it is normally not tax-free; however, this rule may not apply to benefit taxation. The maximum portion of the Social Security benefit that may be subjected to taxes is 85%, any excess income beyond this amount is not subject to SSBT. So, if you manage to avoid benefit taxation this year you may never have to pay taxes on these non-taxed benefits in the future if you do a little tax planning.

SSBT Considerations:

If you're planning to take a large capital gain, try to do it when you know you'll be well over the SSBT MAGI (Modified AGI) limits.

Tax-Deferred income is not included in the SSBT formula. Retirement and IRA income should be examined to determine if it should be shifted or postponed.

If you're taxed on interest that's compounding and not used for current income, remember interest that compounds within a tax-deferred annuity is not included in the SSBT formula.

If you're reinvesting capital gains, capital gains reinvested within a variable annuity are not included in the SSBT formula

Fixed Index Annuities Instead Of Certificates Of Deposit

An index annuity offers a conservative method for pursuing higher potential returns. In a rising market the annuity could substantially outperform other savings vehicles - like CD's, and if the market falls the buyer is protected against market risk to principal. Index annuities are an excellent alternative especially for bank customers desiring the ability to reach higher yields.

However, for some bank savers the minimum guaranteed return is not high enough. Even though certificates of deposit do not have minimum rates and have recently credited less than 2%, these index annuity prospects may object to the effective 1% to 3% minimum rates on indexed annuities. Instead of looking at an index annuity's interest potential the bank saver gets hung up on the possibility that they might earn less. But there is a way to provide the higher minimum returns that these savers require and still provide a vehicle that could beat CD yields.

Split Annuity Premium

Say that a bank saver has $100,000 and could earn 3%. If nothing changed the $100,000 would grow to $134,392 in ten years. Instead let's say we could find a fixed rate annuity earning 4% and put half the money there, and we found an index annuity with a minimum guarantee based on 90% of premium compounding at 3% and put half the money there. If nothing changed our split annuity would have a minimum value of $134,485 in ten years. If the index increased we could substantially outperform the CD (and in over 80% of historic ten year periods the index would have increased more than the index annuity's minimum guaranteed rate).

The split premium idea is a no loss way to convince a bank saver to put at least a toe in the index annuity water. All you are doing is figuring out what combination of guaranteed index annuity return and fixed rate annuity yield will match the bank return. The strategy is a way to attract the saver that desires the potential for higher interest, but worries about low returns.

Index Annuities As Supercharged Fixed Annuities

You can often find fixed rate annuities that yield more than U.S. Treasury bonds, and certificate of deposit yields, but what if you want more? You could put your money into equity mutual funds or variable annuity equity sub-accounts, but stocks can go down. You could buy high yield bond mutual funds, but bond funds do not react favorably if interest rates go up and can be just as risky as stocks. You could put all your money into a fixed index annuity offering the potential for a higher index-linked yield, but in a poor market you might only receive the minimum guaranteed return.

Or, you could Supercharge your fixed annuity by placing part of your money in a fixed rate annuity and the balance in a fixed index annuity. A supercharged fixed annuity gives you a higher minimum return than the index annuity, and the potential for more interest than you would receive from the fixed rate annuity. Although the rates used in the following example were available when this was written, they may not reflect the real world at the moment you are reading this, but the concept still works in almost every environment.

SuperCharged Fixed Annuity

Put two-thirds of the money in the 6.00% fixed rate annuity and one-third in the index annuity. Say the index annuity selected participates in 85% of index growth over a nine year term and averages the final year's closing values. The index annuity's annualized guaranteed return is 1.80%.

The lowest overall return from this model is calculated as follows: the fixed 6.00% rate is multiplied by two-thirds producing a sum of 4.00%; the index annuity 1.80% minimum return is multiplied by one third producing a sum of 0.60%. The 4.00% fixed portion is added to the 0.60% index portion producing a worst-case return of 4.60%. If we plug in our new supercharged index annuity model into nine-year index periods over the last 30 years, our chart of hypothetical annual returns now looks like this.

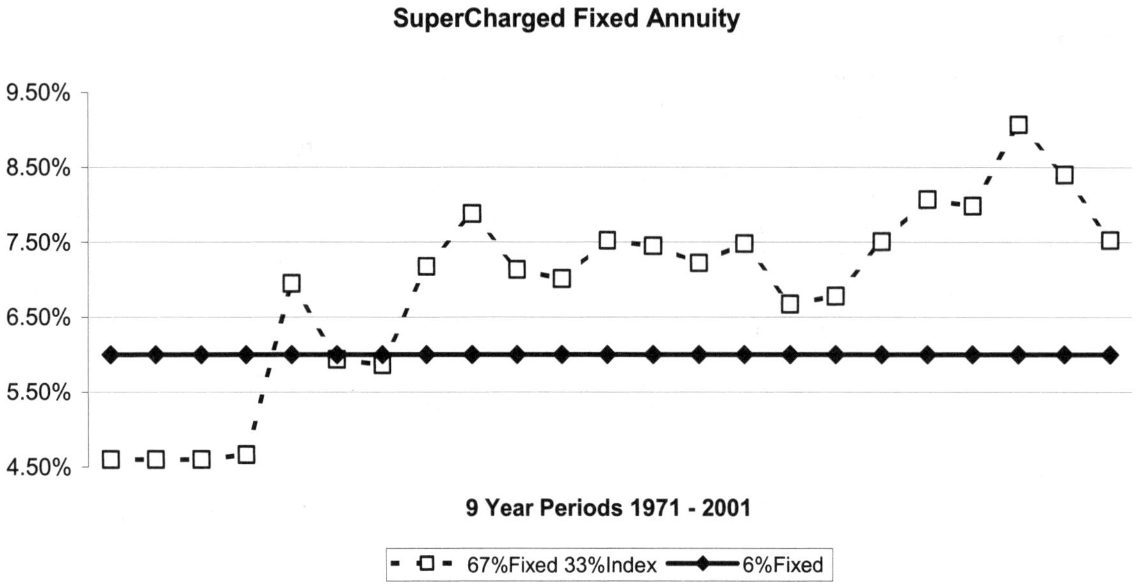

As we already determined, the worst return for any nine-year period is 4.60% and that's what we would have earned in four of the terms, but in 19 out of 23 periods we would have earned more with the Supercharged Fixed Annuity than if we had only bought the fixed rate annuity. In this example our risk is that we'll earn 4.60% instead of the safe 6.00% fixed rate return, but if the stock market cooperates we could earn 6.50%, 7.00%, 7.50% or even more.

What is the ideal balance of fixed rate and fixed index components? It depends on the minimum market risk-free rate you're willing to accept. If you place more money in the fixed index side you increase the potential for higher interest. If you place more money in the fixed rate side you maximize your minimum return. In addition, the minimum guaranteed return of the fixed index annuity would also affect your final returns.

The Supercharged Fixed Annuity offers the potential for enhanced returns with the certainty of knowing the worst-case outcome. The annuity buyer determines the lowest acceptable minimum return and positions premium dollars accordingly. The Supercharged Fixed Annuity is an alternative to the volatility of bonds and bond funds and is positioned as the safe element in a portfolio. It is a simple concept providing a high level of return stability.

Balancing Language

Index annuities offer consumers a long-term savings vehicle with the potential for a higher return than they might realize from other conservative alternatives. However, index annuities are not equity investments nor are they an index mutual fund. No index annuity realizes gains from reinvested dividends and capital gains. But in a falling market, no index fund provides the protection of principal realized with an index annuity.

A balanced picture of the strengths and weaknesses of an index annuity needs to be presented. You could say that an index annuity, unlike a mutual fund, preserves the principal if the market declines, but you should also say that the index annuity does not have the same upside potential of a fund. You could say that an index annuity has the potential for higher interest than a CD, but you also need to state that the return could be as low as the minimum guarantee.

"This is a fixed index annuity. Because it is a fixed annuity it provides minimum guaranteed interest. Because the annuity is linked to an index, excess interest may be earned. What will your return be? I don't know, because it depends on how the equity index performs and how much of the performance you are able to capture. Some years will be good and some years could be zero, but the objective of the fixed index annuity is to offer the potential to earn more interest than you'd receive from a fixed rate annuity."

Balancing language needs to disclose the positives and negatives of both index annuities and the interest crediting structures and product features. For example, it is fair to say that averaging methodologies eliminate the risk of locking in a period's lowest value, however you also need to say that averaging prevents you from getting the highest value as well.

They're Not Mutual Funds

At current index participation no index annuity will come close to matching average equity mutual fund returns over the long haul. This does not mean that index annuities will not produce double-digit returns. If the stock market acts again as it did in the '90s many index annuities will generate 10% or higher annual gains, but they will not keep pace with the average stock fund.

However, if we have an extended period of market turmoil as in the '70s, index annuities could realize substantially higher returns than mutual funds. When market factors allow participation rates to rise, index annuities could match or exceed mutual fund returns, but not at today's rates. Index annuities should be positioned as complements or alternatives to other savings vehicles that also protect principal from market risk.

Who Shouldn't Buy This Stuff?

Index annuities are an extremely versatile financial tool, but there are some situations where they do not work very well. These are not rules, because I can find exceptions for everyone of them, but more like generalities that usually apply.

Too Short A Time Frame – Since most index annuity returns are equity-linked, you need to give them time to respond or recover from a bad market. If you are going to need your money within five years you should probably consider something else.

Going For Maximum Returns – If you have enough time, direct equity investments give you a better shot at hitting mega returns. If you want long-term 15%, 20% or 30% annual returns you are not going to get them in an index annuity.

Must Be FDIC Insured – No, can't help you. Have you considered an indexed CD?

Funding A College Education – Index annuities probably should not be used because of the "under age 59½" IRS penalty that applies to all annuities.

Required Minimum Distributions – Depending on product design withdrawals from an index annuity may lose previous index gains. In any event you are going to want flexibility in choosing when to take money out of an index annuity so that you do not withdraw funds at the wrong time.

Portfolio Tinkerers – If you feel compelled to adjust your portfolio positions on a regular basis, try to time the market, or are bored by guarantees, then index annuities are not a good fit.

Cheat Sheet

Index Annuity Stats*

The average age of an index annuity buyer is 57

51% of the buyers were males

53% of the premium is qualified

The average index annuity sales premium reported was $37,958

Sales By Distribution Channel

96.8% Independent Insurance Agents
1.6% Banks
0.5% Through Broker/Dealers
1.1% Career Agents

55% of index annuity premium comes from existing variable and fixed annuities

Depending how you look at them there are

131 Index Annuities - Segmented By Surrender Period & Methodology
137 Index Annuities - Previous Segments Plus Bonus Rates, Cap/No Cap Option
203 Index Annuities - Previous Segments Plus Other Available Indices

* from the ***Advantage 2002 Index Product Sales & Market Report***

Discussion Questions

1. What problems do you see in creating realistic index annuity return expectations?

2. Which is better – bond funds or index annuities?

3. When might you choose a variable annuity instead of an index annuity and why?

Chapter Quiz

1. Index annuities are designed for people

A. That want stock market gains without risk of loss
B. That are interested in performance over safety
C. That are averse to risk
D. All of the above

2. A reason one might choose an index annuity instead of a bond mutual fund might be

A. Bonds can be extremely volatile
B. Interest rates are expected to rise
C. Equity returns have historically averaged higher than bonds
D. All of the above

3. Variable annuities

A. Should always outperform index annuities
B. Offer principal protection in the event of death
C. Work like annual reset index annuities
D. All of the above

4. The two main reasons for having inadequate funds at retirement are

A. Not saving enough and investing too conservatively
B. Not saving enough and taking too many risks
C. Inflation and taxes
D. Risk and taxes

5. The wrong reason to buy an index annuity is

A. Like the concept of indexing, but don't want the risks of an index fund
B. As a bridge if you've never invested in the stock market
C. To maximize returns
D. To supercharge a fixed rate annuity

Chapter 9 – Sales & Marketing Tips

Index Annuities Are For People Who Are

Part Bull

Part Bear

Part Chicken

Your Home

Let's say two identical houses were available for $100,000. If you buy the first house you have all the rights and obligations of ownership. If the house goes up in value you'll get 100% of the gain. But what if a hog rendering plant is built across the street and next summer's breezes bring the scent of slaughtered pigs through your windows. If the house goes down in value you'll suffer 100% of the losses.

Which house would you buy?

If you buy the second house an insurance company takes over the obligations. Even if they build a slaughterhouse across the street the insurance company guarantees you can still walk away with your $100,000. In fact, the insurance company will guarantee your house will always go up in value a little each year regardless. For this protection the insurance company will share in 10% to 50% of any gain.

The Millionaire

The most successful television show a couple of years ago was *Who Wants To Be A Millionaire*. Through a demonstration of knowledge and nerves contestants could increase their monetary gains until they reached their ultimate goal. The game even provided ways to lower risk - three lifelines and insurance stages that locked in gains once certain levels are reached.

Some players quickly lost their lifelines and showed that due to a lack of knowledge or nerves that they really should not have been in the game in the first place, but even the better players in the game developed a crisis of confidence as the stakes go up and they realized they risked losing much of what they had gained. Because of this, contestants often withdrew from the game before they reached their final goal - even when they know they should keep playing, due to the risk of loss.

The stock market is a lot like the game show. There are people that due to temperament or training probably shouldn't be in the market and there are many other people with an unrealistic view of the risks of the stock market. Index annuities may be an answer for both because they provide unlimited lifelines if the market goes down. And, index annuities even let you bring in money from another game and protect any transferred gains from market declines. Index annuities lock in gains and still let you play the game.

Tic Tac Dough

Financial vehicles are selected based on their "risk/reward" merits. Certificates of deposit are very low on the risk spectrum because the principal is protected from market risk, but the reward is limited.

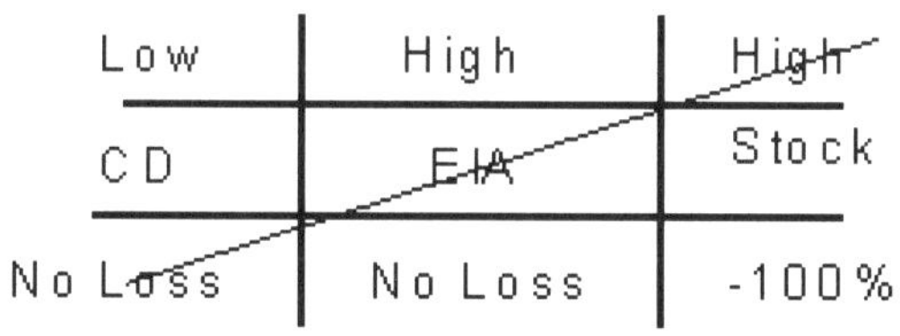

Stock investments have an unlimited upside, but the possibility exists that one could lose all of their money. Index annuities protect the principal from market risk (they even provide at least a minimum return if the market goes down), and a potential return that is significantly higher than the CD.

Index Annuity Hockey

An analogy of where index annuities fit in retirement planning might be to compare the investment world with a hockey game. Many people would agree that the most important player on the ice is the goalie. The goalie's job is to protect the net, to safeguard the team. The goalie's task is similar to the fixed rate investments in a portfolio. These fixed investments protect the portfolio from market risk. However, goalies very seldom score goals. Their job is protection, not performance.

SAFETY **PERFORMANCE**

Fixed Interest

Index Annuities

Mutual Funds

There are other players on the ice like wingers. Their job is to take the offense and score goals. They're flashier than the other players and they go for the big plays. They would be like the mutual funds or stocks in a portfolio. Their main job is performance, not protecting their goal.

But, there are other players on the ice - the defense and center. They skate up and down the rink. Sometimes they help in scoring points and other times they help protect their own goal. Index annuities are like these players. At times they'll be helping the overall performance of the portfolio, but when they're needed they'll be there to help the goalie protect the goal.

Index Annuity Blackjack

Blackjack is a simple game to play. If you win you get back double your money. If you do not win you lose all of your money. Index annuity Blackjack is played a little differently.

You cannot go bust playing index annuity Blackjack. As long as you stay in the game long enough you will always get back what you started with, plus maybe a few extra pennies. Now, the house charges for this no loss provision; so what percentage would you be willing to give up of your winnings if you knew you couldn't lose?

If you ask people this question the most common answer is that they'd be willing to give up half of the potential gain to be protected against loss. Depending on the index annuity you have chosen the "give up" could be less.

Jeffrey Hines, a financial consultant in Las Vegas uses a slightly different twist. "Suppose you were invited to play some roulette, craps or blackjack at a reputable casino (or a highly rated company). The casino host makes you the following offer to entice you to give her casino a try.

You buy in for $10,000 worth of chips and agree to play for a specified time. At the end of the gaming session you tally up. If you are down, the casino will give you everything you lost plus dinner and drinks on the house (the minimum guarantee). If you win, you get to keep all of your winnings up to a certain level (reflecting the participation rate or cap).

When I ask prospects how they would feel about such an offer, they often respond that it's too good to be true or impossible, which of course it is in the gaming world! They often ask what's the catch? I go on to explain that the catch is you must leave your money at the casino for a number of years. If you wish to take your money early, withdrawal charges come into play, but if you leave it with the house, you'll get all of your money back plus either your winnings, or dinner and drinks on the house, whenever you play.

This casino analogy seems to give prospects a general idea of how an Equity Index Annuity works and gives them a sense of the "give and take" involved with this type of savings vehicle."

Baseball Has Been Good To Me

Babe Ruth was one of the greatest home run hitters of all time; he also struck out a great deal. Investing in the stock market is similar. There are times when swinging for the fences results in a high batting average, but you can wind up striking out and a slump or bear market can ruin your career.

Index annuity baseball guarantees you cannot strike out and the worst you can get is a single due to the minimum guarantees. And although you probably will not hit a home run you have a real shot at punching out some doubles and triples. CD owners never get off the bench.

1040 Form

Remind folks of the wonderful tax benefits of all deferred annuities by highlighting a Form 1040. Ask how much interest income they are reporting on Line 8a and whether they are spending the interest or letting it compound.

1040		Department of the Treasury—Internal Revenue Service **U.S. Individual Income Tax Return**		**2002**
Income **Attach Forms W-2 and W-2G here.** **Also attach Form(s) 1099-R**	7	Wages, salaries, tips, etc. Attach Form(s) W-2	7	
	8a	**Taxable** interest. Attach Schedule B if required	8a	
	b	**Tax-exempt** interest. **Do not** include on line 8a **8b**		
	9	Ordinary dividends. Attach Schedule B if required	9	

If it is being saved for future use describe how annuity interest left inside the contract is not subject to current taxation and thus reduces current tax bills. If interest is listed on line 8b ask if they knew that tax-deferred annuity interest, unlike municipal bond interest, does not contribute to Social Security Benefit Taxation (SSBT). If there are figures on line 9 inquire whether they are comfortable with the risk to principal found in stocks and funds and would they be interested in learning about a vehicle that protected principal and credited returns from stock market risk (and might reduce their current taxes too).

Cross of Gold

The Cross of Gold is an excellent way to convey the protection-potential story of index annuities that don't place a cap on interest earned. Draw a cross. In the top left corner place the symbol for infinity (∞), this represents the unlimited upside of the stock market. In the bottom left corner write –100%, this shows how much of your money you could lose in the stock market.

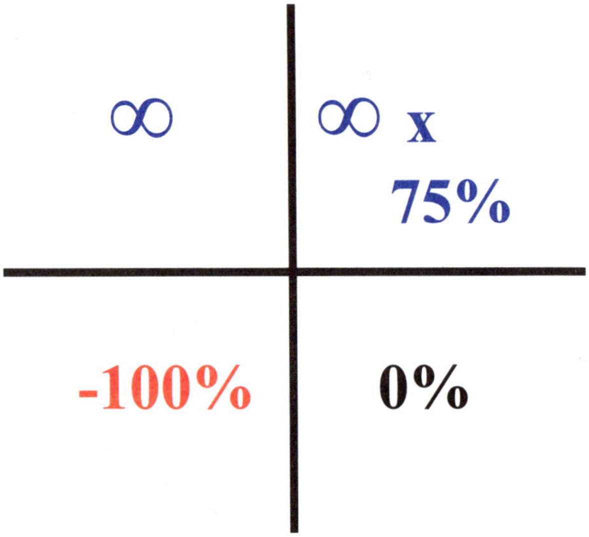

In the bottom right corner of the cross write 0%, this shows how much money you could lose in an index annuity if the stock index went down. In the top right corner place the symbol for infinity and complete the corner with either an "x" for times and fill in the participation rate, or a "-" for minus and complete the line with the yield spread or asset fee of the annuity you've selected.

The cross is a graphic example of the range of returns you can expect. The stock market has unlimited potential, but 100% of your money is at risk. An index annuity eliminates the market risk and you still get most of the unlimited upside of the index.

Index Annuity Potion

Index annuities are the Viagra® of financial products because they never go down.

Index Annuity Algebra

If you are talking with teachers or engineers, you could explain the benefits of index annuities by using a math equation.

One could express a mutual fund or variable annuity return as

M - E = R

Where M is the fund or variable annuity gain or loss for a period, from which you subtract E, representing fees and expenses, and the resulting number is R, or the return. So, if a mutual fund moved up 10%(M) by the end of a period, and the management fee was 2%(E) then the return is 8%(R).

You could use a similar formula to compute an index annuity return. Index annuities do not have fees in the same way that mutual funds and variable annuities do, but you could say that the E in the equation represents the yield spread in an index annuity. So, if an index moved up 10%(M), and the yield spread was 2%(E), you could show a return of 8%(R) for the index annuity as well.

And it does not take much imagination to change the formula so that it works with index annuities using a Participation rate, rather than a yield spread: M x P = R would do the trick. So, if the index moved up 10% (M) and the participation rate was 80% (P), then the index annuity return is 8% (R).

Now we get to the ooh and aah part of the lesson. The mutual fund and variable equation look like this.

M - E = R

But the index annuity formulas are *conditional equations*. A conditional equation means the variable value depends on the value substituted. In the index annuity equation zero is substituted if R is negative:

M - E = R If R<0 Then R=0
or
M x P = R If R<0 Then R=0

And the index annuity formula becomes a very strong equation.

Let's say the mutual fund or variable annuity actually goes down, say, 20%. The formula would show [-20% - 2% = -22%] or a loss of 22%. Indeed, the minimum value in a fund or variable annuity for R is -100%, representing a total loss of all principal.

On the other hand, let's say an index annuity with a 2% yield spread is linked to an index posting a 20% decline. Due to the conditional value the formula would show [-20% - 2% = 0].

What if the index annuity had an 80% participation rate and the index dropped 20%? The formula would show [-20% x 80% = 0]. The minimum value for an index annuity R is 0.

Think about the ramifications of If R<0 Then R=0. In an interest crediting period the worst that can happen is you don't lose any money. Take this a step further. Since R can never be less than zero, this means that returns credited in previous periods cannot be lost either.

Since R can never be negative, index annuities do not lose ground and will not give back credited interest. In fact, because all index annuities are fixed annuities with minimum guaranteed returns, R will ultimately be greater than zero, so the worst the index annuity can produce is a positive return, and that is a very favorable condition indeed. This is one algebra lesson that should be shared.

Bear Tamer – Annual Reset Index Annuities

Do you have a prospect that thinks we are in a prolonged bear market? Great! Meet the bear tamer.

The worst bear market since the Great Depression, with the exception of the Millennium Bear Market, was the awe inspiring 73-74 bear market that took 90-months before the level of the previous high was regained.

In 1972 the S&P 500 closed at the highest end of the year value up to that time and it did not reach that level again until 1980. If you would have bought the index at the end of 1972 you were underwater for the remainder of the '70s. At the end of 1979, seven-years after it had reached a new high, the S&P 500 was still 9% below where it was in 1972.

However, index annuities using an annual reset crediting method lock in any gain. A significant advantage of annual reset annuities in a choppy market is that they do just that, they reset. If the index drops 20%, the annual reset annuity would record no growth for the year, but growth for the future would start at the lower level. If next year the index returned to where it was, the annual reset owner would participate in a 25% gain, but the stock index owner would merely be back to where they started.

The '70s - Annual Reset Point-to-Point Approach

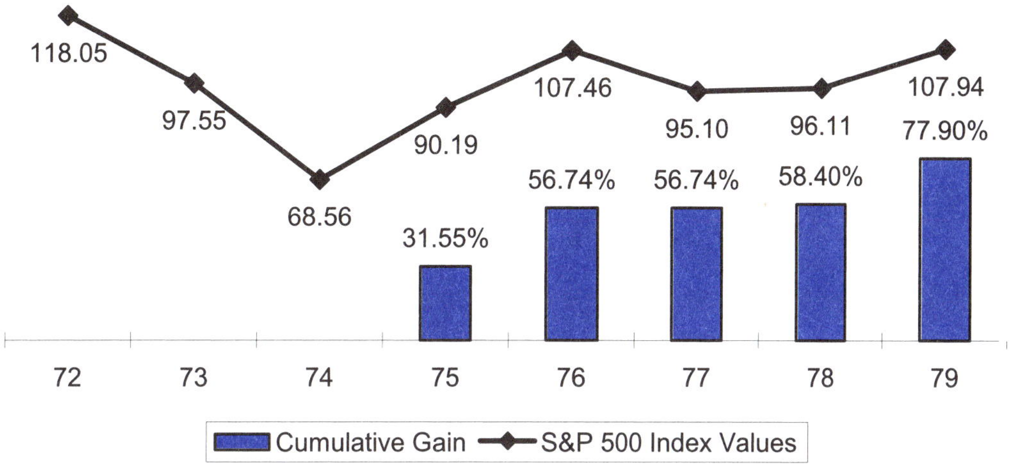

If you look at the index and apply an annual reset structure you would have realized a total return of over 77% even though the index never broke even.

The above graph shows the total return from 1972 through 1979 if you apply an annual reset point-to-point approach to the index. But the power of the annual reset methods holds up when you apply daily averaging to the annual index movements...

The '70s - Annual Reset Daily Averaging Approach

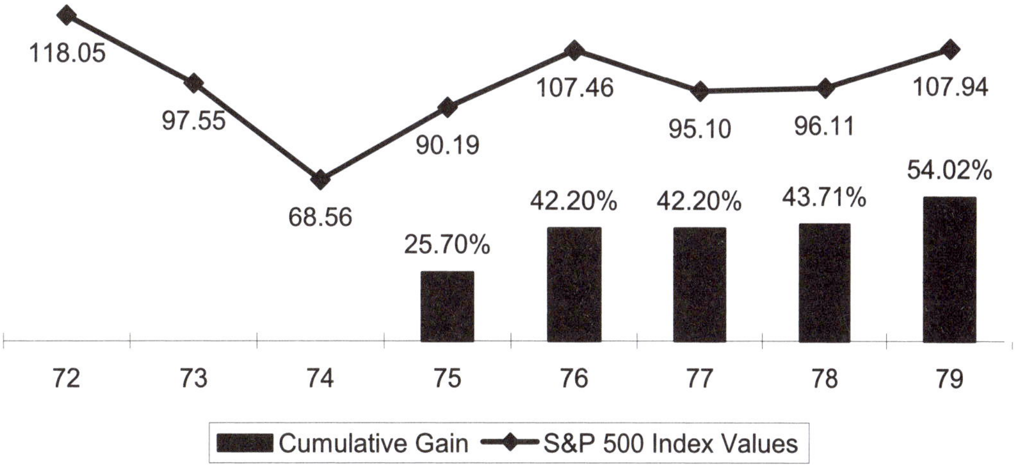

...Or monthly averaging using an annual reset format. Annual reset structured index annuities take advantage of bad markets.

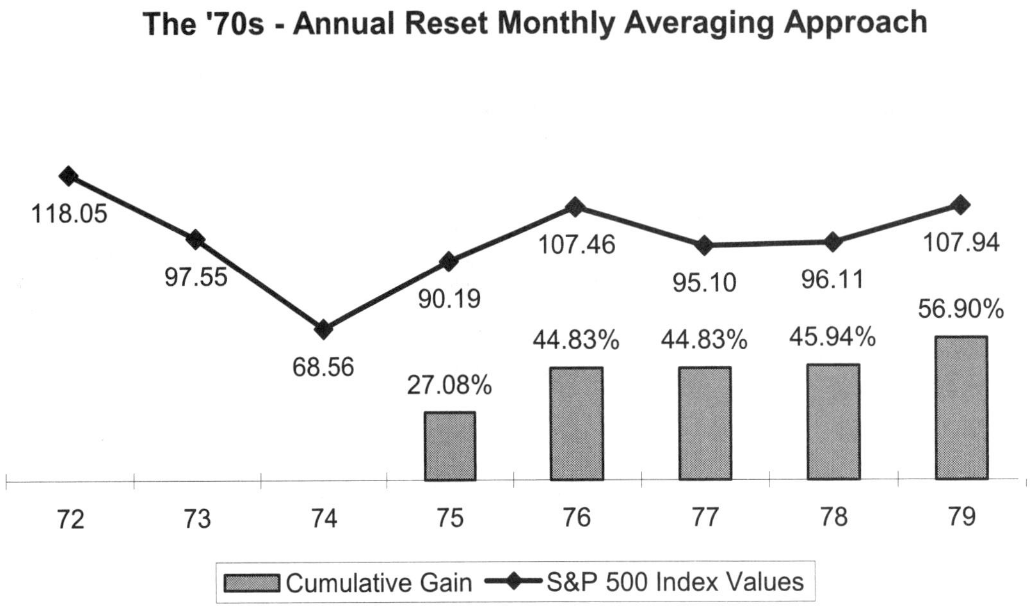

Bag of Stocks

Even though more people own stocks and mutual funds, there are many people that are still uncomfortable and a mite intimidated by the investment world. For these folks stocks and stock indexes are some esoteric intangible pieces of watermarked paper, or a gaggle of symbols appearing on some computer or television screen. These people do not understand the potential of stocks because for them stocks have no real form in their everyday lives. Here is how to help folks understand just what a stock is and why a stock index might go up. (For safety sake, you might want to preface your presentation with the disclaimer that this is for illustrative purposes only, is not an inducement to buy or sell any security, and past results do not predict future performance).

Go out and buy a Hershey's Kiss, a Swiss Miss hot chocolate packet, a single-wash box of Tide detergent and a paper lunch bag at your local Wal-Mart. Put the three items in the bag. The next time you are sitting with a consumer that says the stock market is a bunch of hooey, bring out your bag and say this:

"This is a Hershey's Kiss. They are made by Hershey Foods in Hershey, Pennsylvania. If you owned a hundred shares of Hershey stock in 1985 your quarterly dividend check was $38. If you had done nothing and left the stock alone and spent the dividend checks, your 2002 quarterly check from Hershey was $198. In that seventeen-year period your interest income from certificates of deposit dropped 80%, but the income from your Hershey's stock increased fivefold.

Tide is made by The Procter & Gamble Company who manufactures and markets more than 250 products to more than five billion consumers in 130 countries throughout the world. On 1 October 1987 100 shares of P&G was worth around $10,000. Fifteen years later it had morphed into 800 shares with a market value of over $70,000.

Swiss Miss is made by ConAgra Foods. ConAgra also makes Peter Pan peanut butter, Chef Boyardee, La Choy, and a hundred other easy-to-prepare foods that you've probably used. In the last ten years ConAgra has raised it's dividend eleven times.

The big question with an index annuity is will stock indices continue to go up? Stock indexes are made up of the stocks of individual companies. So I'll ask you...

Will people in the future eat less chocolate?

Will clothes still need to be washed?

Will the demand for easy-to-prepare food increase or will people start making everything they eat from scratch?

A stock index benefits every time someone purchases the goods or services of the companies whose stocks comprise the index. A stock index is not a column of electronic squiggles and hieroglyphics, but a scorecard of every good and service purchased within the index components. Index growth does not result from some magic formula, but is the direct consequence of people buying more food, more gas, better health care, improved consumer goods, and a thousand other tangibles that increase earnings and income.

This bag is made by International Paper. International Paper is traded on the New York Stock Exchange and pays an annual dividend of $1. I purchased all of this at Wal-Mart. At the start of 2002 Wal-Mart operated 3,244 stores in the United States, and 1,151 stores in eight countries, and is expanding in China. The stock symbol for Wal-Mart is WMT.

The stock market is not talking heads, it is not analysts, and it is not pieces of paper. The stock market is people consuming and creating income and wealth."

Because CDs Don't Pay Enough

Over the last thirty years the average interest paid on certificates of deposit has ranged from less than 2% to almost 18%. During the last ten-years a CD's return has averaged around 5% a year; a respectable yield. However, you do not get to keep all of that interest because income taxes takes a cut of the yield and inflation is constantly nibbling at the purchasing power of that CD.

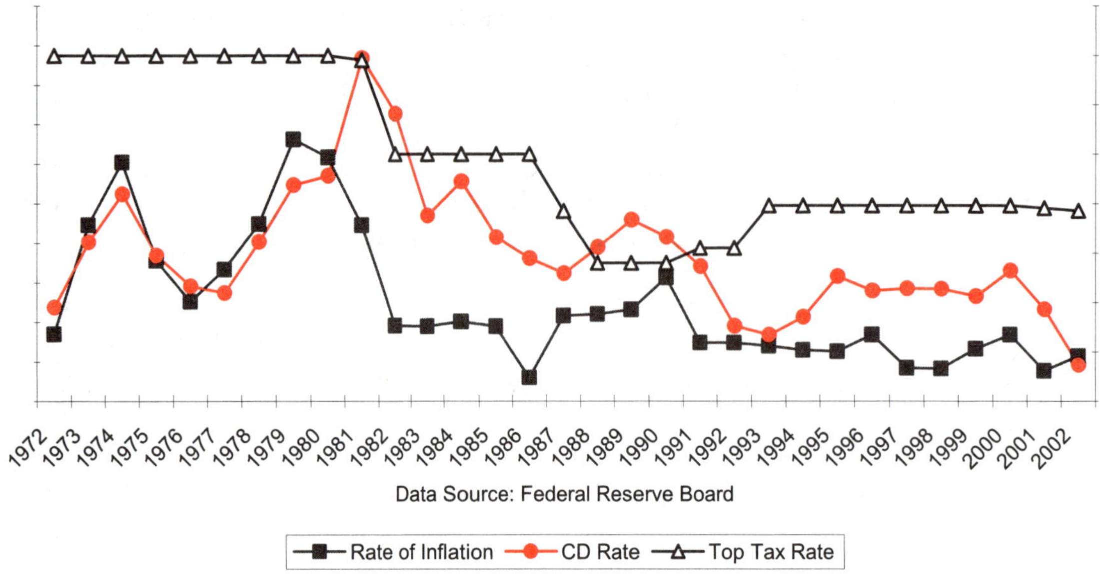

If you look back over the last thirty years, and take into account the ravages of inflation and the top marginal income tax rate, your real CD return after taxes and inflation was negative over half the time. Even with the lower inflation and tax rates of the last ten years your real average return was not 5%, but only 0.5% a year.

CD Real Returns (after taxes & inflation)

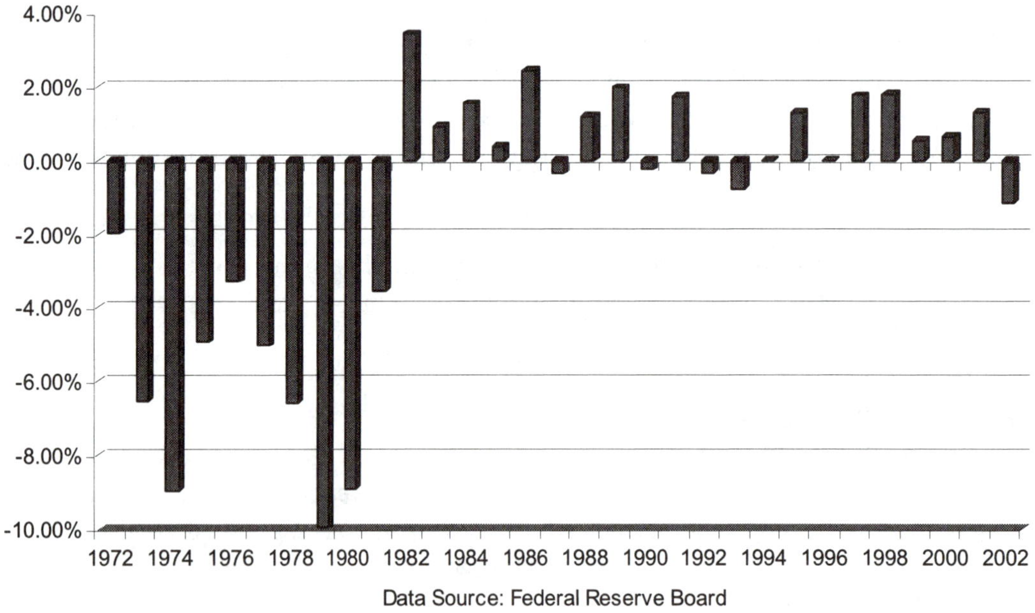

Index Annuities offer the potential for higher interest than certificates of deposit, and still protect principal and credited interest from stock market risk, all on a tax-deferred basis. Index annuities offer a realistic opportunity for real returns.

Earning Just 2% More

The magic of index annuities is not because they might have periods where they credit double digit interest; the real story is they might credit a little more interest than other instruments offering the same principal protection from market risk. And even a 2% increase can mean much more money down the road.

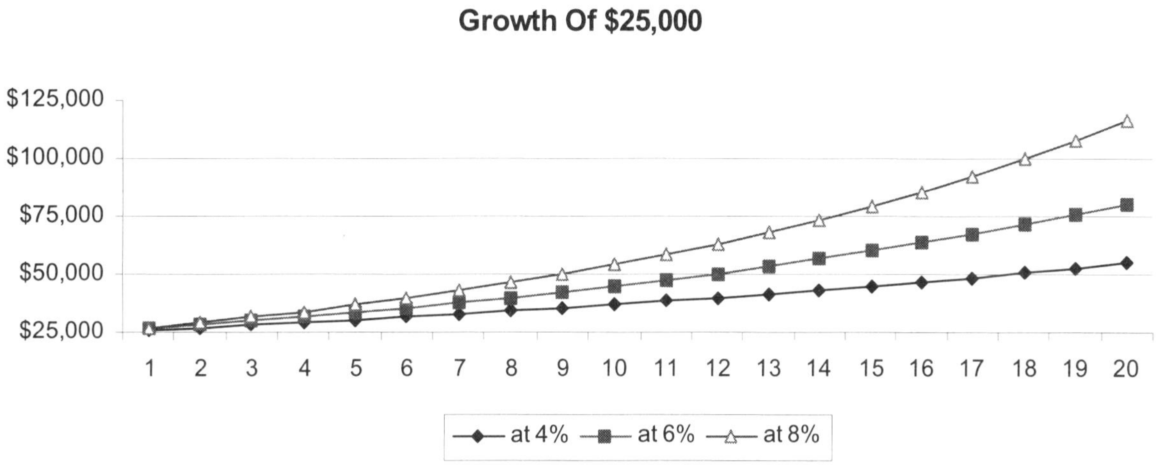

If you begin with $25,000 earning 4% interest you have $37,006 in ten-years. But if you can earn just 2% more you have over $44,000. A 6% return over twenty-years results in over $80,000, but just 2% becomes a six digit $116,524. Index annuities provide the potential for that extra 2%.

Seeing If Your Prospect Qualifies

Maybe it is because we are all three year olds at heart, but almost everyone hates to hear that somebody else might get something they do not. This technique uses the sense of loss approach by describing the requirements a prospect must meet to purchase an index annuity.

"Mr. Smith, index annuities are not for everyone, and I am not sure if you fit the profile. Well, since you insist on knowing, these are the acceptable parameters for an index annuity owner:

An index annuity owner has a strong aversion to losing principal. Index annuity owners are not gamblers, they are savers, and if you want to bet the house on trying to get the maximum return then you are not right for index annuities.

Index annuity owners are in it for the long term. They know that looking only at the short term is a losing proposition because marathon runners, not sprinters, make the real money. Unless you are willing to give your money time to make money, then you are not right for index annuities.

Index annuity owners can handle some bad times because they know they are ultimately protected. Even though index annuities protect your principal and credited interest from market loss, there will be periods of lousy returns. An index annuity owner realizes that the index does not always go up, but takes a longer view of economic trends. If you'd be upset by a year with a poor return, then you are not right for index annuities.

Index annuity owners take an incremental approach. They know that the ultimate winners are those people that try to earn a couple percent more without risking principal, rather than the folks who swing for the fences and more often strike out, or even more sadly sit on the bench and never take a swing. An index annuity owner goes for singles.

Mr. Smith, do you feel you meet the requirements to become an index annuity owner?"

Cueing The Prospect

A behavioral economist at MIT, Dan Ariely, has conducted several studies to determine how people really think about money. Classic economic theory says people are rational economic beings, Professor Ariely's research suggests otherwise. The axiom that consumers can determine the real value of a product was tested by having consumers price items that have a wide range of prices in the real world (like wine). The study asked if the subjects would be willing to buy the wine for a price determined by converting the last two digits of their Social Security numbers to dollars (23 becomes $23, 09 becomes $9, etc.). Although the price produced by the Social Security numbers was arbitrary, and the subjects knew their suggested price was totally random, subjects with high Social Security numbers said they'd pay almost twice as much for the wine as those folks with low numbers.

The implication from this for financial counselors is that they can strongly influence the return expectations of consumers, and thus influence the success of their presentation, by cueing the consumer. Here's what I mean: If an agent begins talking about the 2% yields on CDs and then mentions the 4% fixed rate annuity yield, the consumer will be more receptive than if the agent starts right off talking about the 4% annuity rate. The 4% annuity rate offered may not even be a competitive annuity rate – other annuities might be paying 5%, or the annuity rate could be very competitive but the consumer had a mental image of 6% when you sat down. By cueing or grounding the consumer on the lower rate of another product the agent establishes a reference point for the consumer to use in making a perception of value on the product being presented.

The same cueing can be done to minimize current or future complaints about performance. As an example, just before the consumer receives an index annuity statement showing a zero credited in the index-linked interest column, the financial counselor could talk about the one year losses of index funds, to place a no-loss return in its proper perspective. Cueing can help to reset price or return expectations in comparative situations, but it's much less effective in resolving perceptions of cost.

A recent study* by the Wharton School found that consumers are not motivated to pay more if a business's cost of doing business increases, because the consumer figures the business is making way too much profit anyway. The study showed consumers dramatically underestimate the costs of doing business and overstate profits. As an example, the average subject believed a typical grocery store had a net profit of 27% when the reality is around 1% to 2%. Similar "fat cat" beliefs were held about other industries and cueing these subjects about economic realities did not help change opinions.

The implication from the Wharton study is that an agent is wasting their time explaining to a consumer that the reason index annuity participation is 60% instead of 100% is due to the effects of higher volatility and lower interest rates, because the consumer figures the insurance company is either making even more money at the lower rate or still has a huge profit built in even if costs went up. It would be more effective if the index participation rates of several products were compared to establish a value reference, or showed competitive returns could still hypothetically happen at the lower rate and create a value perception. Cue your customers and sell value, not how much it costs.

**Consumer Perceptions of Price (Un)Fairness*, Bolton, Warlop & Alba, Wharton School, University of Pennsylvania, 2002

Opportunity Cost

In Economics you are told that an *Opportunity Cost* is the theoretical cost of forgoing a profitable alternative. One example of this is selecting a certificate of deposit with a stated rate instead of a fixed index annuity with an unknown return. If the index annuity returns more than the CD the cost is the opportunity lost by not selecting the annuity. If the index annuity is selected but pays less, the cost is the difference between the CD yield and the annuity.

At the turn of the century certificates of deposit were yielding nearly 7%, some traditional fixed annuity rates were even higher, and the S&P 500 index was near its all-time high. Although index annuities have credited double digit interest rates, there can also be years of zero, or near zero, returns. A few years ago the opportunity cost of selecting the potential returns of an index annuity over the stated returns of a certificate of deposit or traditional fixed annuity was high.

Recently the opportunity cost of selecting the index annuity over these other saving vehicles was much lower. In 2002 the average one-year CD yield was under 2.5%. This means that even if the index annuity credited zero, the cost of selecting the index annuity opportunity was under 2.5%; a very low cost by historical standards.

The potential opportunity cost of selecting an index annuity is the rate that can be earned on alternatives. If alternative returns are low, the potential cost is low. However, the opportunity cost of <u>not</u> selecting the index annuity can be very high. Which opportunity would you select?

Meeting Objections

Annuities Are Not FDIC Insured

Annuities are only underwritten by insurance companies and are backed by the assets of the insurance company. Your annuity carriers meet high standards for financial stability. Every state has a guaranty fund (which an agent cannot tell a buyer about unless asked for some perverse reason) providing at least some protection if the insurance company fails. If all else fails, try to get a little annuity piece today and try for more later.

The FDIC – Annuity Challenge

I was on the panel at a gathering awhile back and one of the other speakers was offering suggestions on overcoming objections. Two of the points he said to raise when people asked if annuities were FDIC insured were that banks failed in the 1930s and there's not enough money in the FDIC fund if a lot of banks failed today.

I've heard these same tired excuses used to try to sell against FDIC for 20 years and they've never convinced a consumer to move money into an annuity. If economic conditions resulted in the failure of many banks and exhausted the fund, Congress would simply authorize the government to put more money into it. To suggest that a bank deposit within the FDIC limits won't be covered if the bank fails insults the consumer's intelligence and makes the agent look desperate.

What is the consumer really asking? Although some are actually in love with FDIC – it took me two years to convince my folks to buy government bonds because they weren't FDIC insured – the vast majority of consumers are really saying that they are scared to death of losing money. The only financial products that are more protected from principal risk are cash in hand and government bonds, and many people will never own anything other than FDIC insured savings. However, some of those savers might be convinced to purchase an annuity if they believe it too is safe, but the way you show the safety of an annuity is not by trashing FDIC.

I agree that several annuity carriers have failed in the last two decades, however; I have been unable to find hard evidence that any annuity customer received back less than 100 cents on the dollar because of the failure if they didn't bolt. Am I saying that every fixed annuity customer that stayed the course throughout the regulatory relief process of every busted carrier got back all of their principal? No. I'm saying that I can't find any proof that they didn't.

If your potential annuity buyer is concerned about safety, ask them to tell you if they know any person that has lost principal in a fixed annuity because the insurance company went under. I doubt if they can.

The Advantage Group, an independent research and consulting firm, upon completion of a study in 2002 said, "No index annuity owner has ever lost money because the insurer failed. I didn't say most people didn't lose...I didn't say almost nobody lost money...I said nobody has ever lost money in an index annuity because the carrier failed, not no how, not no where, not no one."

I Don't Want To Tie Up My Money

There are people that think green bananas are a long-term commitment, so you need to uncover the buyer's real concern. Your answers should reflect actual contract provisions and carrier policy, but some possible initial responses are:

I could lose money – *This carrier meets high standards for financial stability.*

I could lose money – *Tell me someone you know that lost money in a fixed annuity.*

I want liquidity – *If you withdraw money from the annuity this carrier typically sends the proceeds within ___ weeks.*

I might have an emergency – *If you cash in the annuity this carrier typically sends the proceeds within ___ weeks.*

I might have an emergency – *This is why we left $195,000 sitting in the 2% passbook saving account and only committed $5,000 to the annuity.*

The rates are too low – *Compared to what? What other instrument provides the same degree of protection with this rate or potential interest.*

The rates are too low – *I can get you a higher rate. How much of your principal can you afford to risk?*

The surrender period is too long - *When you renew your CD a new interest rate is declared and a new penalty period begins. Even if you stay with one bank and keep renewing CDs for 30 years you will always have a six-month interest penalty. The penalty period on this annuity is based on the date of the premium and eventually goes completely away.*

Avoiding Returned Policies

Whether you call it buyer's remorse or post-decision indigestion, many people wonder whether they did the right thing after making a purchase. You can help avoid broken sales and returned policies by doing two things.

First, tell them they may experience buyer's remorse. Tell them it's normal and restate why the buy decision was a good one. Then when they get the queasy feeling, they'll be reminded that you had warned this might happen and rationalize the feeling away.

Second, send them a letter reaffirming the reasons they made the purchase, but do not include new selling points. For example, if the client liked the tax-deferral aspect you might mention that money left inside the annuity means they won't get a Form 1099 in the mail next January. But do not introduce new selling points if they were not covered before. Telling a client previously unconcerned about financial strength that their new insurer has the highest financial ratings and therefore a very low likelihood of going out of business could introduce a new fear. Restate the positives; do not keep selling.

Annuities Have Temporary Liquidity Costs

A fixed annuity typically deducts a surrender charge if the contract is liquidated prior to the end of a predetermined period. However, it may be more accurate to replace the term "surrender charge" with temporary and voluntary liquidity cost.

Surrender charge implies an ongoing expense and has resulted in agents referring to annuity products as having a "seven year term" or being a "ten year product " with the stated years representing the period during which liquidity costs are assessed. In fact, the expense associated with liquidating the contract usually disappears after an agreed upon duration and the "term" of an annuity is from date of purchase until maturity.

Indeed, a forty year old owner's annuity may have a fifty year "term" until the policy matures and may also have a seven percent cost, but only if the contract is voluntarily liquidated in the next eight years.

There are annuities that measure index movement over a multiple of years whose ending point coincides with the last year of the temporary liquidity cost, but the annuities typically don't require the annuity balance to be distributed at this point.

The 2x4 Close

"Mr. & Mrs. Consumer,

►This annuity provides tax deferral, which means your money grows three ways (simple interest, compound interest & tax-advantaged interest) your CD can't do this.

►This annuity has a minimum interest guarantee which means regardless of how low interest rates may fall you are guaranteed you can't earn less - your bank can't do this.

►This annuity may be converted, at your discretion, into a stream of guaranteed income that you can never outlive - your bank CD can't do this.

►If you elect not to spend the interest and let the annuity grow you will not receive a Form 1099 - you can't do this with your bank CD.

In fact, Mr. & Mrs. Consumer, the annuity's benefits so outweigh the CD's benefits that the bank should pay you 2% more interest than the annuity pays. If they're not, why are you still at the bank?"

Unconventional Marketing

The section on unconventional marketing is based on successful use. A decade ago I owned a broker/dealer with offices in nine states. Our financial counselors were doing okay, but not setting the sales world on fire. One year after I began teaching our people unconventional marketing, the average production level and commission income had tripled. It takes a while longer than "smiling and dialing" but the typical client is higher quality.

People often confuse the marketing process with its parts. An ad agency says that running an ad is marketing. A salesperson says that sitting down with a prospect and getting the order is marketing. A store manager setting up an end of the aisle display of goods says this is marketing. These are all parts of the marketing function.

Marketing is the interaction of various activities with the goal of satisfying specific customer needs. Its ultimate purpose is to position a product whereby it creates demand and then shows how the product satisfies that demand. However, a problem that many agents have is that they confuse the marketing of physical products with the real goal of marketing themselves.

An agent may say that they market annuities. They will run an ad showing the current rate of an annuity and give their phone number. But, this is not marketing it is selling. Selling assumes that the prospect already demands the product and knows how the product will satisfy this demand. The ad simply shows where the product is available. It does nothing to market the agent.

What is wrong with an agent saying that they sell fixed annuities? First, you are counting on the customer to realize that they need a fixed annuity and hoping they pick you as the fixed annuity seller. Second, you are typecasting yourself into a very small box. If all you sell, and are going to sell, are fixed annuities, then maybe being recognized as a "fixed annuity salesperson" is okay. Your customers will be people that realize they need a fixed annuity and you will be known as the fixed annuity store.

But, what if the prospect does not realize they need a fixed annuity? Being the "annuity store" will not help if the prospect does not recognize their need. And, what if you offer other products that would meet their demands but you are only perceived as the annuity store - prospects won't come to your door for solutions to other needs.

As the financial counselor, you are the product. And, you need to position yourself so that potential customers know how you can satisfy their demands. To do this you need to think in terms of customer needs and providing solutions.

Needs Based Solutions
Problem-Solving not *Product-Pushing* Approach
Traditional Selling Says *Features-Benefits*
Unconventional Selling Says *Goal-Solutions*

Needs Based Solutions uses a problem-solving not product pushing approach. Traditional selling says that you talk to a customer in terms of features and benefits. Feature - this annuity grows tax deferred; Benefit - while the interest is compounding in the annuity you will not pay taxes so your value grows faster and you have more money down the road.

Unconventional selling says that you listen to a prospect's goals or needs and provide a solution. "Mr. & Mrs. Client, you've told me that your goals are to not lose principal - solutions for this goal are CD's, fixed rate annuities and fixed index annuities. You also want to avoid Social Security Benefit Taxation on the interest while it's compounding - this can be accomplished with a fixed rate or index annuity. You want to earn a higher rate of interest than you're currently getting - a solution for this goal is an indexed annuity. And, you want a 20% return - this goal is not realistic based on your other goals. Do you want to change the other goals or just this one?"

With Needs Based Solutions you're not positioning yourself as the annuity store. You are providing a solution to a customer's needs. The bottom line is still the same – you have sold an annuity, but the customer perceives you as a problem solver.

People Hate to be Sold But They Love to Learn

Needs based solutions is still selling, it is not marketing. But the image you create with needs based solutions should define your marketing efforts. Both are based on a simple premise - People Hate to be Sold But They Love to Learn. With Needs Based Solutions you didn't sell the customer an annuity. You taught the customer that an annuity was a solution to their goals. Unconventional marketing is designed to teach prospects to become your customers.

Unconventional Marketing Methods

People are more likely to believe a newspaper article than a newspaper ad. Consumers place higher credibility on the words of a professor than a salesperson, and more people will buy a stock based on what they saw on *Wall Street Week* than if their broker gives them the tip. Why? The first sources are perceived as teachers not sellers. People enjoy learning new things and using their newfound knowledge to better themselves. But, they do not want to be sold. Unconventional marketing gets past the sales defense screen so that your message gets through because you are perceived as the teacher.

Four avenues are used in unconventional marketing - teaching, speaking, writing and hosting. All of them portrayed the agent as the reluctant salesperson.

Reluctant Salesperson — you never talk about a product - except as a general solution to a problem. You never ask for an appointment - but you would be willing to see the prospect when you can spare the time. You never hand out product materials - but you make it clear what solutions you can provide.

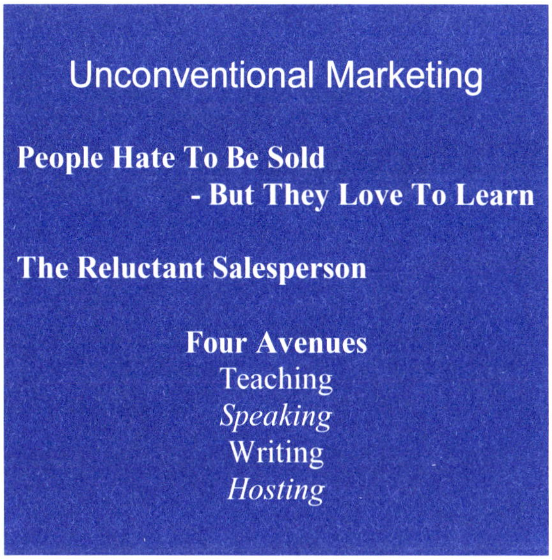

In fact, if you are asked for an appointment you do not give out your business card, just write your name and phone number on a piece of paper and ask if they could call you tomorrow - and you will juggle your schedule to fit them in.

I realize this flies in the face of every sales article that tells you to distribute business cards like snowflakes and press for the appointment. But you are not selling; you are teaching prospects to become customers. The four avenues:

Teaching

The best place to teach is in school. Many community colleges and school systems offer adult classes in a variety of areas. Offer your services to teach a general investment course or talk about the "financial needs of seniors". The ultimate goal is not to convert students to clients, though occasionally you'll have a student with a lump sum pension plan distribution or with $100,000 stuck in a passbook savings account earning 2%. The objective is building a referral network of former students.

Another method is to teach a two or three part course addressing the needs of the prospects you are targeting using a school or library as the location. Many schools, colleges or libraries rent out meeting rooms. These sites convey learning rather than selling.

Try not to hold these classes at a hotel. Every prospect knows that classes at hotels – whether they are called workshops or symposiums – are designed to sell them something.

Another way to teach is to offer continuing education courses for accountants and attorneys. Every state requires these professionals to complete a certain number of CE hours to remain in good standing. In many states it isn't difficult to get a session approved for CE credit.

Does this work? Yes. At first you'll get an occasional call from accountants or lawyers asking for the address of an insurance company or asking for the definition of some policy feature; eventually you get referrals.

Many companies have me speak about index annuities at their top producer conferences where the attendees are agents that are personally selling $3 to $10 million of annuities. I ask everyone of these agents "Where is your business coming from?" Nine out of ten tell me that consumer appointments made from trust & estate planning seminars are the reason for their big production.

Speaking

Business clubs like the Lions, Exchange Club and Rotary are always looking for speakers. Contact your Chamber of Commerce for a list of local club presidents and offer your services on a general topic like "protecting retirement plan principal". Establish an emergency speaker service where the club can call you at the last minute and you'll step in if there is a cancellation.

Writing

Every time I ran an ad it cost me a few hundred dollars and generated one or two calls. Every article written costs me nothing and generates four or five calls. The article may contain the same information as the ad, but it's received as a teaching tool and not a sales implement.

Writing an article and getting it printed are two different things. Try to build a relationship with your local newspaper. In the meantime, submit your work to your suburban or community newspapers. And, there are dozens of newsletters produced by civic clubs, trade organizations and community groups that may welcome an article on a financial topic of interest to their readers

If you cannot get published, get quoted. If a reporter can rely on you for immediate and accurate comments on a topic, they'll use you again and again. Remember deadlines – if a reporter can't get hold of you they'll find a different source.

Hosting

One hundred cable TV channels means a lot of airtime to fill. One can strike very reasonable deals on sponsoring and starring in a regularly scheduled cable TV show. If you believe that agents should be heard and not seen, a weekly radio show time slot on a local station can be purchased at low cost. Even though people are cynical about the media, appearing on TV or radio enhances your image as an expert. And, many people like to boast that they are customers of a celebrity.

But I Can't...Speak...Talk...Act!

Then you had better learn. If you don't want to develop your own materials there are a number of sources that provide packaged scripts and articles on a number of topics. But, you will still need to be able to talk. Take public speaking courses, join Toastmasters, take a drama course or hire a communications consultant.

Do not worry that you will never be as good as Dale Carnegie. Practice creates competency. You do not need to be an ace, just okay.

Other Unconventional Ideas

Plan A Campaign - Find a solution for a need and tell everyone about it for the next 30 days. Maybe the need is avoiding market risk to principal and the solution is an instrument that has outperformed both bond funds and certificates of deposit.

Hit The Road - Drop by small businesses to let them know of your upcoming course on small business pension plans or offer a free subscription to your newsletter (that is prepared and personalized by a newsletter publishing service).

Play Golf - Sponsor a local charity golf tournament.

Cross-Sell - Review your current customer files to see if they may have a need that you have not addressed.

Awaken The Dead - Go through last year's "no-sales" or "no-shows" and give them a call.

Sponsor A Team - Having your name on the back of a kid's baseball, softball or soccer jersey gives you visibility. Show up at least once with soda pop at the end of a game to meet the parents.

3 Letter Drips - Can't get an executive to return your calls? Send them an article about their industry with the handwritten note "Thought this might be of interest". Send them an article about their company or local business news with the note "Thought this might be of interest". Send them an article about a financial problem that you have a solution for with a note "I will call next week". Next time they'll answer your call.

Where You Are The Customer - Talk to the owner of the restaurant where you have your morning coffee, your barber or hairdresser, and your florist about their SEP plan.

"Good News Mrs. Smith" - Call existing customers about the current rate of interest on their fixed or index annuity. Congratulate them on their wise decision.

"Ready for my close-up" - Be creative. One practitioner decorated the office in gauze and bandages, donned surgical scrubs, and roamed the halls of her office building. She told prospects she was making appointments for financial checkups.

Cheat Sheet

Tomorrow I Will Begin To

1. Contact each client every 90 days - It doesn't have to be a sales call.
2. Review 10 client files a day to see if changes should be made and set an appointment with the client.
3. Ask for 2 referrals a day.
4. Schedule a "How To Cope With Falling Interest Rates" seminar. Use a local library or school, notify the newspaper of this service event and call existing clients and prospects.
5. Schedule a "Supercharge Your IRA" meeting with prospects, clients and their guests. Talk about IRA strategies in a turbulent market and how the new rules on distribution will affect them.
6. Plan a campaign. Pick a product you really like, learn all about it, and tell everyone you meet about the product for the next 30 days.
7. Schedule a 2 hour weekly planning appointment. Sit down and determine the 10 things you most want to accomplish for the week.
8. Start a newsletter. There are several sources that provide customer newsletters that can be personalized. Send them to your clients and prospects each quarter, they are an effective prospecting tool.
9. Send a handwritten note to each client that purchased a fixed annuity from you last year. Tell them that they're doing well and current interest rates are at X%.
10. Send handwritten letters to prospects that didn't buy from you last year. Thank them for their consideration and tell them you hope you may be of service at some time.
11. Call your tax-free municipal bond mutual fund clients. Congratulate them on choosing an investment that pays tax-free dividends (and probably generated a gain in value as well).
12. Join an organization that will expand your horizons. It could be a professional association to increase your knowledge or a business club to increase your centers of influence.
13. Ask your best clients "If there was just one thing you could change about doing business with me what would it be?" Your clients will help you improve your business if you ask them for input.
14. Read or reread "The Sale Begins When The Customer Says NO" by Elmer Leterman and "How I Raised Myself From Failure to Success in Selling" by Frank Bettger.
15. Give time or money to a charity you've always wanted to help.

Discussion Questions

1. What is your most effective index annuity sales method?

2. What other points might be used to address annuity related safety concerns?

3. What would be other unconventional marketing approaches?

Chapter Quiz

1. Tax-deferred annuity interest is reported on Form 1040

A. Line 8a
B. Line 8b
C. Line 9
D. None of the above

2. The algebra term for an equation where the variable value depends on the value substituted is

A. A conditional equation
B. Minimum value equation
C. Guaranteed value equation
D. Linked equation

3. If you apply an annual reset approach to the S&P 500 looking at the calendar years from 1972 through 1979 the cumulative return is

A. –9%
B. 0%
C. 77%
D. 100%

4. If you look back over the last 30 years the net return from certificates of deposit, after the effects of inflation and taxes

A. Were negative over half the time
B. Ranged from less than 2% to over 18%
C. Both A and B
D. Neither A nor B

5. Cueing a customer means
A. Cold calling lists of theatre patrons
B. Establishing a reference point for the consumer to use in making a perception of value
C. Beating objections
D. Not selling costs

Chapter 10 – Index Life Insurance (and other things)

Life insurance provides unique benefits that are unmatched by other financial planning instruments. Although the primary benefit of life insurance is to provide cash upon death, in the final analysis life insurance is for the living. Permanent life insurance gives you a solid foundation.

Life Insurance Is For

* Paying Final Expenses - Bills, medical costs, funeral needs	*Dream Fulfillment - Ensuring the mortgage will be paid off or the children will go to college
* Spouse Income - Benefits may be used to replace salary or pension income	* Estate Planning - Covering estate taxes and completing bequeaths

* Emergency Fund - Any cash values may be withdrawn or borrowed against if needed

Only life insurance can provide an immediate estate. If others are economically dependent upon you, life insurance can provide the cash to take care of those needs. Life insurance may also be used to preserve an estate by providing cash to pay estate settlement costs.

Permanent Insurance

There are really only two types of life insurance - insurance that does build cash value or insurance that does not build cash value, otherwise known as term insurance. Term insurance provides a specified benefit for a specified period of time; when the time is up the coverage expires. One example of term coverage is flight insurance. We pay a few dollars at the airport kiosk for an insurance policy. If the plane successfully completes the flight our policy expires. This is how term insurance works. One difference between flight insurance and regular term insurance is that the cost goes up as we get older. You can delay the increase in premium by selecting a policy that levels the premium for a period of time, but if you still want the coverage to continue at the end of the period you will pay more.

Permanent insurance is designed to provide lifetime insurance protection. The premium you pay covers the current costs of the insurance protection with the balance used to build up a cash value. This cash value helps to keep premiums level for the life of the policy or may even eliminate the need for premiums at some point down the road.

Universal Life

A popular type of permanent life insurance is Universal Life or UL. UL gives you more control and greater flexibility than traditional whole life insurance. UL permits you to increase or decrease the specified benefit if your situation changes (increases are usually subject to evidence of insurability) and premiums can be adjusted. If your cash value growth is sufficient it may even be possible for you to quit paying premiums at some future date. Of course, if cash value growth is below expectations you may need to continue paying at least the minimum required premium.

Variable Universal Life

Another type of permanent insurance is Variable Universal Life or VUL. Over time stock investments have generated higher returns than fixed interest instruments like bonds. VUL uses part of the premium to cover the current costs of the insurance protection with the balance invested in subaccounts containing diverse portfolios of equities.

It is hoped that these VUL accounts will increase cash value growth at a faster rate than typical fixed rate UL. One risk of VUL is that the accounts are fully exposed to the swings of the stock market. In a declining market cash values could decrease and additional premiums be required.

Equity Indexed Universal Life

The dynamics of the last few years resulted in a new approach to permanent life insurance. Consumers liked the higher return potential of linking cash value growth to equity markets in VUL, but didn't like the possibility of losing cash value if the market went down. To meet these needs insurance companies developed equity indexed universal life or EIUL.

EIUL shares the coverage and premium flexibility of other universal life policies, but the crediting of interest is unique. Typically, cash value increases are linked to positive changes in an equity index. If the index is higher at the end of the policy year the interest credited to the cash value will reflect this. So, if the calculated index is higher at the end of the year the cash value will participate in a percentage of this increase.

What if the index goes down? If the index stays flat or declines the cash value is still credited with a minimum guaranteed interest rate. This is the attraction of EIUL. When the index goes up the policy owner shares in the increase, but if the index goes down the policy still earns at least a minimum interest rate.

It should be noted that the cash value will probably not reflect all of the increase in the index nor are dividends or capital gains included in the index calculation. Protecting the cash value from market loss and guaranteeing a minimum return costs money, and money used to protect the cash value means a reduction in maximum potential returns. Even so, EIUL offers many features:

Index Universal Life Offers	
Tax-deferral of interest earnings	Tax-deferral of interest earnings
Equity indexed linked returns	*Cash value protection against market declines*
Guaranteed minimum annual returns	Annual lock-in of earnings
Premium flexibility	*Cash value access*
Accumulation Fund to Supplement Retirement	Provide income through policy loans

How Interest Is Credited

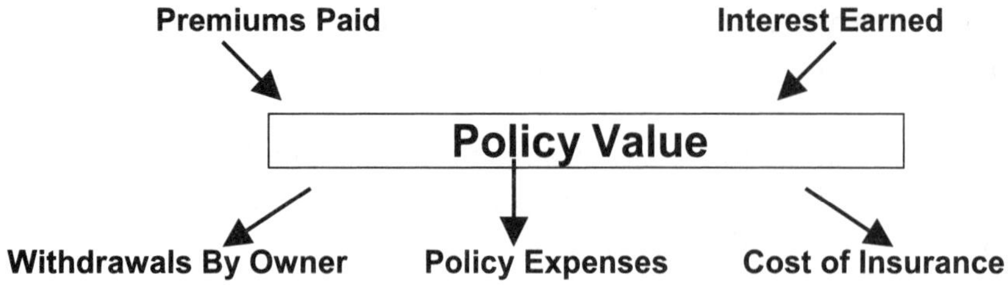

An EIUL policy works like other universal life policies. Premium paid and interest earned are added to the policy value, and policy expenses and the cost of insurance are subtracted. The only difference is interest earnings are linked to the performance of an external index.

Let's say that we have an accumulated value of $10,000 and a minimum interest rate of 2%. We'll further assume that we receive 60% of the calculated index gain for the year. At the end of the year the calculated index gain is 15%. The accumulated value would earn 9% for the year (15% x 60%) or $900. So, our accumulated value would now be worth $10,900 ($10,000 plus $900).

After Cost of Insurance is Deducted	
Calculated Index Gain	15%
Participation Rate	x 60%
Excess Interest Credited	9%
Minimum Interest Rate	2%
Interest Credited to Policy	9%

But what if the market dropped 10% the following year? The locked-in value of $10,900 would be unaffected by the market decline and would earn 2% or $218 ($10,900 time 2%) leaving an accumulated value of $11,118. The policy receives the greater of minimum guaranteed interest rate or the excess interest earned from the calculated index gain.

Calculated Index Gain	0%
Participation Rate	x 60%
Excess Interest Credited	0%
Minimum Interest Rate	2%
Interest Credited to Policy	2%

Why Would I Consider EIUL?

Equity Indexed Universal Life is for people that need life insurance and desire permanent protection. They want greater flexibility and greater control than is available with traditional insurance. EIUL owners:

Like the opportunity for higher potential interest with equity linked returns

Don't like the volatility and risks of VUL

Want the certainty of knowing they'll earn at least a minimum return in good times and bad

EIUL is available as a flexible premium personal insurance plan with premiums typically paid monthly or yearly. EIUL is also available for estate planning purposes as survivorship life. And, EIUL is available as a single premium insurance instrument.

Immediate (Income) Index Annuities

There is only one remaining carrier offering an immediate annuity with a base income that has payment of additional income linked to index performance. The concept is an interesting marriage of fixed rate and index linkage and will grow.

Indexed Certificates of Deposit

In 1999 equity-linked CDs were introduced by a handful of banks. The FDIC insured products used a term-end point crediting design and promised to pay a percentage of any index increase typically over a 5 year period, but 7 and 9 year periods were also available. No interest was paid until maturity; however, the IRS calculated an annual phantom interest income. Unless the equity-linked CDs were held within a qualified account, taxes on the phantom interest were due each year. Index-linked certificates of deposit never caught on, although the concept is valid.

Variable Annuities With Features Borrowed From Index Annuities

A few variable annuities have index-linked accounts promising to protect against principal loss if held until the end of the period. They typically work like term-end point styled index annuities and determining whether the VA or index annuity could produce the highest return depends on respective net index participation.

Guaranteed return or principal protection features come in a variety of flavors. One clean version simply charges an additional 0.25% a year and guarantees at least principal back at the end of 10 years. I am sure the carrier is betting on the fact that markets do not usually lose money over ten year periods.

Another variable annuity automatically transfers money from the equity accounts to the fixed account when they feel this is needed and guarantees at least the original premium will be there at the end of the period if their formula is in error. However, an overly cautious approach by the insurer could hamstring total returns in a rising market. And another VA promises to keep the owner whole if annual withdrawals are limited to a certain (low) percentage of assets, my guess is the limits are designed to make time work for the insurer because historically if you wait long enough the market always comes back.

Principal Protection From Wall Street

Brokerage houses do an excellent job of creating investment opportunities with the potential to build wealth, but whenever they start saying how they are now concerned about safety of principal, I wonder if they are not really trying to fit the bull and the bear into sheep's clothing and become something they are not.

Principal Protection Funds

Principal protection funds and equity-linked notes use a split-investment concept that has been around a long time. The concept involves buying zero coupon bonds that mature in 5 to 10 years with an ending value equal to the original principal and any money that isn't needed for bonds is used to buy stocks. You could do this yourself, but Wall Street puts it all together in a nice pretty package and charges additional management fees plus typically a front end load or deferred sales charge. If you hold the fund to maturity you get back your money plus any gains from the stocks.

These principal protection funds are traded, so you can sell them before they mature and get the market value of the bonds and stocks on the day you sell, which could be more or less than you paid. And, unless the fund is inside a qualified retirement account it will create phantom taxable income from the bonds and possible taxable dividend or capital gains income from the stocks.

Equity-Linked Certificates

Equity-linked certificates say they will give you at least a minimum return if you hold them to maturity, but will let you participate in the upward equity movement. What they do is calculate monthly or quarterly index gains – up to a cap, and subtract monthly or quarterly index losses – without a cap. The problem is that "no cap on downside" bit.

For example, let's say you had a cap wherein the most you'd gain in any month is 3%. The marketing spin on this is you could make up to 36% a year and still get at least your principal back plus a little interest if the market tanked. The reality is a little different. Say the market increased 10% a month for five months. The market would be up 50%. The certificate would be up 15%, that's 3% a month cap times 5 months. But what happens if the index drops 15% in month six? Even though over that six month period the index rose 50% and then fell 15% so that its still up 35% from 6 months before, the 15% loss wipes out the 15% capped gain so the certificate gain is back to zero even though the index is way up.

Market Index Securities

They promise a guarantee of principal if held to a 5 or 7 year maturity and act like term yield spread styled index annuities. Essentially, you lock in the index value today and see where the index is at the end of the term. If there's a gain, a retroactive annual asset fee is deducted and the security buyer gets back the greater of original principal or the new index gain. These securities are traded, so they are liquid, but of course the selling price before maturity could be more or less than paid.

Cheat Sheet

- All of the index annuity alternatives use a variation of term end point crediting; none take an annual reset approach. The protection benefits offered by annual reset styled index annuities has not been matched by securities.

Discussion Questions

1. When might one use equity-indexed life insurance instead of universal or variable life?

2. Why didn't equity-indexed certificates of deposit catch on?

3. Do the principal protection offerings from brokerage houses offer the same benefits of index annuities?

Chapter Quiz

1. Life insurance

A. Provides unique benefits
B. In the final analysis is for the living
C. Can provide an immediate estate
D. All of the above

2. Equity index life differs from variable life in that

A. Cash value can't be lost if the market goes down
B. Costs are guaranteed never to increase
C. The index life policy can never lapse
D. All of the above

3. Methods used to guarantee VA principal from loss are

A. Carrier offers 100% principal guarantee at end of period and charges a fee for the protection
B. Carrier offers 100% principal guarantee if withdrawals are restricted
C. Both A and B
D. Neither A nor B

4. Securities sold as principal protection products include

A. Market index securities
B. Principal protection funds
C. Equity-linked certificates
D. All of the above

5. What can be said about securities sold as principal protection products

A. They offer the protection of annual reset styled index annuities
B. They all measure index movement over a number of years
C. They offer minimum interest guarantees
D. They don't charge commissions, fees or loads

Index annuity earned interest is based on participation in movements of an external index. Equity index movements depend on the individual company stocks making up the index. Why do stocks go up and down? Read on.

An Investment Primer

Mary has decided that an ice cream shop at the edge of Yourtowne would be a good business. It would take $10,000 to start the business, but she only has $1,000. Mary forms a corporation and issues ten-shares of stock. Mary invests her $1,000 to buy one-share and finds nine other people willing to invest $1,000 each for a share. The corporation now has $10,000 in capital and Mary's Ice Cream, Inc. opens for business.

At the end of the first year, after paying all operating expenses and taxes, Mary's Ice Cream, Inc. has $2,000 left over in profits. The investors decide to pay out $1,000 in dividends to shareholders and retain $1,000 in the business to spend on a new freezer.

Corporations issue stock in the form of certificates in exchange for money, property or services. Each certificate represents a share in the ownership of the corporation. In the investment world total profits (or losses) are divided by the numbers of shares of ownership to reflect the proportionate financial interest of the investors.

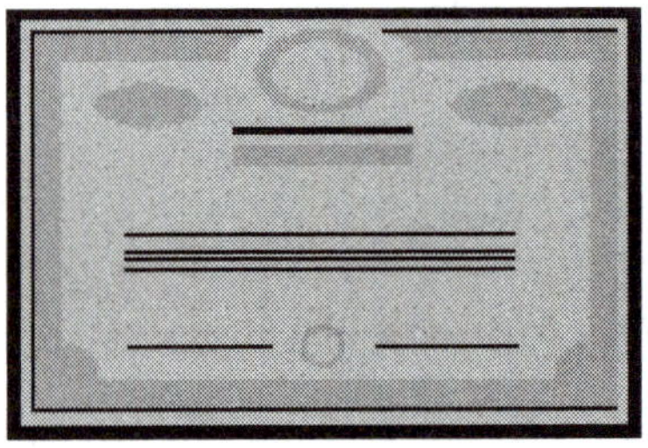

Earnings per Share
Net Corporate Income/
Outstanding Shares
= EPS

To determine the income or loss that each share represents, the net income ($2,000) is divided by the outstanding number of shares (10), which produces a number known as the earnings per share ($200). A corporation may also pay out some of the profits as dividends to the shareholders. To determine the dividend that each share receives the total dividend ($1,000) is divided by the number of shares (10) and thus is known the dividend per share ($100).

For the first year, Mary's Ice Cream, Inc. generated net earnings of $200 per share and paid out a dividend of $100 per share. To figure out how Mary's Ice Cream, Inc. is doing we need to use a couple of financial measuring tools.

The Price/Earnings or P/E Ratio tells us how many years' worth of earnings a share of stock is selling for. The investors paid $1,000 for a share. The earnings per share are $200.

P/E Ratio
Current Share Price/ EPS = Price/Earnings Ratio

If we divide the share price by the earnings per share we see that a share of stock sold at five times earnings. Another way to say this is that the P/E Ratio is 5.

The P/E Ratio for stocks varies greatly depending upon the industry the corporation is in and the outlook for the particular company. A higher P/E Ratio means that investors anticipate that the company's earnings will grow at a faster rate than a stock with a low P/E Ratio. The higher the P/E Ratio, the more confident or bullish investors are that earnings will continue to grow; the lower the ratio, the more pessimistic investors are about future earnings growth.

P/E Ratios indicate optimism about future earnings growth. A high P/E Ratio says investors are very confident that earnings will increase.

A high or low P/E Ratio by itself doesn't mean a stock is better or worse than another. You need to compare the stock against other stocks in the same industry.

Mary's Ice Cream, Inc has a P/E Ratio of 5. To get an idea as to whether the current share price reflects the true value of the company we'd need to compare this stock with the shares of other ice cream companies.

Dividend Yield
Share Dividend/ Share Price = Yield

Dividends represent a portion of the total return that you get from stock ownership, but they are not automatically paid when a company has a profit. Companies in mature industries - utilities would be an example, tend to pay out more of their earnings in dividends. Industries in expanding markets typically retain most or all of the earnings to finance future growth and pay little or no dividends.

Mary's Ice Cream, Inc. paid a dividend of $100 a share. To figure out the dividend yield divide the dividend ($100) by the share price ($1,000). Mary's has a dividend yield of 10%. Mary's Ice Cream, Inc. continues to do well. By the end of the fifth year the corporation's earnings per share are $800 and the dividend is $400. One of the investors wants to sell his share. What is a share of stock in Mary's Ice Cream, Inc. worth?

What Is The Stock Worth?

Mary's Ice Cream, Inc.
Dividend = $400
EPS = $800
Industry P/E Ratio = 6

Would you pay $2,000 for that share of stock? At $2,000 the stock has a dividend yield of 20% ($400/$2000) and would sell at a P/E Ratio of 2.5 when shares of other ice cream industry stocks are selling at a P/E ratio of 6!

Would you pay $4,000 for that share of stock? At $4,000 the stock has a dividend yield of 10% ($400/$2000) and sells at a P/E Ratio of 5, which is still below the industry average.

Let's look at the track record. The company has steadily increased earnings each year and the future looks promising. The price of a share of stock depends upon what someone is willing to sell it at and another is willing to pay. The price is based on the current and potential earnings of the company.

Day-to-Day stock prices are affected by emotions and changes in assumptions of future earnings.

The long-term performance of individual stocks, and the stock market overall, is based on actual earnings. If earnings continue to grow the price of a stock - or value of a stock index, will trend upward reflecting the economic facts. However, on any given day the price of the stock may be higher or lower than its long-term value based on emotions and assumptions.

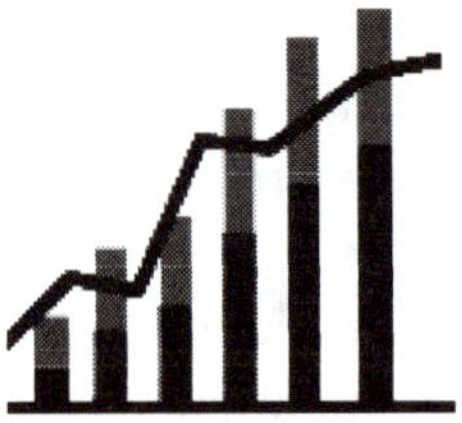

What would happen to the share price if I told you that a new municipal swimming pool is being built right across the street from Mary's Ice Cream, Inc. Hundreds of hot, hungry, thirsty children will cross the sidewalk in front of the store every day. An investor might pay a little more for a share of the corporation because their assumptions about future earnings would have increased.

What if I told you that another ice cream shop was thinking of opening up right next door to Mary's. An investor might offer a little less for a share of stock than they normally would have because if the rumor's true, future earnings could be harmed. But, if the rumor was not true the price of the stock would return to near its long-term value.

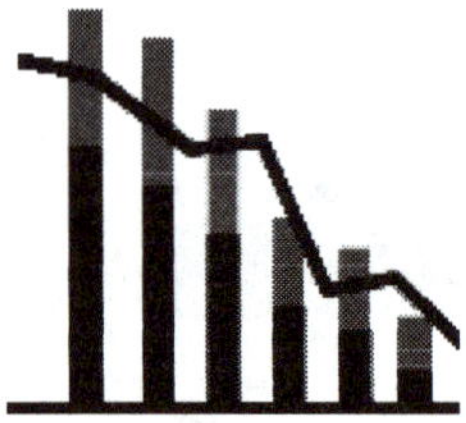

The daily movements of the stock market react the same way. A rumor or announcement of events that could increase earnings - like the possibility of lower interest rates on business loans, causes stock prices to move up. Negative rumors or events, like recession fears, cause stock prices to move down.

The First Stock Exchange

One of the first stock exchanges was founded in Holland in the 17th century. A group of Dutch merchants would invest in the cargo of a ship. If the ship survived the storms and the pirates, and sold the cargo at a profit, the merchants would receive their share of the riches. If a merchant needed money before the cargo was sold they would offer their share for sale to others and the new owner would then be entitled to any profits (or could lose their money if the ship sank).

The Dutch brought this financial medium to the New World when they settled New Amsterdam and they conducted their share exchanges near the fencing that contained the pigsty. The street with the fencing became known as Wall Street, and over two hundred years ago under a Buttonwood tree on Wall Street, in a city renamed New York, the New York Stock Exchange was founded. The origins of the site of the Exchange gave rise to a Wall Street saying "Bulls may make money on Wall Street and Bears may make money on Wall Street, but hogs always get slaughtered."

In the final analysis, stock prices and returns are based on actual earnings over time. If the earnings of a company grows over time the price of the company's shares will grow. If you believe that the nation's economy will continue to expand, stock indexes will increase in value.

Basic Financial Math Concepts

Recovering A Loss

If you had $100 and lost 20% you'd have $80 remaining. What growth is required to get back to $100? No, it is not 20%, even though $20 is 20% of $100; $80 needs to grow 25% before you're back to $100. This table shows how much you need to grown to recover what you lost.

If You Lost	*You'd Need To Gain*
10%	11%
20%	25%
30%	43%
40%	67%
50%	100%
60%	150%
70%	233%
80%	400%
90%	1000%

Rate of Return

In an attempt to compare the annual return of different investments some people will divide the total return by the number of years involved. However, unless the investments are of equal duration, the results may lead to the wrong conclusion.

Say that Investment A returned 30% in three-years, Investment B returned 60% in six-years, and Investment C returned 90% in nine-years. If you divide each investment's total return by the number of years in the period, the answer for each one is 10%. But, the actual annual rate of return for Investment A is 9.13%, the rate of return for Investment B is 8.15%, and the rate of return for Investment C is 7.18%.

The formula to calculate the honest rate of return for an investment without irregular cash flows is this:

$$i = (FV/PV)^{(1/n)} - 1$$

If the **P**resent **V**alue is \$10,000, the **F**uture **V**alue is \$15,000, and the **n**umber of periods is 5. The equation would be $(\$15{,}000/\$10{,}000)^{(1/5)} - 1 = 1.50^{0.2} - 1 = 8.45\%$.

The Real Annual Rate of Return										
Total Return/ No. of Years	**10%**	**20%**	**30%**	**40%**	**50%**	**60%**	**70%**	**80%**	**90%**	**100%**
1	10.00	20.00	30.00	40.00	50.00	60.00	70.00	80.00	90.00	100.0
2	4.88	9.54	14.02	18.32	22.47	26.49	30.38	34.16	37.84	41.42
3	3.23	6.27	9.14	11.87	14.47	16.96	19.35	21.64	23.86	25.99
4	2.41	4.66	6.78	8.78	10.67	12.47	14.19	15.83	17.41	18.92
5	1.92	3.71	5.39	6.96	8.45	9.86	11.20	12.47	13.70	14.87
6	1.60	3.09	4.47	5.77	6.99	8.15	9.25	10.29	11.29	12.25
7	1.37	2.64	3.82	4.92	5.96	6.95	7.87	8.76	9.60	10.41
8	1.20	2.31	3.33	4.30	5.20	6.05	6.86	7.62	8.35	9.05
9	1.06	2.05	2.96	3.81	4.61	5.36	6.07	6.75	7.39	8.01
10	0.96	1.84	2.66	3.42	4.14	4.81	5.45	6.05	6.63	7.18

Effective Rate

The effective rate is the actual rate you earn after taking into consideration the effects of compounding. The formula to convert a nominal or stated rate into an effective rate is

$$ER = [1 + (i/n)]^n - 1$$

Say that you are comparing a fixed rate annuity to a certificate of deposit. The fixed rate annuity has a nominal rate of 6.1% compounded annually, and the certificate of deposit has a nominal rate of 6%, compounded monthly. Because the fixed annuity has only one compounding period the fixed annuity's nominal and effective rate are the same — 6.1%. However, because the CD compounds monthly there are twelve compounding periods. The CD's effective rate is 6.17% computed as follows $[1+(.06/12)]^{12} - 1 = 1.005^{12} - 1 = .0617$.

Compound vs. Simple Interest

Suppose you had \$1 and someone gave you a choice between earning 10% calculated as simple interest or 9% calculated as compound interest. Which one do you choose? It depends on how long you are going to leave your money at work.

At the end of one-year the simple interest method would add a dime to your initial dollar and you'd have \$1.10. The compound interest method would add nine cents and you'd wind up with \$1.09. If you're only looking at one period there's no difference between simple and compound interest.

If you went out two-years, the simple method would add another dime to your \$1.10 giving you a balance of \$1.20. Simple interest means that interest is only earned on the original principal.

Compound interest works a little differently. Compound interest multiples the previous balance - in this case \$1.09, by the interest rate (9%), and adds the numbers together to determine a new value.

So, \$1.09 multiplied by 9% produces not 9 cents but 9.81 cents. This is added to the previous balance (1.09 + .0981) to produce a second year total of \$1.1881. A short hand way to figure the results of compounding is to put a one in front of the interest rate (\$1.0 x 1.09 = \$1.09).

At the end of five years the Simple Method would have produced a total of \$1.50 (\$1+ 0.1+ 0.1+ 0.1+ 0.1+ 0.1)

But, the Compound Method generated \$1.54 (\$1 x 1.09 x 1.09 x 1.09 x 1.09 x 1.09)

If you are only looking at a few periods there is not a lot of difference between the effects of simple and compound interest. However, the benefits of compound interest become proportionately greater with each passing period.

Compound vs. Simple \$10,000 at 8% Interest

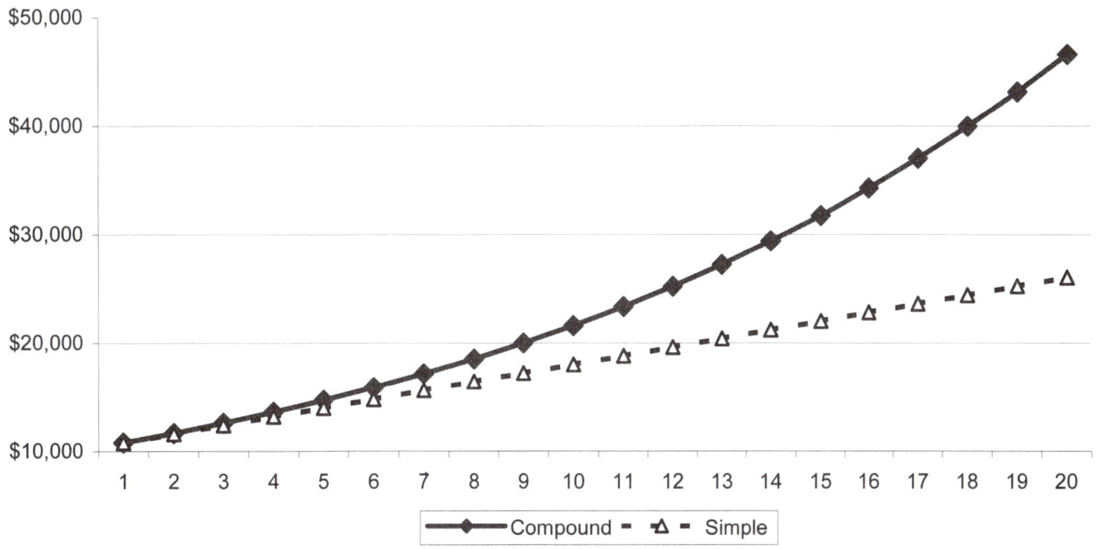

Rule of 72-50-2

Rule of 72
72 / 6% =
12 Years

The Rule of 72 tells you approximately how many years it takes a sum to double at a given rate. It is handy to be able to figure out, without using a calculator that if you are earning a 6% return, dividing 6% into 72 says it takes about 12-years for money to double. But the Rule of 72 can also be expanded to illustrate the potential earnings power of index annuities.

The Rule of 72-50-2 says that if you can increase the return 50% you will wind up with twice as much by the end of the second lower rate term. Let's say that a fixed rate annuity is paying 6% and we put in $10,000 today. Using the Rule of 72 our $10,000 would grow to $20,000 in 12-years and $40,000 in 24-years.

At 6% The Rule of 72 Says $10,000 becomes $20,000 in 12 years & $40,000 in 24 years $10,000 > $20,0000 > $40,0000

Now let's say that we believe the fixed index annuity will average a 9% annual return – 50% more than the traditional fixed rate annuity. The Rule of 72 says our money will now double in eight years [72/9% = 8]. Using the Rule of 72 our $10,000 grows to $20,000 in eight years, to $40,000 in sixteen years, and to $80,000 in twenty-four years – double the total return of the other annuity.

At 9% $10,000 becomes $20,000 in 8 years, $40,000 in 16-years & $80,000 in 24 years $10,000 > $20,0000 > $40,0000 > $80,000

Even though the index annuity only earned 3% more than the fixed rate instrument we wound up with double the money.

Rule of 72-50-2

Year	8	12	16	24
at 6%		$20,000		$40,000
at 9%	$20,000		$40,000	$80,000

The Rule of 72-50-2 illustrates that even a modest increase in your return can reap big rewards over time.

How To Read The Stock Page

The high and low trading price of the stock for the 52 weeks before the last trading day

The annual dividend rate. XYX pays a $1.20 dividend

Price Earnings Ratio divides share price by last 4 quarters earnings (dd means no earnings)

This reflects the price of the last trade of the day & the change from the previous session

52 Weeks							Vol				Net
Hi	Lo	Stock	Sym	Div	Yld %	PE	100s	Hi	Lo	Close	Chg
41.25	22.25	XYZ	X1A	1.2	4.0	15	899	30.25	29.50	30.00	+0.25
9.10	1.50	Yaga	Y1BA	...	...	dd	1100	1.55	1.53	1.53	-0.02
16.00	11.80	Zatru	ZZ1	0.3	2.0%	30	7	15.00	14.50	15.01	+1.00

The name of the company and the ticker symbol used. 4 or 5 letters are Nasdaq (real symbols don't use numbers)

The Yield is the dividend divided by the closing price

Volume is shares traded in hundreds in last session

These are the highest and lowest prices the stock traded at in the last session.

Understanding An Annual Report

Corporate Consolidated Statements Of Income	**2002**	**2001**	**2000**
Net Revenues ***(1)***	$20,847	$12,202	$11,521
Cost of Sales ***(2)***	9,164	7,811	5,576
Research and development	1,808	1,296	1,111
Marketing, general, administrative	2,322	1,843	1,447
Operating Costs and Expenses	13,294	10,950	8,134
Operating Income***(3)***	**$ 7,553**	**$ 1,252**	**$ 3,387**
Interest Expense	(25)	(29)	(57)
Interest and investment income***(4)***	406	4,415	273
Income Before Taxes	**7,934**	**5,638**	**3,603**
Taxes	2,777	2,072	1,315
Net Income***(5)***	**$5,157**	**$3,566**	**$2,288**
Earnings per share***(6***	$ 5.81	$ 4.03	$ 2.62
Weighted average shares outstanding***(7)***	888	884	874

(1) Sales and Revenues. Are they growing and are they in line with rest of industry. This company's revenues grew 34% averaged over the last two years.

(2) Cost of sales was a larger part of revenues in 2001. In 2000 they were 48% of revenues, in 2001 they were 64% of revenues. Although they were back down in 2002 to 44%, why the spike in 2001?

(3) To determine operating margin – which is the cash the company has after paying the day-to-day bills, divide operating income by revenue. This company's operating margin is 36%. Healthy companies are usually over 10%.

(4) What business are you in? A large income from other areas could mean the company isn't focusing on core competencies. With an insurance company it could mask lower operating profits.

(5) Earnings growth has been steady. Compare it to the price of the stock to determine p/e ratio

(6)(7) A sharp increase in number of shares could dilute earnings...that's not happening.

Corporate Consolidated Balance Sheet		
Assets	**2002**	**2001**
Current Assets ***(8)***		
Cash and cash equivalents	4,165	1,463
Short term investments	3,829	995
Accounts Receivable ***(9)***	3,723	3,116
Inventories ***(10)***	1,293	2,004
Other current assets - deferred costs ***(11)***	674	519
Total Current Assets	13,684	8,097
Property, plant, equipment, net	10,051	9,407
Total Assets ***(12)***	**23,735**	**17,504**
Total Current Liabilities ***(13)***	4,863	3,619
Long Term Debt ***(14)***	1,725	1,020
Stockholder Equity ***(15)***	17,147	12,865
Total Liabilities and Equity	**23,735**	**17,504**

(8) Big increase in cash and short-term investments. Is company looking to acquire or be acquired?

(9) Accounts Receivable - We can determine Day Sales Outstanding (DSOs). Divide accounts receivable (9) by revenue (1), then multiply by 365 [3723/20847 = 0.1786 x 365 = 65.18 days]. The company is getting paid on their sales in 65 days. Last year it took 93 days to collect the bills. Look for DSO's of 45 to 90 days. This means the company is getting their money in 6 to 12 weeks. If a lot of the business is overseas you can allow for longer DSOs. If there is a big jump in account receivables and/or in DSO it means that business may be selling to bad credit risk customers just to pump up short-term sales.

(10) To determine how fast inventory is turning over divide annual cost of sales (2) by inventories(10) [9164/1293= 7.08]. This calculation shows company is turning over inventories 7 times a year. Inventories usually rise in tandem with sales; if inventories rise faster goods aren't selling.

(11) Deferred costs. This is one of the areas the SEC is getting all heated up about. Deferred costs may be a current cost that would impact current earnings. A deferred cost is not recognized as a current cost and may overstate current earnings.

Book value is Assets (12) minus Liabilities (13)(14) divided by Outstanding Shares (7) [23735 – 4863 – 1725 = 17147/888 = $19.31 book value per share]

.

Return on Equity (ROE) divide net income (5) by stockholder equity (15) [5157/17147]. ROE is 30%.

Certificates of Deposit

The financial media often talks about derivatives in the investment world. A bank derivative investment is called a certificate of deposit. Fixed rate and fixed index annuities appeal to the same people that buy CD's. Why do people buy CD's? Certificates of deposit are regarded by people as safe investments, but let's look a little closer.

One of the most volatile areas in the financial world is the movement of interest rates. The yields on six month and one year certificates of deposit may swing violently between one period and the next. As an example, if you were retired and living off CD interest in the fall of 1991, you saw your income plummet 44% by the fall of 1992. Even more dramatic was the 69% drop in CD rates from the fall of 2000 to the fall of 2001.

Certificate of Deposit Rates 1/81 - 1/03

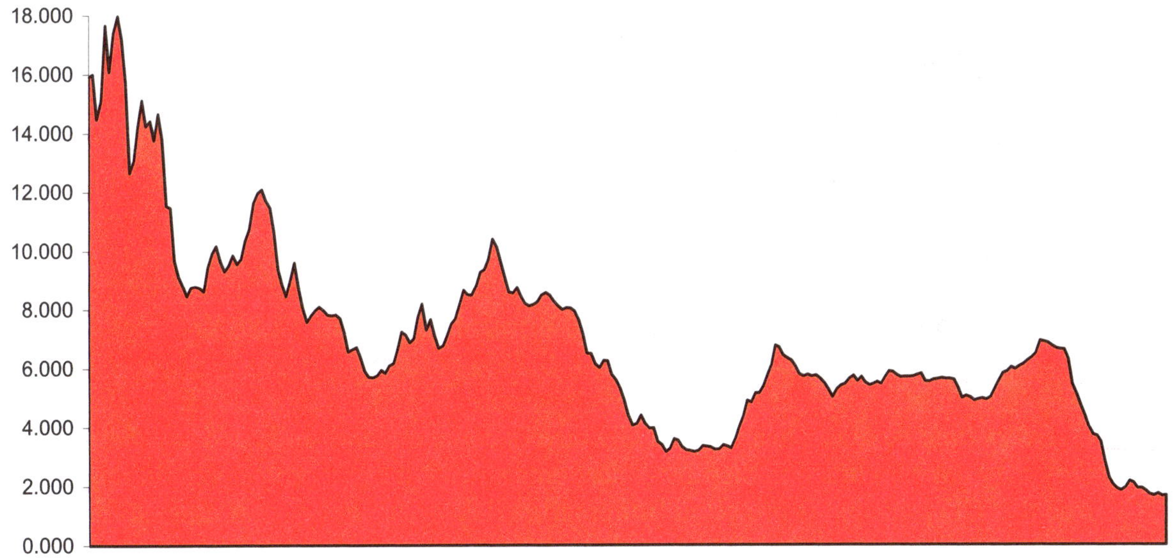

Data Source: Federal Reserve Board

If someone has been using CDs to fund their retirement they will probably need to work a few more years. While the average annual return in the '80s for short term CDs was 10.03%, the average return in the '90s was 5.41%. And the current decade is averaging less than 3% annualized return. Unfortunately, CDs do not have minimum guarantees. If the future for interest rates is low, then there is nothing to preclude CD yields from staying below 3% as they did for a time in the mid 1990s and in 2001 and 2002. The viability of certificates of deposit as long-term savings vehicles is doubtful. And yet, many people continue to place retirement savings in CDs instead of equity instruments because they mistake volatility for risk.

In the short term the direction of the stock market is every bit as volatile as interest rate movements and stocks pose a greater risk than CDs because you can lose principal. But, over time the volatility of the stock market smoothes out and the risk of principal loss goes down. If you intend to remain in the market for at least five-years, the probability of loss greatly declines, and the odds of a loss becomes statistically unrealistic the further you get past a ten-year holding period. While the odds of a loss decline as the period lengthens the potential for higher returns increases.

CD Volatility & Risk

Volatility is an aspect of all financial instruments; risk is a function of financial goals

Here is a key concept. Volatility is an aspect of all financial instruments; risk is a function of financial goals. It would be risky to invest money in the stock market that you're going to need in a year because volatility could produce a loss. However, using CDs as a long-term financial vehicle has a high degree of risk because of the strong probability of inferior returns.

If you own certificates of deposit you are already in a volatile vehicle. Even though a CD is federally insured up to certain limits and has virtually no investment risk, the money is still subject to inflation risk (loss of purchasing power), earnings risk (rate guarantees are of limited duration), and volatility (interest rates will fluctuate). If your investment horizon is of sufficient length you should consider an instrument – like an index annuity - that takes advantage of volatility to generate returns while protecting the principal from market risk.

**From 1991-2000 the S&P 500 annual gain was 14.86%;
CDs averaged a 5.26% return**

Every time there is a bear market CD buyers come out and smile and say that while they may not earn much in their bank accounts at least they're protected. Although it is true that CD principal is protected from market risk we have seen that interest earnings can wildly fluctuate. Since 1970 there have been eight-times when CD interest rates fell more than 20% from the previous high in the cycle. On average, the lowest rate in each cycle was 50% of the previous high. If you had been retired and using CD interest to help pay the bills you saw your income cut in half. Bank instruments do provide stability of principal, but the trade-off is return volatility.

6 Month Certificate of Deposit Rates - Decline From Previous Cycle High		
Cycle High	*Cycle Low*	*% Decline From High*
1/70	3/71	(55.41%)
8/74	12/76	(60.53%)
3/80	6/80	(53.04%)
8/81	1/83	(52.98%)
7/84	10/86	(52.81%)
3/87	4/93	(69.61%)
1/95	1/99	(21.73%)
5/00	11/02	(78.80%)

Fixed rate and fixed index annuities provide protection of principal from market risk. Fixed rate annuity returns are affected by the same interest rate cycles as CDs, but provide the safety of a minimum return floor.

Before you purchase that Certificate of Deposit please read this disclosure

Inflation

I realize that the yields on CD's have been less than the rate of inflation in one out of every five years.

I realize after subtracting taxes and the rate of inflation that the return on my CD has been negative 50% of the time

Returns

I realize that the average return on equity investments has been more than double that of CD's.

I realize that a reliance on CD's to fund my retirement could result in a 40% shortfall at retirement and require me to work after age 65.

Risk

I realize that the purchase of this CD subjects me to interest rate risk and inflation risk.

I realize that while my principal will not fluctuate, my income could drop as much as 69% in any given year without prior notice.

Taxes

I realize that the interest earned is subject to federal and state income taxes whether I use the income or let it accumulate.

Liquidity

I realize that the bank is not required to give me access to my CD principal during the term of the CD and may prevent me from making early withdrawals.

Although my account is FDIC insured I realize that in the event of a bank failure FDIC may delay in returning my CD principal to me.

I fully understand the risks of buying this CD.

____

CD Buyer

None of this is meant to imply that certificates of deposit should never be used. CD funds are very safe and are an excellent parking place for short-term money. But bank savings instruments will continue to be volatile. It makes sense to have volatility work for you over the long term while protecting the principal.

Risk & Return

An investment maxim is potential returns should increase as risk to your money increases. In the grand scheme of things Treasury bills pose the lowest risk to principal because they are liquid, of short maturity, and are backed by the full faith and credit of the United States. Insured certificates of deposit are essentially in the same risk category. Due to their low risk, T-bills and CDs offer low returns.

Stocks and stock mutual funds are at the other end of the spectrum. The relative risk and potential returns can be managed to some extent with proper diversification, but all stock investments pose much higher risk than government issued or insured vehicles.

Bonds fall somewhere in the middle. At the head there are sound corporate and municipal bonds that entail extremely limited risk of the borrower being unable to pay; at the feet there are junk bonds with high returns and one toe dangling over bankruptcy. Even with highly rated bonds the risk always exists that if you need the money before the bond matures and sell it, that you might get back less than you put in.

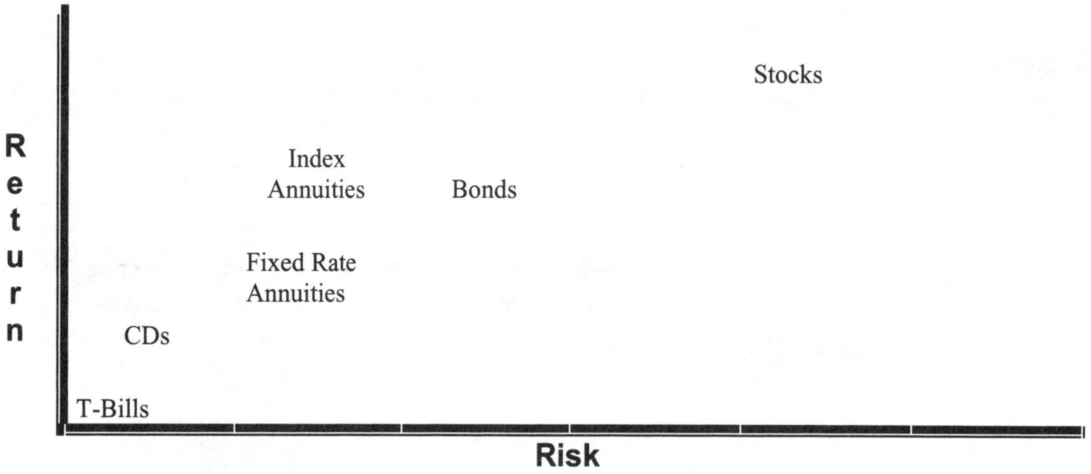

Fixed annuities are neither government insured nor government backed, but the risk of losing principal due to the insurance company failing is very low. Insurance companies must meet strong reserve requirements, and as an additional safeguard every state has a guaranty fund, which offers a little bit of protection if an insurer crashes.

In exchange for a modicum of increased risk, fixed annuities offer the potential for higher returns. In the past, fixed rate annuities have credited one to three percent more interest than CDs or T-bills. Fixed index annuities provide the same "reserve" protection of principal and the potential for higher returns. I believe index annuities may provide similar returns to bonds, but with lower risk to principal

Tax Deferral

If you compare annuities with other savings vehicles there is a tendency to focus on the relative yields or interest rates and ignore the really incredible benefit of annuities - the ability of the owner to defer taxes on the earnings.

Annuities Get Triple Interest Crediting

Money that remains inside the annuity grows free from current income taxes. Not only does the principal earn interest (simple interest at work), and the interest earns interest (compound interest at work), but the money that would have gone to Uncle Sam also earns interest (tax-advantaged interest at work)

Suppose we had $50,000 and were in a combined federal and state tax bracket of 33%. We will say both a taxable account and the annuity are earning 6%. The annuity benefits from triple interest crediting and works with the full 6% interest. However, the taxable account produces an IRS Form 1099 every year that says part of the interest must be paid in taxes, whether it is being used or left for later. If we are earning 6%, but have a 33% tax rate, a third of that 6% - or 2%, goes for taxes. This means we only have 4% working for us in the taxable account. Here is what the accumulated values of the taxable account and the annuity would look like down the road.

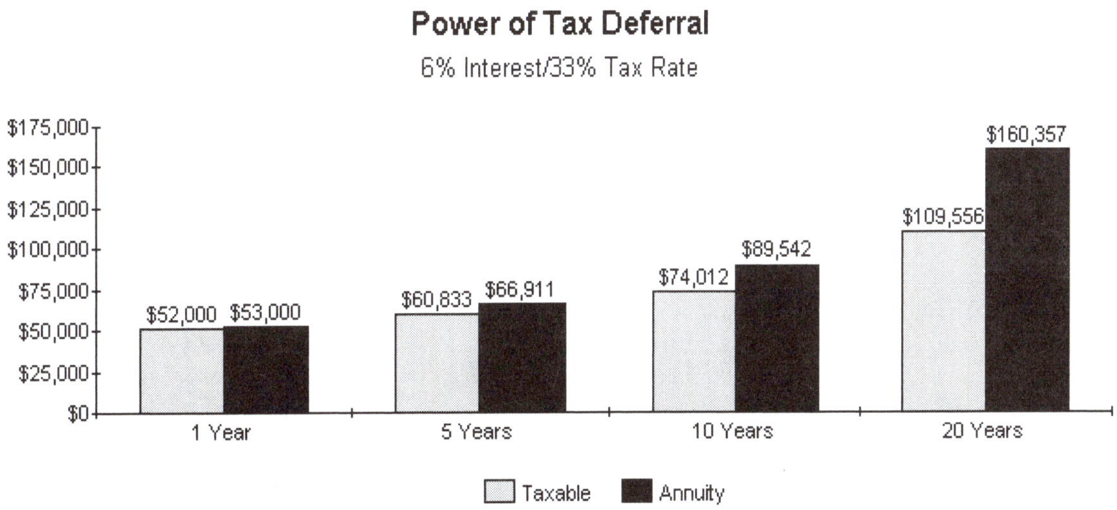

More Interest Income

The annuity advantage continues growing with each passing year. Tax-deferred growth means more money is available for future needs. Say that you wanted to begin spending the interest down the road. If we kept earning 6% here's the interest that would be generated by the taxable and annuity accounts.

Comparison - Interest Earned			
After Year	*Taxable Account Interest*	*AAnnuity Interest*	*Annuity Advantage*
1	$3,120	$3,180	2%
5	$3,650	$4,015	10%
10	$4,441	$5,372	21%
20	$6,573	$9,621	46%

The annuity advantage means we would have over 20% more interest available to spend in only ten-years and an amazing 46% more interest from the annuity than we would get from the taxable account in twenty-years. An annuity could mean the difference between enjoying retirement or just getting by.

One of the fears in retirement is outliving our money; an annuity can help overcome this fear. The power of tax-deferral means we have a higher accumulated value in the annuity from which to draw. Suppose it's twenty years from now and we need to take $9,500 out each year from our accounts. If we are earning 6% our taxable account runs out of money in 21 years while the annuity has actually grown.

Tax-deferred does not mean tax free. Taxes have to be paid on the interest when withdrawn or paid out at death.* However, tax-deferral still means more dollars. Let's look at our previous example and assume we surrendered the annuity and paid the taxes. Here is what we'd have in our hands.

After-Tax Values

6% Interest/33% Tax Rate

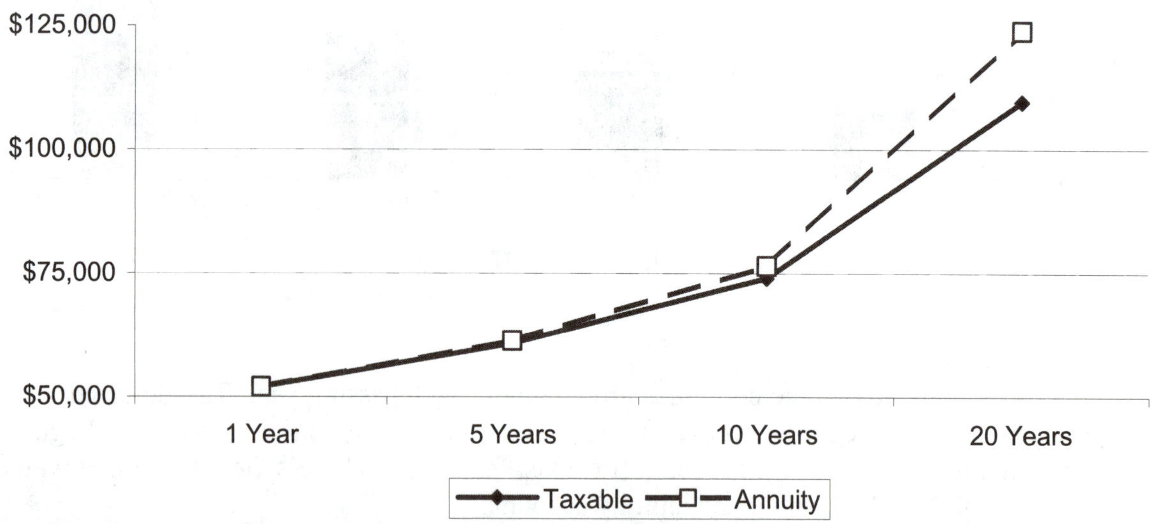

*In addition to regular income taxes there is a 10% penalty on withdrawals from an annuity before age 59 1/2. The penalty only applies to interest earned and doesn't affect the premium, but withdrawals are taxed on an "interest out first" basis. The penalty does not apply upon the death or disability of the owner, or if substantially equal payments are made. Consult your tax advisor for more information

Even after paying taxes the annuity still gives us more money in our pocket. There are other ways to look at the power of tax-deferral.

Interest-Free Loan

If someone told you they would loan you $10,000 and said you did not have to pay it back for 10, 20 or 30 years and you would not have to pay any interest on the loan, but you could earn interest on the money w*ould you be interested?*

Annuities offer tax deferral. In essence this means you are getting to use money that should have gone to pay taxes. Someday, that money has to be paid back. However, you get to keep the after-tax portion of the interest you earned from those tax dollars and, if you are in a lower tax bracket when you do repay the "loan", you could pay back fewer dollars. There's no limit on the amount of taxes or the length of time you can defer, but interest is taxable when withdrawn or at death of the owner.

Tax Control

If you have a taxable account every January you receive IRS Form 1099 that says you must pay taxes on any interest earned, even if that interest is being saved for future use. An annuity gives you tax control. You decide when to take the interest and pay the taxes - not the IRS.

Avoiding Social Security Benefit Taxation (SSBT)

If your pension, taxable interest income, tax-free municipal bond interest and social security income is over a threshold amount you can be forced to pay taxes on your social security benefits. However, interest compounding within an annuity is not counted in the calculation. If you move dollars generating compounding interest from a taxable account to an annuity you may lower or avoid SSBT.

Missouri Bucket

Having your money in a taxable account is kind of like putting it in a bucket. The problem is every year the IRS punches a hole in your bucket and drains off some of that interest in taxes. However, placing your money in an annuity is like adding a faucet to the bucket. The only time you pay taxes is when you decide to open the faucet and take out some of that interest.

Tax-Deferral Example

Whether it is in connection with a pension plan, an IRA or an annuity, we have all seen charts showing the power of tax-deferral. Usually the chart shows a sum accumulating on a tax-deferred basis and another sum growing on a taxable one. The two lines begin together, but by the time twenty or thirty years has passed the tax-deferred growth line has surged into the stratosphere while the taxable line is struggling to maintain altitude, thus illustrating that tax-deferred growth really adds up. However, you do not have to wait years and years to see the positive effects of tax-deferral.

Tax-Deferral Means Tax Control

One of the great benefits of a deferred annuity is that it gives the buyer tax control. Tax control means that you decide when to spend the interest and pay the taxes - not the IRS. Tax control lets you earn money on taxes instead of the government.

Let's say you bought a deferred annuity instead of opening a taxable account. Let's also say that out of all the annuity interest you earned this year that you did not need $100 of it to live on. Instead you left that $100 inside the annuity for future use. I know that you could leave more interest in the annuity for future use, but let's simply use $100.

If you were in the 20% combined federal and state tax bracket, deferring that $100 in interest would save you $20 today in taxes. I know that you are probably in a higher tax bracket and that the annuity would save you even more in taxes, but let's simply use 20%.

If you could earn 5% on those tax dollars you'd have an extra dollar at the end of one year. Even if you decided to then spend that $100 from the previous year and pay the $20 of deferred taxes back, you'd still keep most of that dollar. So, tax control has made you about a buck, enough to buy you a cup of coffee.

If you left that $100 of interest in the annuity for two-years you would have $2 - enough for a hamburger. At the end of three-years you would have $3 - enough extra to add fries and after five-years you would have $5 - which would get you a combo meal. That is almost $5 in your hand even after you spend the interest and pay back the taxes you deferred. If you deferred $100 in each of the next five-years and earned 5% you would have $15 in your pocket thanks to tax control.

I realize $5 or $15 isn't much, but we are not doing anything special, we have simply decided to take control and not pay taxes on interest we are not using. And what if instead of talking about $100 of interest, we have regained tax control over a $1,000 or $10,000 of interest? And instead of talking about one-year or five-years, maybe we will not need the interest for ten or fifteen years? How much more money would you have in your pocket with the annuity?

Tax-deferral gives you tax control because you decide when to take the interest and pay the taxes - not the IRS, and while tax-deferred is not tax-free you get to keep most of the interest earned from taxes postponed. Tax-deferral is a simple yet powerful financial tool.

Cheat Sheet

- An understanding of financial and investment concepts helps in comparing index annuities with alternative instruments and provides a basis for a realistic evaluation of choices.

Discussion Questions

1. Do actual earnings or anticipated earnings have the most bearing on the price of a stock?

2. Do consumers really understand the risks of owning certificates of deposit?

3. Think of different financial instruments and rank where they would appear on a Risk/Return chart relative to index annuities.

Chapter Quiz

1. A P/E Ratio

A. Relates to the numbers of towels to students in gym class
B. Is used to compute the dividend yield of a share of stock
C. Should be compared against other stocks in the same industry
D. A high P/E ratio means investors are pessimistic about increasing earnings

2. If you had $100 and lost 25%, what percentage growth is needed to get you back to $100

A. 20%
B. 25%
C. 33%
D. 50%

3. When talking about simple and compound interest it is true to say that

A. Merely dividing the total return by the number of periods can give you a misleading answer
B. They produce identical returns over a single period
C. The benefits of compound interest over simple interest grow as time passes
D. All of the above

4. Certificate of Deposits

A. Are FDIC Insured
B. Aren't volatile
C. Do not have withdrawal penalties
D. All of the above

5. On the topic of tax deferral you could say
A. Although safe from current income tax, tax-deferred interest is subject to Social Security benefit taxation
B. Tax-deferral means triple interest crediting
C. Tax-deferred interest becomes tax-free at death because of stepped-up tax basis
D. All of the above

Chapter 12 – Stories & Fables

A Financial Fable

A wonderful feature of indexed annuities is that the crediting of excess interest above the minimum guarantee is linked to the movements of an equity index. The use of an equity index provides for a potential return that is greater than one might realize from other fixed rate long term savings vehicles.

Many index annuities use an annual reset or annual ratchet structure. This structure locks in any gains each contract year and treats years of negative index movement as "years without growth'. Previous credited gains are maintained and negative years are simply noted with a zero. A growing number of index annuities permit the owner to move the accumulated value on each policy anniversary between the equity index crediting method and a fixed rate account. This flexibility gives owners more control over the future of their annuity.

On January 1, 1950 Mr. and Mrs. Smith decided to invest $1,000 for each of their four children. The only requirements were that the children can't touch the money until January 1, 2000 and that the same investment style must be used for the entire period. How did the children do?

*The first child's money was invested in one year U.S. Treasury Bills. On New Years Day Two Thousand the $1,000 invested in T-bills had grown to $15,393.13. **

*The second child's money was invested in an index that became the Standard & Poor's 500 index. In fifty years the starting point of $1,000 became an end point of $87,669.76.**

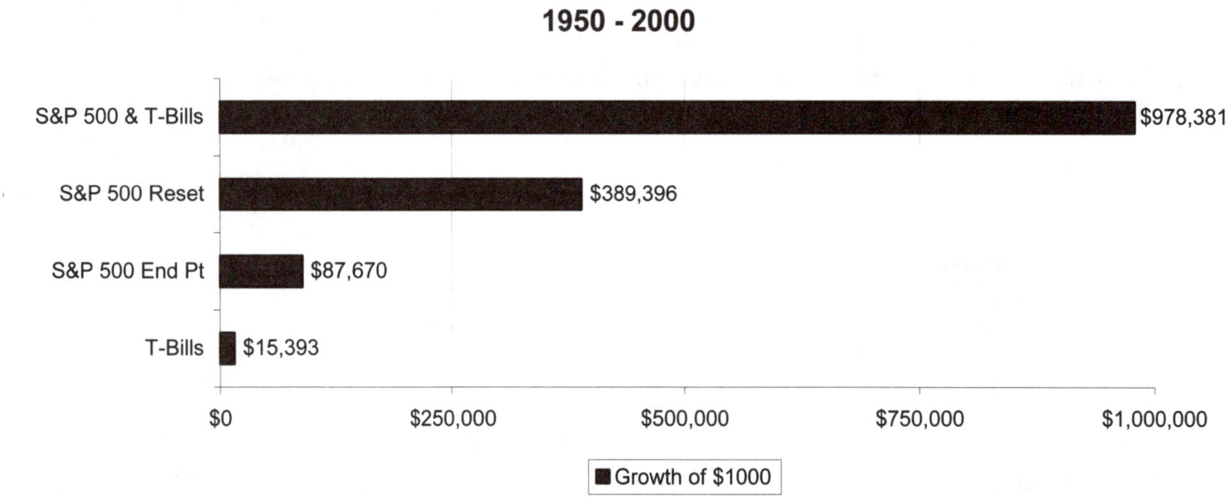

*The third child used an S&P 500 index with a difference. While the account recognized any years with positive index movements it treated down years as years with zero growth. A half century later these positive reset years resulted in $1,000 becoming $389,396.54.**

*The final child was prescient and used both the T-bills and the S&P 500 index; each year determining which alternative would provide the highest return and positioning the money accordingly. On January 1, 2000 the original $1,000 had grown to 978,381.09.**

The last half century witnessed double digit interest rates as well as double digit inflation, the greatest bull market of the century as well as the most severe bear market since the 1930's, and times of opportunity and setback. Two aspects of this period should be noted. The first is that equity instruments achieved far greater returns than fixed rate vehicles. The second is that attempting to minimize the risk of loss of equity instruments can substantially enhance those returns.

Index annuities eliminate market risk to principal and market risk to realized returns. Even if one had only participated in a fraction of the equity index's growth over this period the return would still have outdistanced the returns of the other savings vehicles. Index annuities can be a vehicle for the next half century.

*Source: 1 Year Treasury Constant Maturity Rate, Federal Reserve Board; Standard & Poor's 500 and S&P 500 are trademarks of The McGraw-Hill Companies, Inc and must be licensed for use. S&P does not sponsor, endorse, sell or promote any index-linked products. S&P 500 data does not include reinvested dividends and is for informational purposes only.

A Fistful of Annuities

Fiery dawn rays streaked the iron red rock of the mesa as I rode over the crest and had my first look at the town of Real Vida. As I neared boot hill the words of the mayor's telegram that I had received the day before returned to my mind, "COME TO REAL VIDA. FUTURE SHOCK GANG IS RUNNING WILD. SHERIFF HURT. DEPUTY IN HIDING. HURRY."

I had just passed the general store when I heard "psst, psst". Either my horse had sprung a leak or someone was trying to get my attention; it was the later. A man with a pale face and a ten gallon hat was hissing and beckoning me his way. I got down and walked over to him. It was the mayor.

"Marshall, I sure am glad you showed up," said the mayor.

"What seems to the trouble?" I asked.

The mayor began his story, "This has always been a quiet little town. People felt if they just lived their lives and did what the banker told them to do, then everything would be all right. Two days ago the Future Shock Gang rode into town and it all changed. Before you knew it all heck had broken loose. People's piggybanks were stampeded, savings accounts were corralled, and our oldest dance hall girl, Ms. Ira, was forced out of retirement and put back to work."

I've heard about this gang," I replied, "if I remember correctly, the leader is a difficult hombre called Retirement Needs. His right hand man is Market Risk, and the other gang members are Inflation and Taxes. I'd like to talk to the banker and get his take on what I'm up against."

The mayor sneered, "As soon as they showed up the banker lit out of here shouting 'every asset for himself'. He was absolutely no good."

"Bankers usually aren't any good when facing up to Retirement Needs." I went on, "I believe I met your sheriff, Variable Annuity, once in Dodge City. What happened to him?"

"Our sheriff, everybody calls him V.A., was quick on the draw and was able to put Taxes away, so Taxes won't be a problem anytime soon. And he wounded Inflation. But Market Risk got to V.A. and dropped him out of sight. As long as Market Risk is formidable, V.A.'s out of the fight." continued the mayor.

"And the deputy?" I asked.

The mayor answered, "The deputy is the sheriff's kid, Fixed Annuity, Fixed Annuity was simply outgunned and is hiding in the stable waiting for you to arrive."

"I guess I'd better go over and get the deputy, I could use the help," said I.

The mayor asked, "What are you gonna use against the gang? A Winchester?"
"Nope."
The Mayor continued, "You going to go in with your six shooters a blazing?
"Nope."
"Then you must be using a sawed off shotgun," puzzled the mayor.
"Nope," I Cooperishly replied.
Exasperatedly the mayor said, "Then what are you going to use to subdue the Future Shock Gang?"
"Fixed rate and fixed index annuities," I concluded.

I moseyed over to the stable and spied the deputy hiding in the third stall back. I explained what needed to be done. The deputy took a big gulp and said that she was with me all the way. I wasn't surprised by the deputy's response; I've found that Fixed Annuities can always be counted on when you need them.

The deputy and I strode over to the saloon where the mayor said the gang was. As I pushed open the swinging doors I saw the gang seated in the center of the room. Market Risk had a pair of scissors and was cutting mutual fund statements to bits. Inflation was feeding a pile of dollar bills into the flame of a kerosene lamp and laughing every time another George turned to ashes. The leader, Retirement Needs, had the townspeople busy trying to build a retirement plan out of sand. But every time one wall of the retirement plan seemed to be complete, the others collapsed back to the ground, a sight that gave Retirement Needs great amusement.

The leader spotted us, "What are you here for?"
"A showdown," I responded.
"I don't see any pistols, where are your weapons?" the gang leader queried.
"We're packing annuities," I replied with steel in my voice.
"Annuities," squeaked Market Risk, "We don't need no stinking annuities!"

"Oh yeah," says I, "Fixed rate and fixed index annuities protect principal from market risk." Market Risk yelled and grabbed his shoulder.

"And fixed rate and fixed index annuities preserve credited interest from market loss," added the Deputy. Market Risk screamed and put one hand on his leg.

"In addition, fixed annuities provide a guaranteed minimum return regardless of how the market performs," the deputy and I said in unison.

Market Risk clutched his stomach like he'd been gut shot and rolled onto the floor – Market Risk was no more.

Inflation had already been beat up by Sheriff V.A. and it didn't take much more to put it away. "Equity-linked vehicles," I soliloquized, "typically outdistance inflation providing a real return that keeps up with the cost of living and preserves retirement assets." Inflation sighed, "You got me," and his eyes rolled back. Inflation was whipped.

Retirement Needs smirked, "I won't be as easy to defeat. It'll take more weapons that you've got."

"The only weapon we need to face Retirement Needs is knowledge," and with that the Deputy and I opened up the saddlebags I'd retrieved from my horse, and pulled out fixed rate and fixed index annuity sales materials, illustrations and product disclosures, which we gave to the townspeople. By using this annuity knowledge the townspeople were able to build a solid base for the retirement plan and keep their goals from crumbling.

Retirement Needs slinked out the door saying, "Curses, annuitized again. I may have met my match here but there are other towns that don't know about annuities, I'm not finished yet." And with that, the threat from the Future Shock gang was history in Real Vida.

"My champion," breathed Ms. Ira as she batted her eyes, "Now I can go back to my well deserved retirement." "Aw shucks, Ma'am," I modestly replied, "It was annuities that defeated Taxes, Inflation, Market Risk and faced up to Retirement Needs. I am only a Marshall in their service."

I got back on my horse, tipped my hat to the townspeople, and slowly rode out of town. As I was almost out of earshot I heard the deputy ask the mayor "Who was that stranger that rode in here and saved the day?" The mayor replied, "That was the agent with no name". Yippee-Ki-A.

Talking Pictures

Although *The Jazz Singer* movie is usually credited as being the first talking picture, the truth is the first movie with an actual soundtrack was invented in 1905, twenty years before *The Jazz Singer* premiered. This cinematic treasure, whose title has been lost to the ages, was directed by Steven Stereoski, who also invented the sound system that bears his name.

1905 audiences greeted Steven Stereoski's film with great enthusiasm. The problem is the audience had no way to convey to others how wonderful sound movies were. Exit surveys found viewer after viewer saying "Talking pictures are the greatest thing since...." but the viewers were unable to finish the sentence.

Because moviegoers couldn't explain the magic of sound on the silver screen, Stereoski's film was a box office disaster and silent movies reigned for another two decades.

The reason you have never heard of Steven Stereoski, and another inventor is given the credit Stereoski rightfully deserves, is because another individual, O. F. Rohwedder, had not yet created the invention that was responsible for the technological explosion of the twentieth century. You see, Otto Frederick Rohwedder invented an automatic bread slicer in the 1920's.

Coinciding with the announcement of Rohwedder's invention *The Jazz Singer* premiered. The voice of Al Jolson filling the theatre thrilled audiences, and thanks to Mr. Rohwedder's invention these people had something to say. Now when asked "How was it?" The moviegoer could remark "Talking pictures are the greatest thing since sliced bread" and an industry was reborn.

The sliced bread metaphor became the most popular advertising comparison used in the western world and resulted in a proliferation of inventions, consumer products, and played a major role in the final triumph of capitalism over communism. Otto Rohwedder lived to a ripe old age amid the adoration of marketing people everywhere. Steve Stereoski died in 1930, ironically, after falling into a kneading machine at a local bakery.

The lesson to be learned from all of this is it's not enough to simply create a better product, to make dough you also knead to be able to relate the product benefits to something the customer already understands.

Goldilocks And Modern Portfolio Theory

Once upon a time

there were three bears that dreamed of a honey filled retirement. Year after year they contributed to their Bear Retirement Accounts with each utilizing a different investment vehicle from the other.

One day after saving for a number of years the three bears decided to ask a financial consultant if they were on track for retirement.

The people at Goldilocks Financial Advisors reviewed the portfolios of the three bears and came back with these projections.

The first bear had gone to a banker for retirement advice and so the money was deposited in certificates of deposit and although the principal was very safe from loss it wasn't earning very much. Goldilocks projected that at the current rate of return the first bear's retirement would be spent sitting in a cabin on the Red River near Fargo.

The second bear used the internet for financial advice and was invested 100% in stocks. Although the second bear's portfolio had certainly outperformed the first bear's it was subject to the full risk of the stock market and in fact it had dropped over 35% in the last year and a half. Goldilocks was unable to make a projection due to the extreme volatility of the portfolio. Goldilocks told the second bear that with the lack of safeguards in the portfolio retirement could be relaxing on a yacht on the Riviera or a twilight career greeting people at the local discount store.

The third bear was a prudent bear. This bear wanted the opportunity for more than the bank would allow and yet protection of the principal and credited gains from market loss. The third bear had used indexed annuities to plan for retirement. Goldilocks congratulated the third bear and projected a retirement filled with sweetness and light due to the potential & safety of indexed annuities.

The moral of the story is even bears benefit from index annuities.

Retirement Lost (and found)

"The stock market dropped for the fourth straight day as the major indexes continued to plummet. This market can't seem to find a bottom and no one knows how much further stocks will fall," reported the television anchor as the evening news began. Phyllis just shook her head because she didn't want to think about what was happening to her retirement savings.

A few years ago everything was perfect. In 1999 alone the increase in the value of her IRA was more than she had earned from her job. Back then she knew that she'd be able to retire on time and do more of the volunteer work that was becoming her passion, but now? The ringing phone interrupted her thoughts.

"Phyllis, this is Bill," it was her friend from work calling. "Did you happen to catch the financial news?"

"Oh Bill I did, isn't it terrible?" Phyllis replied.

"Yeah" said Bill. "As near as I can figure I've lost 35% of my retirement money in this market, and I was hoping to pull the plug next year and play golf all day. I guess I'll be working a lot longer then I planned. How are you holding up?"

"I don't know," said Phyllis, "Early last year my advisor helped me move my IRA into some index that she said offered more protection from market loss."

Bill opined "Phyllis, I guarantee you there's no such thing as an index that protects you from market loss. If there were everyone would own one. I guess we'll both be working at our jobs a lot longer than either of us planned."

As Phyllis got off the phone she felt her stomach knot. All of her goals and dreams were going to disappear in this bear market. Last spring when it appeared that this downturn was only going to last a few months was one thing, but it now seemed like the market would never go back up. Well, she might as well schedule an appointment with her financial advisor and see how badly she'd been hurt. Phyllis found her advisor's card and dialed the number.

"Barbara," she began "This is Phyllis. I'm sorry to call you this late, but I was hoping to come in and see you tomorrow to talk about how much money I've lost."

"Phyllis, of course I'd be happy to see you, but I'm a little confused. What lost money?" asked Barbara.

"Well" Phyllis continued, "The stock market has been awful this last year and my friends tell me they've lost thousands and thousands of dollars. I felt I should face the music and see how long I'll have to delay my retirement."

"Oh, I see," responded Barbara, "Perhaps I can ease your mind a little. During our annual review of your portfolio in the spring of last year do you remember telling me that even though your IRA was going up in value, that you were still very uncomfortable with the volatility of the stock market?"

"Yes. I didn't like the fact that I could lose what I gained if the stock market went down," said Phyllis.

"Exactly" Barbara replied, "You told me that you were willing to accept a lower potential return if your principal was protected from market risk, correct?"

"Yes."

"So, last year we transferred your IRA money into a combination of fixed interest annuities and fixed indexed annuities. The fixed interest annuities produce a guaranteed interest rate and the fixed indexed annuities give you the potential for a higher return because the interest earned is linked to an equity index. Since this equity-linked interest is earned inside a fixed annuity neither the interest credited to it nor the original principal can ever be lost if the market goes down."

"I haven't lost any money?"

"No, the fixed interest annuity paid a guaranteed interest rate and the indexed annuities credited zero interest due to the bear market, but of course when the index goes back up you'll share in the growth and over the coming years the indexed annuity can produce a lot more interest."

"So, I didn't lose any money?"

"No, you didn't lose any money," said Barbara smiling as the call ended and Phyllis said goodbye.

When Barbara reached her office the next morning there was a rather large chocolate cake sitting on her desk. On the cake was written "Thank you for saving my retirement". Barbara didn't need a card to tell her whom the cake was from. As Barbara prepared for her first client meeting of the day the phone rang "This is Bill, I work with Phyllis. When can I come into see you about these indexed annuities…?"

Quotations for the Insurance Industry

On Selling

"The most important secret of salesmanship is
to find out what the other fellow wants, then
help him find the best way to get it. When you show a man what he wants,
he will move heaven and earth to get it"

-Frank Bettger

How I Raised Myself From Failure to Success In Selling, Chapter 6

On Overcoming Objections

"There is no excuse for an excuse, but there
is always a reason for it. Nothing is as
objectionable as an excuse masquerading
as an objection! Let's make it an objective to meet every objection."

- Elmer G. Leterman

The Sales Begins When The Customer Says "No", Chapter VIII

For an Actuary's Resume

"I'm very well acquainted too with matters
mathematical,
I understand equations, both the simple and
quadratical,
About binomial theorem I'm teeming with a
lot o' news -
With many cheerful facts about the square of
the hypotenuse.

- Major-General Stanley

Gilbert & Sullivan, The Pirates of Penzance, Act I,

For www.indexannuity.org

"Happy is the man who finds wisdom and the man who gets understanding,
for the gain from it is better than gain from silver and its
profit better than gold."

- Bible, Proverbs verse 3

For the Marketing Director to Compliance

"The first thing we do, let's kill all the lawyers"

- Dick Butcher

King Henry VI - Second Part, Act IV, Scene II

On Selling Ideas

"I can remember when a guy once told me
that he bought insurance from a particular
agent because he was told that if he became
disabled, that particular company would pay the premiums on his policy for him.
He didn't tell him that 1,854 other companies will do the same thing...An idea was sold."

- Joe M. Gandolfo

Robert Shook, Ten Greatest Salespersons

For a Sales Manager to the Field

"It isn't enough! See! You've got to get more money out of our customers.
See! I want you to go to the butchers, the tailors, laundrys
and the rest and milk 'em dry. See!"

- Boss Zucco

Detective Comics No. 38

On Time Management

"Remember that TIME is Money. He that can earn Ten Shillings a Day
by his Labour and...sits idle one half of that Day...
has really spent or thrown away Five Shillings."

- Benjamin Franklin

On The Effects Of Compounding

"Remember that Money is of a prolific generating Nature,
Money can beget Money, and its Offspring can beget more"

- Benjamin Franklin

On Taxes

"Neighbors, the Taxes are indeed very heavy,
and if those laid on by the Government were the only Ones we had to pay,
we might more easily discharge them
(but) we are taxed twice as much by our *Idleness*,
three times as much by our *Pride*,
and four times as much by our *Folly*".

- Benjamin Franklin

On the Need For Market Research

"Do you hear something?"

- General George Armstrong Custer

Tale of the Safe Money Regatta

Lo, there were many pretenders to the safe money throne with differing sycophants singing the praises of each. And so the guardians of financial safety decided that the winner of a royal regatta would claim the title. Ships would depart at the morrow's first light and the first ship to reach the shores of the Safe Money Place would claim the throne. The claimants made ready their vessels, and so at dawn on an overcast day, as bears watched from the woods ashore, the flotilla journeyed forth with every boat's crew clutching separate dreams of victory.

Loud noises had been made of the prospects of the vessel offered by the Street of Wall with her builders saying that the good ship *Principal Preservation Fund* would enable her owner to sleep at night while still growing richer. But when the morning fog burned off it was revealed that this ship was in truth simply a bond barge lashed to an equity sloop. The resultant craft was unwieldy and slow, and was often forced to stop and pay tribute at the locks along the seaway owned by the ogre named IRS. The Street of Wall often attempts to wed two vessels into a single leviathan, but usually the marriage brings out the worst traits in both and submerges the best.

The Keeper of the Banks entrant, *CD,* also attempted the challenge. But alas, the interest currents had severely lessened during the long previous night and *CD*'s progress was very slow. Harmful too, she was often forced to stop and also pay tribute at the locks along the seaway owned by the ogre named IRS.

The Guild of Traditional Insurers launched the good ship *Fixed Annuity*. Although she too was subject to the ebbs and flows of interest currents, the ship *Fixed Annuity* was able to avoid the ogre's locks and thus travel faster than boat *CD*.

Shipwrights from the Insurer Guild and Street of Wall had combined to launch the bark *Variable Annuity*. This fine vessel avoided the IRS locks and was able to ride the investment winds ever faster than the other boats. The builders had even covered her keel with principal protection plating, so that if she were grounded on shoals or reefs she would still remain afloat. However, if the investment winds were becalmed the vessel would not go forward, and if gales pushed against her *Variable Annuity* could lose the progress she'd gained.

The last vessel in the armada was the proud clipper *Index Annuity* planked by Innovative Insurers. Like the crafts *Fixed Annuity* and *Variable Annuity*, *Index Annuity* avoided the locks of the IRS ogre. And like *Variable Annuity*, this ship used investment winds to her advantage. But *Index Annuity*'s special design meant she wouldn't retreat in a foul wind when advantage had been gained, and her hull was also protected from all shoals and reefs. Even if becalmed *Index Annuity* would still move forward by catching at least a minimum of the interest currents.

Alas, we know not who the winner of this regatta is because the race is still being run. Though a question to the reader poised, at journey's end which ship do you think will have won?

Activity Pages

Hey Kids! Show your parents how index annuities can help them navigate through financial uncertainties and achieve security. After all, you don't want them moving in with you when they're old and wrinkled. Yuck!

Index Annuity Road To Riches

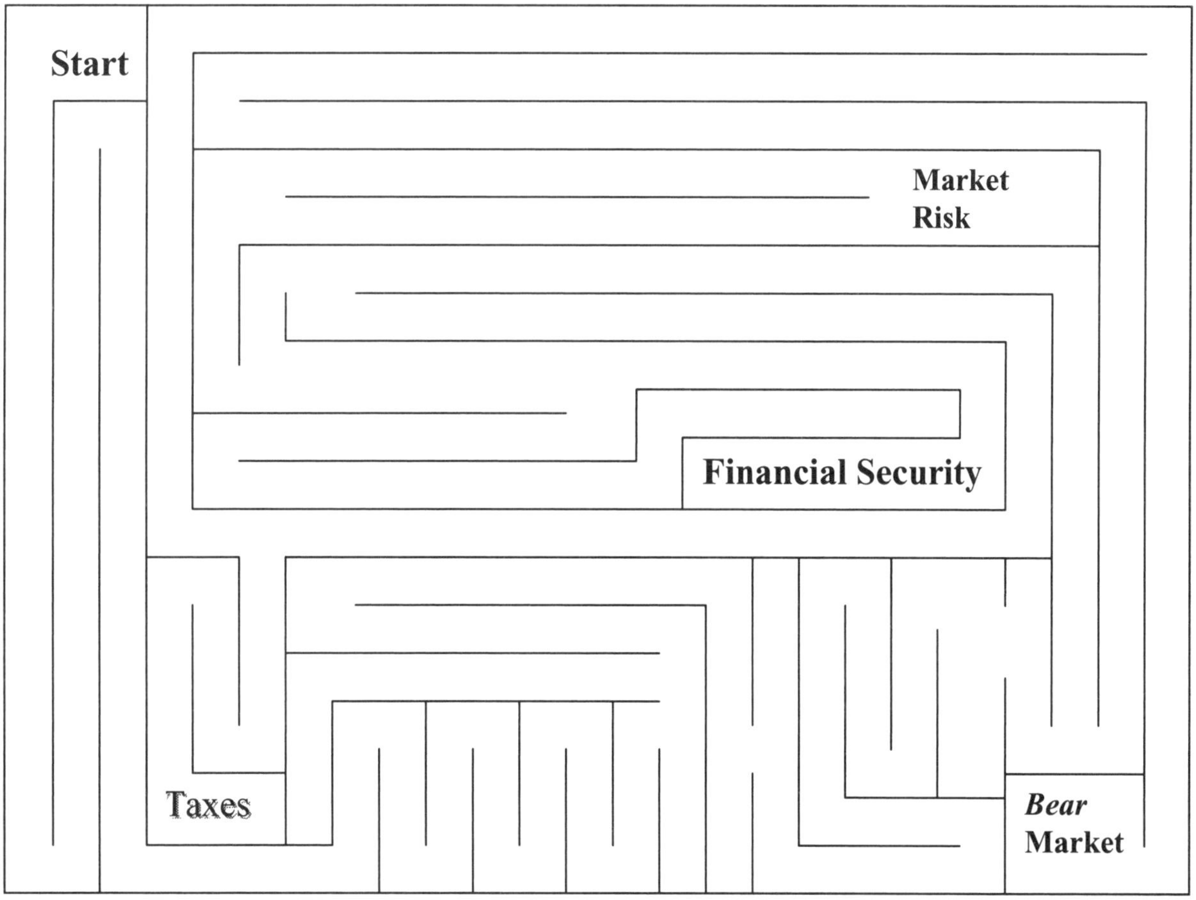

Appendix

Chapter Quiz Answers

Chapter 1
1. A
2. C
3. D
4. C
5. A

Chapter 2
1. A
2. C
3. A
4. B
5. C

Chapter 3
1. B
2. B
3. A
4. D
5. D

Chapter 4
1. D
2. C
3. A
4. D
5. A

Chapter 5
1. A
2. A
3. A
4. C
5. B

Chapter 6
1. D
2. A
3. C
4. D
5. C

Chapter 7
1. C
2. B
3. A
4. D
5. A

Chapter 8
1. C
2. D
3. B
4. A
5. C

Chapter 9
1. D
2. A
3. C
4. C
5. B

Chapter 10
1. D
2. A
3. C
4. D
5. B

Chapter 11
1. C
2. C
3. D
4. A
5. B

Glossary

Accumulated Value – the original premium plus any interest credited.

American-style option – may be exercised at any time before it expires. A European-style option may only be exercised on its expiration date.

Annual Reset (annual ratchet, cliquet) – crediting methods measuring index movement over a one year period. Positive interest is calculated and credited at the end of each contract year and cannot be lost if the index subsequently declines. *Say that the index increased from 100 to 110 in one year and the index annuity had an 80% participation rate. The insurance company would take the 10% gross index gain for the year (110-100/100), apply the participation rate (10% index gain x 80% rate) and credit 8% interest to the annuity. But, what if in the following year the index declined back to 100? The individual would keep the 8% interest earned and simply receive zero interest for the down year.* An annual reset structure preserves credited gains and treats negative index periods as years with zero growth.

Annuitant – the person upon whose life expectancy a life income is based upon annuitization.

Annuitization – converting an annuity's value into an income.

Averaging – index values may either be measured from a start point to an end point (point-to-point) or values between the start point and end point may added up, divided by the number of periods used, and this average becomes the end point. Index values may be averaged over the days, weeks, months, or quarters of the period.

Call Option (also see put option) – gives the option buyer the right to buy an underlying security or index at a specified price on or before a given date.

Cap – the maximum interest rate that will be credited to the annuity for the year or period, or the maximum index growth upon which interest will be calculated. The Cap usually refers to the maximum interest credited after applying the participation rate or yield spread. *If the index methodology showed a 20% increase, the participation rate was 60% and the maximum interest cap was 10%, the contract would credit 10% interest.* Other annuities use a maximum index cap instead of a maximum interest cap with the participation rate or yield spread applied to the lesser of the gain or the cap. *If the index methodology showed a 20% increase, the participation rate was 60% and the maximum gain cap was 10%, the contract would credit 6% interest.*

Cash Value (contract value, surrender value) – the minimum amount the annuity owner receives if the contract is surrendered.

Certificate of deposit – a bank investment derivative product without a minimum guaranteed interest rate, tax-deferral or life income options.

Cherry Picking – strengthening a hypothetical illustration by picking time periods that make a particular crediting method look better than it really is by using extreme examples.

Compound Interest – interest is earned on both the original principal and on previous interest. If you're only looking at a few periods there isn't a lot of difference between the effects of simple and compound interest. However, the effects of compound interest become proportionately greater with each passing period.

Crediting Method (also see methodology) – the formula(s) used to determine the excess interest that is credited above the minimum interest guarantee.

Deferred Annuity – an annuity whereby at least a year will elapse between when the premium or premiums are paid and the annuity is annuitized with a stream of income produced.

Defined Liquidity - Unlike stocks or bonds, index annuities have defined liquidity. Regardless of how the market performs you usually know exactly what your surrender value is at any time.

Equity Index Universal Life – shares the coverage and premium flexibility of other universal life policies, but the crediting of interest is linked to an equity index.

European-style option - may only be exercised on its expiration date. An American-style option may be exercised at any time before it expires

Excess Interest – interest credited to the annuity contract above the minimum guaranteed interest rate. In an index annuity the excess interest is determined by applying a stated crediting method to a specific index or indexes.

Exercise - to use an option to buy or sell the underlying security or index.

Extrapolation – where one infers unknown information by projecting known information. It is used with great accuracy in mathematics and much worse accuracy in financial and economic forecasting.

Fixed Annuity – a contract issued by an insurance company guaranteeing a minimum interest rate with the crediting of excess interest determined by the performance of the insurer's general account. Index annuities are fixed annuities.

Floor – the minimum participation rate or minimum cap that could be applied at future renewals.

Free Withdrawals – withdrawals that are free of surrender charges, however loss of excess interest or premature distribution penalties could apply.

Index – the underlying external benchmark upon which the crediting of excess interest is based; a measure of the prices of a group of securities.

Indexing – matching the performance of a specified group of annuities. Indexing does not attempt to beat the market, but to be the market.

Market Index Securities – a security promising a guarantee of principal if held to a 5 or 7 year maturity with upside index potential (see term yield spread index annuities).

Market Risk – the possibility to lose past gains or even principal. The original principal and credited interest of an index annuity are not subject to market risk. Even if the index declines the annuity owner would receive no less than their original principal back if they decided to cash in the policy at the end of the surrender period. Unlike a security, index annuities guarantee the original premium and the premium is backed by the insurance company that issued it.

Maturity Date – the maturity date is the longest one can keep annuity interest deferred before it must be taken out. Maturity dates usually occur when the annuitant celebrates their 80th to 90th birthday.

Methodology (crediting method, crediting structure) – the way index movement becomes interest crediting is calculated. There are currently 40 different methods used to determine how index movement becomes interest credited.

Minimum Guaranteed Return (minimum interest rate) – the minimum interest guarantee. If *the annuity guaranteed 3% a year based on 100% of the premium. This means that at the end of a seven year term the minimum guaranteed return would be $1.23 for each $1 of premium. If the external index increased so that the index annuity interest crediting method resulted in a 30 cent interest gain for the entire period the annuity contract would credit 30 cents- not 30 cents plus 23 cents.* If the calculated index gain was zero for a year, the typical index annuity would not credit the minimum guarantee of 3% for that specific year, the contract would record 0% interest. Most index annuities compute the minimum guarantee on 90% of premium.

Option – a contract which conveys to its buyer the right, but not the obligation, to buy or sell something at a specified price on or before a given date; after this given date the option ceases to exist. Insurers typically buy options to provide the index linkage for the excess interest potential. Options may be American styled whereby they may be exercised at anytime prior to the given date, or they may have to be exercised only during a specified window. Options that may only be exercised during a specified period are European styled options.

Price/Earnings or P/E Ratio – tells how many years' worth of earnings a share of stock is selling.

Participation Floor – a crediting factor minimum guarantee.

Participation Rate – the percentage of positive index movement credited to the annuity. *If the index methodology determined that the index increased 10% and the index annuity participated in 60% of the increase, it would be said that the contract has a 60% participation rate.* Participation rates may also be expressed as asset fees or yield spreads.

Point-to-Point – a crediting method measuring index movement from an absolute initial point to the absolute end point for a period. An index had a period starting value of 100 and a period ending value of 120. A point-to-point method would record a positive index movement of 20 [120-100] or a 20% positive movement [(120-100)/100]. Point-to-point usually refers to annual periods, however the phrase is also used instead of term end point to refer to multiple year periods.

Principal Protection Funds – a security using a split-investment concept involving bonds and equities.

Put Option (also see call option) – gives the buyer the right to sell an underlying security or index at a specified price on or before a given date.

Return Floor – another way of saying minimum guaranteed return.

Rule of 72 – formula for determining approximately how many years it takes a sum to double at a given rate. 72 is divided by the return percentage and the answer is approximately the time it takes money to double at that rate.

Simple Interest (also see compound interest) – interest is only earned on the original principal.

Standard & Poor's 500® (S&P 500®) – most widely used index annuity external index. The index does not include reinvested dividends of the underlying stocks

Strike Price (also see option, exercise price) – the specified share price or index value at which the shares or interest may be bought or sold. If the strike price of a call option is less than the current market price of the underlying security the call is said to be in-the-money. Conversely, if the strike price of a call option is greater than the current market price it is out-of-the-money and would not be exercised.

Surrender Charge (surrender penalty) – a charge imposed for withdrawing funds or terminating the annuity contract usually within a specified number of years. The charge is usually expressed as a declining percentage of the total contract value.

Surrender Value (cash value, contract value) – the minimum amount the annuity owner receives if the contract is surrendered.

Term Average Highest Anniversary – a crediting method where a rolling annual average of monthly index values is calculated and the highest averaged anniversary value used as an end point. It is <u>not</u> a high water mark methodology.

Term End Point – crediting methods measuring index movements over a greater timeframe than a year or two; the opposite of an annual reset method. Also referred to as a term point-to-point method. *Say that the index value was at 100 on the first day of the period. If the calculated index value were at 150 at the end of the period the positive index movement would be 50% (150-100/100). The company would credit a percentage of this movement as excess interest.* Index movement is calculated and interest credited at the end of the term and interim movements during the period are ignored.

Term High Point (High Water Mark) – a type of term end point structure that uses the highest anniversary index level as the end point. *Say that the index value was at 100 on the first day of the period, reached a value of 160 at the end of a contract year during the period, and ended the period at 150. A term high point method would use the 160 value - the highest contract anniversary point reached during the period, as the end point and the gross index gain would be 60% (160-100/100).* The company would then apply a participation rate to the gain.

Term Yield Spread – a type of term end point structure which calculates the total index gain for a period, computes the annual compound rate of return, or internal rate of return, deducts a yield spread from the annual rate of return, and then recalculates the total index gain for the period based on the net annual rate. *Say that an index increased from 100 to 200 by the end of a nine year period. This is the equivalent of an 8% compound annual interest rate. If the annuity had a 2% term yield spread this would be deducted from the annual interest rate (8%-2%) and the net rate would be credited to the contract (6%) for each of the nine years.* Total index gain may also be computed by using the highest anniversary index level as the end point.

Variable Annuity – a contract issued by an insurance company offering separate accounts invested in a wide variety of stocks and/or bonds. The investment risk is borne by the annuity owner. Variable annuities are considered securities and require appropriate securities registration.

Vesting – typically used with term high point methods a portion of any gain is locked in each year and this vested portion is available for withdrawal.

	S&P 500		Daily Average Of Index	
	12/31	**Annual**	**Ending**	**% Change From**
Year	**Index**	**Return**	**Average**	**Previous Year**
1952	26.57	11.78%	24.450	2.86%
1953	24.81	-6.62%	24.720	-6.96%
1954	35.98	45.02%	29.723	19.80%
1955	45.48	26.40%	40.488	12.53%
1956	46.67	2.62%	46.650	2.57%
1957	39.99	-14.31%	44.429	-4.80%
1958	55.21	38.06%	46.199	15.53%
1959	59.89	8.48%	57.401	3.97%
1960	58.11	-2.97%	55.846	-6.75%
1961	71.55	23.13%	66.272	14.05%
1962	63.10	-11.81%	62.322	-12.90%
1963	75.02	18.89%	69.837	10.68%
1964	84.75	12.97%	81.372	8.47%
1965	92.43	9.06%	88.153	4.02%
1966	80.33	-13.09%	85.182	-7.84%
1967	96.47	20.09%	91.960	14.48%
1968	103.86	7.66%	98.375	1.97%
1969	92.06	-11.36%	97.782	-5.85%
1970	92.15	0.10%	83.194	-9.63%
1971	102.09	10.79%	98.321	6.70%
1972	118.05	15.63%	109.135	6.90%
1973	97.55	-17.37%	107.438	-8.99%
1974	68.56	-29.72%	82.780	-15.42%
1975	90.19	31.55%	86.177	25.70%
1976	107.46	19.15%	102.035	13.13%
1977	95.10	-11.50%	98.176	-8.64%
1978	96.11	1.06%	96.112	1.06%
1979	107.94	12.31%	102.999	7.17%
1980	135.76	25.77%	118.710	9.98%
1981	122.55	-9.73%	128.054	-5.68%
1982	140.64	14.76%	119.694	-2.33%
1983	164.93	17.27%	160.474	14.10%
1984	167.24	1.40%	160.460	-2.71%
1985	211.28	26.33%	186.828	11.71%
1986	242.17	14.62%	236.359	11.87%
1987	247.08	2.03%	286.997	18.51%
1988	277.72	12.40%	265.880	7.61%
1989	353.40	27.25%	323.053	16.32%
1990	330.22	-6.56%	334.632	-5.31%
1991	417.09	26.31%	376.186	13.92%
1992	435.71	4.46%	415.749	-0.32%
1993	466.45	7.06%	451.615	3.65%
1994	459.27	-1.54%	460.415	-1.29%
1995	615.93	34.11%	541.720	17.84%
1996	740.74	20.26%	670.495	8.86%
1997	970.43	31.01%	873.428	17.91%
1998	1229.23	26.67%	1085.520	11.91%
1999	1469.25	19.53%	1327.306	7.98%
2000	1320.28	-10.14%	1427.215	-2.86%
2001	1148.08	-13.04%	1194.179	-9.55%
2002	879.82	-23.37%	1026.077	-10.63%

averages daily values for each year for ending value, change from previous year end

All information is for illustrative purposes only, does not provide investment or tax advice. Past performance is no guarantee of future results. "S&P 500®" is a trademark of The McGraw-Hill Companies Inc., and must be licensed for use. Index-linked products are not sponsored, endorsed, sold or promoted by Standard & Poor's and Standard & Poor's makes no representation regarding the advisability of purchasing these Products. Information is from sources believed accurate but is not warranted.

	S&P 500		Monthly Average Of Index	
	12/31	**Annual**	**Ending**	**% Change From**
Year	**Index**	**Return**	**Average**	**Previous Year**
1952	26.57	11.78%	24.636	3.64%
1953	24.81	-6.62%	24.700	-7.04%
1954	35.98	45.02%	30.062	21.17%
1955	45.48	26.40%	40.881	13.62%
1956	46.67	2.62%	46.481	2.20%
1957	39.99	-14.31%	44.246	-5.19%
1958	55.21	38.06%	46.786	16.99%
1959	59.89	8.48%	57.807	4.70%
1960	58.11	-2.97%	55.602	-7.16%
1961	71.55	23.13%	66.653	14.70%
1962	63.10	-11.81%	61.956	-13.41%
1963	75.02	18.89%	70.218	11.28%
1964	84.75	12.97%	81.547	8.70%
1965	92.43	9.06%	88.470	4.39%
1966	80.33	-13.09%	84.458	-8.62%
1967	96.47	20.09%	92.232	14.82%
1968	103.86	7.66%	98.547	2.15%
1969	92.06	-11.36%	97.590	-6.04%
1970	92.15	0.10%	83.443	-9.36%
1971	102.09	10.79%	98.290	6.66%
1972	118.05	15.63%	109.782	7.53%
1973	97.55	-17.37%	106.509	-9.78%
1974	68.56	-29.72%	81.482	-16.47%
1975	90.19	31.55%	87.128	27.08%
1976	107.46	19.15%	102.791	13.97%
1977	95.10	-11.50%	97.477	-9.29%
1978	96.11	1.06%	95.464	0.38%
1979	107.94	12.31%	103.327	7.51%
1980	135.76	25.77%	119.578	10.78%
1981	122.55	-9.73%	127.842	-5.83%
1982	140.64	14.76%	120.276	-1.86%
1983	164.93	17.27%	160.762	14.31%
1984	167.24	1.40%	160.315	-2.80%
1985	211.28	26.33%	188.967	12.99%
1986	242.17	14.62%	238.921	13.08%
1987	247.08	2.03%	285.992	18.10%
1988	277.72	12.40%	268.051	8.49%
1989	353.40	27.25%	326.314	17.50%
1990	330.22	-6.56%	332.680	-5.86%
1991	417.09	26.31%	381.536	15.54%
1992	435.71	4.46%	417.117	0.01%
1993	466.45	7.06%	453.452	4.07%
1994	459.27	-1.54%	460.662	-1.24%
1995	615.93	34.11%	546.877	19.08%
1996	740.74	20.26%	674.846	9.57%
1997	970.43	31.01%	875.862	18.24%
1998	1229.23	26.67%	1087.860	12.10%
1999	1469.25	19.53%	1330.600	8.25%
2000	1320.28	-10.14%	1419.728	-3.37%
2001	1148.08	-13.04%	1185.371	-10.22%
2002	879.82	-23.37%	988.58	-13.89

averages monthly values for each year for ending value, change from previous year end

All information is for illustrative purposes only, does not provide investment or tax advice. Past performance is no guarantee of future results. "S&P 500®" is a trademark of The McGraw-Hill Companies Inc., and must be licensed for use. Index-linked products are not sponsored, endorsed, sold or promoted by Standard & Poor's and Standard & Poor's makes no representation regarding the advisability of purchasing these Products. Information is from sources believed accurate but is not warranted.

Year	Personal Savings Rate	Rate of Inflation (Adjusted)	Average 6 Month CD Rate
1952		0.75%	
1953		0.75%	
1954		-0.37%	
1955		0.37%	
1956		2.60%	
1957		3.26%	
1958		1.75%	
1959	7.54%	1.38%	
1960	7.22%	1.36%	
1961	8.33%	0.67%	
1962	8.26%	1.33%	
1963	7.79%	1.64%	
1964	8.76%	1.29%	4.05%
1965	8.55%	1.92%	4.43%
1966	8.25%	3.13%	5.63%
1967	9.30%	3.34%	5.21%
1968	8.43%	4.71%	6.00%
1969	7.78%	5.90%	7.89%
1970	9.42%	5.57%	7.66%
1971	9.59%	3.27%	5.22%
1972	8.84%	3.41%	5.02%
1973	10.45%	8.94%	8.31%
1974	10.67%	12.10%	9.98%
1975	10.58%	7.13%	6.89%
1976	9.40%	5.04%	5.62%
1977	8.73%	6.68%	5.92%
1978	9.01%	8.99%	8.61%
1979	9.17%	13.25%	11.44%
1980	10.18%	12.35%	12.99%
1981	10.82%	8.91%	15.77%
1982	10.91%	3.83%	12.57%
1983	8.83%	3.79%	9.27%
1984	10.61%	4.04%	10.68%
1985	9.16%	3.79%	8.25%
1986	8.22%	1.19%	6.51%
1987	7.30%	4.33%	7.00%
1988	7.78%	4.41%	7.90%
1989	7.53%	4.64%	9.08%
1990	7.78%	6.25%	8.17%
1991	8.31%	2.98%	5.91%
1992	8.69%	2.97%	3.76%
1993	7.11%	2.81%	3.28%
1994	6.10%	2.60%	4.96%
1995	5.58%	2.53%	5.98%
1996	4.80%	3.38%	5.47%
1997	4.24%	1.70%	5.72%
1998	4.74%	1.67%	5.44%
1999	2.66%	2.67%	5.46%
2000	2.84%	3.37%	6.58%
2001	2.29%	1.55%	3.64%
2002	3.83%	2.37%	1.85%

Data sources are Federal Reserve Board and U.S. Department of Labor
Personal Savings Rate and Consumer Price Index are seasonally adjusted

Index

Charts

Advantage Bond Rate Indicator 134
Annual Index Annuity Sales 16
Bear Markets 117